Puppy

Preschool

John Ross and his puppy, Crea.

John Ross and
Barbara McKinney

Puppy
Preschool

Raising Your Puppy Right—

Right from the Start!

Revised Edition

St. Martin's Griffin

New York

This book is dedicated with love to our daughter,
Hannah Louise Ross, born on July 4, 1995

PUPPY PRESCHOOL. Copyright © 1996, 2008 by John Ross and
Barbara McKinney. All rights reserved. Printed in the United
States of America. No part of this book may be used or repro-
duced in any manner whatsoever without written permission
except in the case of brief quotations embodied in critical articles
or reviews. For information, address St. Martin's Press, 175 Fifth
Avenue, New York, N.Y. 10010.

www.stmartins.com

Design by Songhee Kim

Photographs by Jamie Keever and the authors

Library of Congress Cataloging-in-Publication Data

Ross, John.
    Puppy preschool : raising your puppy right—right from
the start! /
    John Ross and Barbara McKinney.
        p.   cm.
    Includes index.
    ISBN-13: 978-0-312-37591-1
    ISBN-10: 0-312-37591-3
    1. Puppies.   I. McKinney, Barbara.   II. Title.
    SF427.R78   1996   95-41346
    636.7'07—dc20   CIP

Revised Edition: March 2008

10 9 8 7 6 5 4 3 2 1

Acknowledgments

Special thanks to Jamie Keever for her hard work in taking many of the photographs; to Chuck Noonan, D.V.M., animal doctor of Weston, Connecticut, for his help with the health chapter; to Chris Benyei, D.V.M., for his continuing support and friendship; and to our great editor, Bob Weil, for believing in our efforts to create responsible dog owners.

We also thank the following for some of our favorite Nantucket Island indulgences: the Ropewalk for shrimp and beers; the Juice Bar for watermelon creams; Steve McCluskey for superb food and ambience at the Company of the Cauldron; and the Melrose gang—Joyce & Ted, Dennis & Wendy, Ecliff & Diana, and Bob & Diane—for those great dinners and fun Melrose Mondays.

From John: Special thanks to Jimmy Buffett for shaking my hand and congratulating me on my wedding day when I met him at Barry Thurston's tackle shop.

Contents

Preface ix

Part I. First Considerations
  1. Is a Puppy Right for You? 3
  2. What Is Puppy Preschool? 14
  3. A Philosophy for Training 19

Part II. Choosing the Right Puppy
  4. Finding Puppies 29
  5. Evaluating a Puppy 41

Part III. Know Your Puppy
  6. Puppy Development: Birth to Adulthood 49

Part IV. Puppy Equipment
  7. The Essentials 63
  8. Safe (and Fun) Toys 72
  9. Your Voice: A Required Training Tool 81

Part V. Starting Off Right
  10. Bonding with Your Puppy 89
  11. Socializing Your Puppy 96
  12. Games Puppies Play 109
  13. Family Matters 116

Part VI. Puppy Preschool Training

14. Housebreaking Your New Puppy   129
15. Canine Separation Anxiety   141
16. Preventing Unwanted Chewing   153
17. Introducing the Leash and Collar   162
18. *"Nhaa!"*—Stopping Unwanted Behavior When You Growl 171
19. Handling Your Puppy   178
20. Introducing Basic Obedience Commands: Part I   186
21. Introducing Basic Obedience Commands: Part II   205

Part VII. Puppy Care

22. Health Issues   223
23. Home Grooming Tips   232
24. Time for Formal Training   243
25. Spoiled Brat or Spoiled with Love?   250

Index   253

Preface

Puppies, puppies, puppies!

Puppy Preschool was originally published in 1996, and at the time, puppies and dogs surrounded my life. Now twelve years have gone by, a new millennium has arrived, and I'm still spending my time with puppies. I guess in an obedience instructor's life, the basics never really change.

Well, a few things have changed. Sadly, my two beloved dogs, Drifter, the Australian shepherd, and Crea, the springer spaniel, both pictured in *Puppy Preschool,* have passed on. I'm now sharing my life with a wonderful field-bred black Labrador retriever, Sophie.

Sophie is four years old and no longer a puppy, although she still sometimes acts like one! When Sophie was a puppy she was a *handful.* Thankfully, she has gone from a high-energy, mouthing, peeing, pooping fur ball into one of the world's great dogs. In fact, she may arguably be the world's best beach dog. If you saw her run, swim, and catch a Frisbee—sometimes all in a single toss—you would know what I mean. She also is perfectly behaved around all the people and dogs we meet on the beach, especially the puppies.

Have you read the wonderful, best-selling book by John Grogan, *Marley and Me*? Well, if Mr. Grogan had owned Sophie and used the same "training approach" that he used with Marley, his book easily could have been titled *Sophie and Me.* As I said, Sophie was a handful.

While I highly recommend *Marley and Me* as a well-told dog story and a great read, I strongly suggest that if you want a well-trained dog, you do what I did with Sophie. Use *Puppy Preschool* as your training approach.

I find it a bit ironic that if Mr. Grogan had read *Puppy Preschool*, he would not have had a national best seller. But he would have had his carpets, his sofa, his arm sockets (not to mention other body parts) intact— and a lot less anxiety in his daily life.

This new edition of *Puppy Preschool* has changed a little bit too, although not too drastically. We added a few new things and dropped a few old ones. I chose to leave out the chapters on "good" and "bad" breed choices for two reasons. For one, the breeds profiled in the original text were popular in 1996. Breed popularity changes. Second and more important, my opinion about breed significance has changed. It is a fact that some breed characteristics can influence behavior. And some breeds tend to fit into the role of "well-behaved family pet" more easily than others. However, I truly believe that if you train and handle your dog properly, any breed of dog (or mix of breeds) can turn out to be a great and wonderful companion.

I've had numerous breeds over the years, and they have all had one common trait: They have been great dogs that I could take anywhere and count on to be well behaved.

What is the formula to my success with dogs? I call it the Canine Triangle. I use natural and positive obedience training methods. I socialize my dogs by integrating them into my household as part of my "pack" and by exposing them correctly to people and places. And I provide my dogs with sufficient physical exercise to keep their bodies healthy and their minds content. Sound simple? It is. Anyone can do it if you make the effort and follow my formula. It's all found in the pages of this book, a formula that's been proved again and again over the past thirty-five years. I've yet to see it fail!

I've also added some important new training insights to this edition of *Puppy Preschool*. One example is a new chapter on separation anxiety. Separation anxiety can manifest itself as out-of-control destructive behavior, but it can be avoided completely with proper handling during puppyhood. Separation anxiety is truly something that you and your puppy do *not* have to suffer with.

Enjoy this new edition of *Puppy Preschool* and enjoy your new puppy. Although puppies require time and attention, raising a dog that you will love and enjoy for the next fourteen years makes the effort well worth it.

It's time to go. Sophie wants to go play Frisbee on the beach. Tails up!

Part One

First Considerations

Congratulations! You have a cute new puppy in your family—or are about to get one. It's a big responsibility. Are you ready for it? The chapters in this section will help you get ready. They describe the joys and trials of raising a puppy and lay the groundwork for all the things you can—and should—do to get your puppy off to a great start.

One

Is a Puppy Right for You?

Few things on earth are more adorable than a puppy. Puppies are warm, cuddly, and cute. They are fun to hold, fun to pet, and simply fun to watch. Children seem to gravitate naturally to puppies. In fact, so do adults. I remember one memorable day bringing my Australian shepherd, Drifter, who was a ten-week-old puppy, to a college campus near my home. I was suddenly surrounded by coeds! Puppies can be irresistible. For this reason, I've learned that you should never look casually at a litter of puppies unless you want to own a dog.*

In addition to being adorable, puppies are also a tremendous amount of work. As a veteran dog-obedience instructor, I find that the phrase I repeat to my clients more than any other is, "You have to live through puppyhood!" That's not an easy thing to do. Despite their cuteness, puppies can be exasperating. Given the chance, they will chew, bark, bite, and eliminate at entirely inappropriate times and places. They may destroy valuable items, terrorize the kids, dig up the garden, run away when called, jump on your friends, and all the other things you *don't* want a dog to do. Mil-

---

*For ease of discussion, puppies and adult dogs are referred to by the male pronoun throughout. In addition, authors John Ross and Barbara McKinney use the voice of John Ross to present much of their information. The word "I" refers to John Ross.

Raising a puppy can be a great experience—or a nightmare. Consider carefully whether puppyhood is right for you.

Don't let that cute expression fool you! Puppyhood is a lot of work.

lions of owners give up their puppies every year because they cannot deal with puppyhood. Puppies require vast amounts of work and attention to raise them right.

Unfortunately, there's no book or training technique that will help you circumvent puppyhood. You've got to live *through* it. Raising a puppy right takes time. But the same holds true when raising a child. You can be the best parent who ever lived, with the patience of a saint and a thorough understanding of child psychology. You may employ the most effective child-raising techniques ever invented, but nothing you do will make your two-year-old behave like a six-year-old. Nothing will get your six-year-old to act thirteen or your thirteen-year-old to act twenty-one. Growing up takes time, and children must go through developmental stages on their way to adulthood. The same is true for puppies.

Does this mean you sit back and do nothing until the pup is an adult? Absolutely not. In fact, that's about the worst thing you could do. Letting an out-of-control puppy stay that way will only produce an out-of-control adult dog. No one wants to live with a nuisance, whether it's 8 pounds or 108 pounds. I'm convinced that if every family with a puppy followed a few basic steps to teach good behavior, we would reduce the amount of unwanted, homeless dogs by the *thousands*. That's because not many people give away sweet, well-trained pets. It's the obnoxious adult dogs—who were once cute, untrained puppies—that end up at the pound on doggie death row.

Puppyhood Is Not Forever

How long does puppyhood last? Not nearly as long as childhood in humans (thank goodness!). Humans are technically considered adults at twenty-one years old, while domestic dogs become adults at about two years old.

There is no magic wand that will zap your baby ball of fur into an adult, so puppyhood is the time to begin proper training. Training can begin the day you bring your puppy home, and if you make an effort to shape your puppy's behavior with training the first two years, you will end up with a dog that you will enjoy for the next ten to twelve years, or longer.

One of my other favorite sayings is that if it were easy, everyone would have a well-trained dog. The truth is, not everyone does, because training isn't easy, but it can be fun. And as thousands of people who have used my programs over the years can attest, the rewards are well worth it.

Should I Get a Puppy or an Adult Dog?

Several times a year I'm asked my opinion about bringing an older dog into the family as opposed to raising a new puppy. Which is the best way to go? What are the virtues and drawbacks with either choice?

When you purchase or adopt an older dog you may be saving a life. There are millions of dogs euthanized in the United States every year. Many of these dogs are sweet, loving creatures who just need a chance. Adopting an older, homeless dog is a wonderful, loving thing to do. Besides saving a dog's life, you usually can avoid the job of housebreaking and training the dog not to chew things in the home.

On the other hand, you may inherit big problems. In my experience I've found that the vast majority of dogs that people "got rid of" did not have a very good start in life. Often these dogs may have been allowed to run loose, which inhibits a dog's ability to bond properly with its human pack members. They may also have been emotionally abused, perhaps by being locked in a cage or chained in the yard for ten or more hours a day. (Social isolation has detrimental effects on a canine's personality.) The dogs may never have been taught to eliminate outside or may have been left unsupervised to trash the house, making your job of training extremely difficult. At worst, these dogs may have been physically abused and are so distrusting of humans that they bite out of fear or have other serious behavioral problems.

My goal in describing these hazards is not to undermine the hard work of thousands of dedicated animal welfare workers trying to place dogs in good homes. In fact, they have my deepest respect for trying to save canine lives against almost impossible odds. I simply want future dog owners to be aware of what I've seen in my years working as a trainer.

If you decide instead to integrate a puppy into your home, one advantage you will have is the opportunity to shape the puppy into the type of dog you want. Although many older dogs do fit in quickly to a new home, the best canine-human bonding happens when a puppy is introduced to its new human pack between the ages of *seven* and *eight* weeks.

At this age you can begin to train your pup to eliminate outdoors by using the system outlined in this book, and you can begin teaching him that behavior such as mouthing on your hands or arms is not acceptable. You can also influence your puppy's behavior so that by around one year old the chewing phase will be over and you will have a dog whom you can trust in the house unsupervised. And if you decide to own a puppy, think of the adorable photos you will cherish in later years. But don't forget: You have to be prepared to live through puppyhood!

What Does Owning a Puppy Really Involve?

Puppyhood is a mixed bag of fun, fur, and frustration. You are essentially taking a nonhuman creature into your home—who doesn't speak your language—and attempting to turn it into a friendly, under-control companion who fits into your family's life. In some ways, that's asking a lot.

On the other hand, dogs by nature are pack animals. They have a strong instinct to bond with fellow pack members (you and your family) and to live with them in a den (your home). That makes dogs uniquely capable of fitting into life with a human family. Of course, some dogs fit in easier than others and some owners make that fit happen better than others. But the fact that domestic dogs accept us at all as members of their pack is amazing to me. In fact, I'm not sure whether dogs think we're canines or they're humans, but I believe they think we're all exactly the same thing.

Consider This Before Getting a Puppy

Because of the challenges described above, I have found that not every household is a good candidate for raising a puppy. This is not to undermine the determination and commitment of a family that truly wants to make it work. But I've seen people with the best of intentions fail with a young dog. In some cases an adult dog would have been a better choice. In some cases a fish aquarium would have been the right choice!

If you find that you or your family fit any of the following descriptions, you should think long and hard about your decision to raise a puppy. I've tried to provide some solutions to each situation, so that with a few changes in your household routine or some outside help, you may be able to make it work. But the odds are stacked against you if any of the following situations apply.

1. Babies or Young Children in the Home

I can't begin to count the number of people who have said to me, "Now that we have children, we want to get a puppy. What kind should we get?" My wise-guy (but truthful) answer is, "A stuffed one."

I do admit that kids and puppies seem to go together. And they certainly like each other. But should you raise small children and a puppy together? Theoretically, it can work. Realistically, it usually doesn't. Why? Raising a

Resist the urge to get a puppy while your children are small. Careful supervision of a puppy *and* a toddler is a Herculean task.

puppy right requires a lot of time and effort. So does raising a child. Not many people can do both well—at the same time.

If several adults are in the home, it may work. Unfortunately, the scenario I see most frequently is "Dad" off at work ten or more hours a day while "Mom" struggles with meeting the demands of a toddler or new baby *and* a rambunctious, mouthing, chewing, urinating puppy. When her time and patience are stretched to the limit, the puppy gets ignored—and grows up to be a rambunctious, mouthing, chewing, urinating adult dog.

I strongly recommend getting a puppy when the kids are schoolchildren—ideally at least eight years old. However, if you do choose to bring a puppy into a home with small children, be sure to get some outside help such as a teenage neighbor who may appreciate a dog-walking job or a nearby family member who may be able to "puppy-sit" on rough days. Also, plan to use every ounce of energy supervising the puppy around the children and teaching the puppy how to behave. And remember, puppyhood is not over in just a few hard weeks or months. Dogs don't get their full adult personalities until they are about two years old, so it's quite possible that your silly, sweet nine-week-old golden retriever will soon be a silly, sweet one-year-old golden retriever, weighing eighty pounds. Without proper training he will still be jumping on your friends, mouthing your kids, chewing your rugs, and having housebreaking accidents all because there was not enough time to deal with him early on.

2. Long Days Spent at the Office

You're never home. Your fast-track career or two-job schedule keeps you away from home ten or more hours a day. You can't check home at lunchtime because you work forty-five minutes away—and you want a puppy? Let's be fair. Owning a puppy means taking care of a puppy. That means providing housebreaking training, frequent meals, exercise, and companionship. Cats can survive long days alone. So can small mammals such as hamsters, guinea pigs, and rabbits, as well as reptiles. But not puppies.

This is not to say that people with jobs can't raise dogs. Of course they can. But people who care about doing it right make some changes in their lives to do so. When the puppy first arrives, you may need to spend your entire two-week vacation at home to get started on a housebreaking routine. You may need to hire a neighbor or pet-sitting service to stop by midday to provide a bathroom break and some playtime. You may have to be willing to take a season off from playing in the after-work softball league or in that month-long racquetball tournament. In other words, you really must make the puppy a priority in your life. If you are unable or unwilling to make those kinds of changes, don't get a puppy. Instead, a better idea may be to offer to serve as a weekend or evening dog-sitter for your friends or relatives. You can have some occasional canine fun without the twenty-four-hour-a-day, seven-day-a-week responsibility.

3. Physical Limitations

What kinds of physical limitations would prevent raising a puppy? Lack of mobility would be the most serious. Raising and training a puppy requires a certain amount of agile movement. Examples include taking the puppy outside (quickly) to prevent housebreaking accidents, correcting and quickly removing the puppy from chewing rugs or furniture (or worse, something dangerous like an electrical cord), catching the puppy if he wanders away from you at home or in the yard, and providing adequate exercise for an energetic young dog.

The most discouraging puppy situations I see are elderly people who have owned and loved dogs their entire lives. When their sixteen-year-old canine companion dies, they do what they have always done—bring another puppy into their home. But often the physical limitations associated with aging prevent them from being good puppy owners. Their hearts are in the right place, but their bodies aren't quite as able as before.

My best advice to people with physical limitations is to get a calm adult dog. The demands of supervising, controlling, and exercising an energetic puppy often are too great. But a sweet-natured adult dog (there are many thousands of them put to death each year in local pounds) makes a great companion to anyone.

4. Frequent Travel

Traveling is not in and of itself a problem when raising a puppy. If you arrange for reliable care while you are away, either in a reputable kennel or with a trustworthy housesitter or friend, a puppy can make it safely through your absences.

However, the problem with being a frequent traveler is that puppies need regular routines and steady companionship to be raised right. If you treat your puppy like a houseplant, shipping it here and there to be fed and watered as needed, you overlook an important aspect of dog owner-ship. Dogs form bonds with those who care for them. If you want your pup to bond with you and to look up to you as the pack leader (essential for obedience training), you need to spend a significant amount of time to-gether. Unless you and your pup travel together, which some people are able to accomplish, being on the road away from your young dog is never an ideal situation.

5. *Allergies*

Some people love dogs, but their immune systems don't. If canine allergies plague you or someone in your family, you are up against a tough situation if you want to own a dog.

My first piece of advice would be to get professional medical advice from an allergist. Simply choosing a breed of dog that "doesn't shed too much" isn't an adequate way to deal with an allergy problem. An allergist may be able to recommend treatment or medicine that will allow you to live comfortably with a dog. However, the advice you get from a medical professional may not necessarily match what a canine expert would ad-vise. For example, an allergist may say that the best place for a dog to live is in a kennel in the backyard. That may help an allergy problem, but it will do nothing toward creating a well-mannered pet who is part of your family.

A few compromises that often do work include keeping the dog off beds and furniture, having the dog sleep downstairs (although small puppies cry when left alone at night), frequent brushing and vacuuming to mini-mize hair around the house, and allergy shots (for humans) to diminish sensitivity to dogs.

Some breeds are less likely than others to aggravate an allergy problem. These include schnauzers, poodles, soft-coated wheaten terriers, and cairn terriers. Your allergist can probably add to this list.

If you have a severe allergy and are strongly advised by a medical profes-sional not to own animals, I can only suggest that you follow that advice. Owning a dog will make you miserable. You won't be able to hug and cud-dle the pup, brush his coat, or give him baths. When your distress be-comes so great that you can't live together, then what? You will have to give away an animal who has become attached to you and your home. From a canine's point of view, being "given away" means being abandoned by his pack. That's the ultimate cruelty.

If you love dogs but can't own one, perhaps you can help raise money for a local animal shelter. Or you can collect supplies that the shelter needs, enlist and coordinate volunteers, write a newsletter, or maintain the grounds with leaf-raking or flower-planting (don't work inside around the dogs—too risky!). I've met some very enthusiastic dog lovers who don't happen to own a dog. And if you can tolerate just a few minutes of allergic sneezing, red eyes, or itchy skin, any hugs and gentle strokes you can give to the homeless dogs you are helping certainly will go a long way to calm some lonely canine hearts.

6. Bad Temperament (Yours, Not the Puppy's)

Not many people admit to being impatient or hot-tempered. Even fewer people like to think of themselves as inconsistent or unable to be a leader. But these personality traits become important issues when you become a dog owner, and they are especially important if you become a puppy owner.

Impatient, angry people don't usually make successful dog owners. They may take out their frustrations and bad feelings on the dog in the form of verbal or physical abuse, or they may ignore the dog when they are in a foul mood. Their relationship to their dog is based on little more than tolerance, and their dog's relationship to them is based essentially on fear. Dogs who live with situations like this rarely trust their owners. The dog may obey obedience commands out of fear, but given the chance, he may be off on his own to hang out with other dogs or the neighbors who are a lot friendlier. If you have enough self-awareness to recognize yourself in the above description, put off buying or adopting a dog.

Another shortcoming that makes for a poor dog owner is inconsistency. Examples of this include sometimes letting the puppy mouth your hand and sometimes telling him "no," or sometimes letting him jump into your lap for a tidbit of food and sometimes correcting him when he tries to jump. Fortunately, I believe this problem can be overcome in most people with the help of good instruction. I've found through my training classes that dog owners often don't realize how inconsistent they are being with their dogs. When given guidance, most owners can "tighten the ship" and become more consistent handlers.

Why is consistency so important? Because to canines, consistency essentially means leadership. I like to use the analogy of the old wolf who is the leader of his pack. He's stronger and tougher than anyone in the group.

When a young upstart tries to take his share of food or claim the best sleeping spot, the dominant wolf consistently fends him off. Because he asserts himself *every time,* he makes it clear that he is in charge.

The same is true with our domestic dogs, although a wolf-style fight is not necessary! Consistency is all you need. By showing your puppy that you will *always* growl when he bites at you, *always* growl and remove him from the room when he chews the rug, and *always* correct him when he jumps all over the kids, you are communicating that you are in charge. This, of course, is essential if you ever expect to have control over your dog.

But what if your puppy doesn't think you are in charge? Even the most submissive dog, when faced with a pack without a leader, will take charge. That means he will listen to no one, come home when he feels like it, growl to protect his bowl of food or space on the sofa, and bite when made to give up a bone or get his nails clipped. Maybe you have known a dog like this. Because of my experience and understanding of dogs, I know that a pet like this is not inherently a "bad dog"; rather, he's the product of owners who do not know how to be "pack leaders."

Two

What Is Puppy Preschool?

The ideal time to begin a puppy's formal obedience education is at four months old. That's when puppies are at the proper developmental stage to concentrate on the more structured approach of formal training. However, most people get puppies at around eight weeks old and must live with the puppy for two months before they are ready to start school. This can be a frustrating and trying two months if you don't know how to handle your puppy. It also is wasted time when you could—and should—be shaping your puppy's behavior.

The best thing you can do with a puppy is get a head start on training through what I call Puppy Preschool. Learning comes easily and naturally to puppies. Between eight weeks and four months, puppies are at just the right age to learn a few ground rules for good behavior. Efforts you make during Puppy Preschool will pay off tenfold when it's time to start obedience class.

What Can I Accomplish?

• One of the most important things you can accomplish during Puppy Preschool is housebreaking. This means conditioning your puppy to go to the bathroom exclusively outdoors. By using the proper system you can avoid weeks or months of accidents in the house. In fact, from the first day your puppy comes home you can have him eliminating outside.

• Curbing mouthing is also an important part of Puppy Preschool. Mouthing means chewing or nipping at hands, arms, or clothes. Sometimes people think this behavior is playing. It is *not* playing. It's the canine way of establishing which individuals in the pack can be dominated and bossed around. Puppies learn this technique between the ages of three and eight weeks by interacting with their littermates and mother. Puppies who are allowed to mouth will, at best, never be obedient and at worst will become aggressive adults. The best time to gently but firmly convince your puppy that you will not tolerate being pushed around is during Puppy Preschool—long before real problems develop.

• During Puppy Preschool I like to get puppies accustomed to being handled. I gently handle their feet so that nail clipping is not a problem. I look into a puppy's ears and eyes. I handle their tails. I open their mouths and examine their teeth. I've seen adult dogs with simple problems—like a stick caught in the roof of their mouth—have to be put under general anesthesia for treatment, all because the dog would not tolerate his mouth being handled. Regular handling of a puppy results in an adult dog who allows his owner and veterinarian to do whatever treatment is needed— without biting or having a "wingding." Teaching the dog this important behavior begins in Puppy Preschool.

Obedience Basics

• Owners also can get a head start on obedience training during Puppy Preschool. This is the time to introduce your pup to a leash and collar. The goal at this stage is simply to get puppies to feel confident wearing a leash and collar, not to teach them leash-walking skills (such as not to pull). When puppies start school at four months they should not be apprehensive about the feel of the leash and collar.

• You can start to teach your puppy to sit and down on command. With older puppies and adult dogs, I teach these behaviors in three phases. Phase one is to show the dog what I want. Phase two is to practice each day so that the dog develops an understanding between the command and the behavior. Phase three is to test the dog. This means

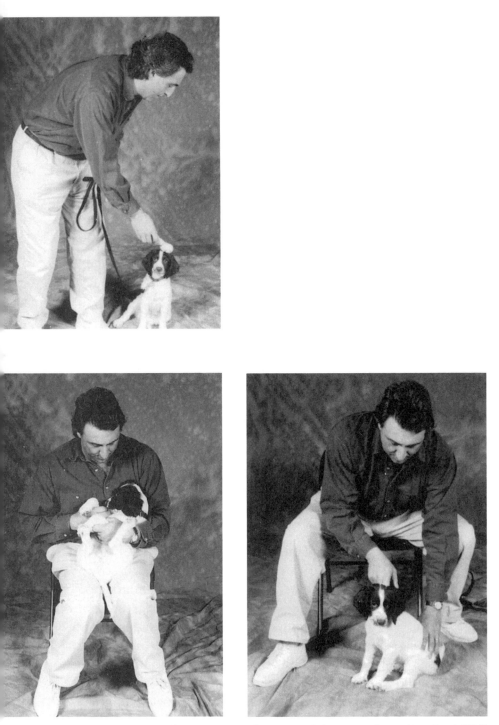

Puppies can start to learn a variety of important behaviors in Puppy Preschool. Walking on a leash, accepting gentle handling, and sitting on command are just three of the many things you can teach.

giving the command and, if the dog does not respond, giving a correction.

During Puppy Preschool I don't test or correct. I simply make the puppy carry out the behavior by gently compelling him to sit or lie down and letting him hear the command. My goal through this period is to show the puppy what I want him to do when he hears the words "sit" and "down." There's plenty of time down the road for testing.

Learning to sit and stay during Puppy Preschool will give your youngster an advantage in obedience school when teaching him to greet people without jumping up on them. Sit-Stay will prevent your pup from shooting out open doorways or over your lap when getting out of the car. It's also a great control mechanism. My Australian shepherd, Drifter, was bred to herd sheep and cattle. Unfortunately for Drifter, my lifestyle did not give him many opportunities to herd livestock. Instead, Drifter thought of people on bicycles as "city sheep." He loved to chase them, biting at their tires and herding them! Because Drifter understood Sit-Stay, I could control him. When we took a walk and I saw someone pedaling a bike down the road, I commanded Drifter to "Sit" and "Stay." It was impossible for him to sit and stay and chase bicycles at the same time.

Staying in a down position is another great control mechanism. Your pup can have a greatly enhanced life if he knows this exercise. Drifter would lie down and stay during dinner parties, baseball games, visits to friends' homes, shopping trips, and a great many other activities. He was part of almost everything I did because he knew to lie down and stay. If my dog could know only one control exercise, it would be Down-Stay. I introduced it early in his life without needing to use harsh corrections or long practice sessions. It's an easy but important part of the Puppy Preschool program.

• In my books, videos, and training classes I put a big emphasis on teaching dogs to come on command reliably. Eight weeks old is not too young for this! Coming on command is one of the most fun exercises we teach in Puppy Preschool. An effective training technique is essential for success, however. Equally important is having an understanding of the many aspects of coming reliably so that owners don't confuse or discourage their puppies. Any dog can be trained to come reliably if owners start early with a good program.

• Last but not least is a crucial aspect of Puppy Preschool: socialization. Puppies who meet people and children, go places on the leash and in the car and experience new sights and sounds grow up to be confident and well-adjusted adult dogs.

In just a week or two, these pups will leave their mother's care and move into their new homes. That's how early Puppy Preschool should start.

*   *   *

It's hard to believe that you can be doing so much with that wiggly ball of puppy fur. Your time will be well spent, however. With luck, you will live with, love, and enjoy your dog for the next ten to sixteen years. Good habits formed now will last a lifetime. Even though your puppy will not be a full adult until he is two years old, now is the time to start shaping behavior. Puppyhood is not an easy time, but it can be a lot of fun. Enjoy it! It goes by quickly, and before you know it, your puppy will be your longtime best friend with a graying muzzle.

Three

A Philosophy for Training

Puppies learn by consistently repeating behaviors. If the behavior they are doing is agreeable to them *as they are doing it,* they will repeat this behavior in the future. If the behavior they are doing is disagreeable *as they are doing it,* puppies will develop an avoidance to this behavior. After repeating this behavior x number of times, puppies will develop a habit, or a conditioned response. A conditioned response is a consistent reaction that a subject has in relation to a specific signal or signals.

Humans react with conditioned responses every day. For example, you may be reading a book and the telephone rings. The sound of the bell is your signal. Your conditioned response is to pick up the telephone and say hello. You may be driving your car down the road when a traffic light turns red. The red light is your signal. Your conditioned response is to stop your car. You also have conditioned avoidances, such as keeping your hands away from a hot oven. After one or more occasions of burnt fingers, you learn to keep your hands away.

An obedience-trained adult dog has conditioned responses to many specific signals. For example, the sound "Sit" is a signal. The trained dog's conditioned response is to put his rear end on the floor. When given the "Stay" command, the trained dog has a conditioned avoidance to movement. That's because whenever he did move in the past, he received a tough *"Nhaa!"* (you learn about the growl in Chapter 19) from the handler. Before long the dog learned to avoid movement during a stay.

You may observe conditioned responses in your dog that you did not intentionally develop. For example, every afternoon you pick up your dog's Frisbee and take him outside for a game. Soon you will see that as you pick up the Frisbee, your dog runs to the door anticipating a game. Picking up the Frisbee has become your dog's signal. Running to the door is now his conditioned response. Your puppy may also develop conditioned avoidances on his own. If he put his nose on the hot oven door and burned himself, you would see that after one or several experiences he would avoid the oven door.

So what does it take to form a conditioned response in a puppy? One important criterion is to consistently repeat the behavior. Puppies rarely develop a conditioned response without many repetitions. But how many repetitions will it take? There are quite a few factors that will influence this number. One important factor is how agreeable or disagreeable the experience was. Another factor would be how closely aligned to the puppy's selectively bred instincts the behavior was. A playful puppy with a strong retrieving instinct and chase reflex will pick up on the routine of that backyard Frisbee game very quickly.

Other factors influencing the process of developing a conditioned response include individual intelligence of the puppy, physical and mental health of the puppy, and the puppy's physical stoicism. All puppies learn different things at different rates of speed. Also keep in mind that one or two successful repetitions of a behavior does not mean that the puppy has a conditioned response. Most habits take weeks or even months to develop. You are setting yourself up for disappointment if you think your puppy has a reliable behavior when he does something two or three times. Help yourself and your puppy by giving good habits time to develop. Training will be a much more positive experience for both of you.

Timing

Probably the most important factor that will help your puppy to learn rapidly (or for that matter to learn anything at all) is timing. What I mean by timing is this: Let's say that your puppy put his nose on the hot oven door. A few minutes later he walked into the dining room, looked at the table, and then felt the burning sensation. He would associate the burning sensation with the table. He would never in a million years associate the disagreeable experience of his burnt nose with the oven door because of the lapse in time.

The same concern for timing holds true when teaching your puppy the rules around your house, such as not to chew the rug. For example, you walk into the living room five minutes after the puppy has finished chewing the rug. You find him sleeping in the corner and drag him over to the rug. You point to the rug and scold him. Your correction is too late! Your pup will never figure out that the disagreeable experience he is having *now* has anything to do with what he did five minutes before.

Anything more than ten seconds after your puppy does a behavior is too late to correct him. He will no longer understand that your correction is related to his previous deed. Of course, even if you come into the room many hours later screaming and yelling about the chewed rug, your puppy is going to cower and act apprehensive. Do not misinterpret apprehension for "guilt." To help your puppy learn rapidly and efficiently it's up to *you* to develop good timing.

So what is good timing? Good timing is correcting or praising your puppy as he is *thinking* about doing a behavior. That's the best way to associate your correction or praise with the behavior you are trying to influence. You do not have to be an experienced dog trainer to know what your puppy is thinking! Puppies are open, honest creatures. Everything they are about to do is written all over their faces.

The ability to anticipate a puppy's next move is called "reading the dog." It's not as hard as it may sound. The more time you spend with your puppy, the better you'll become at "reading" him. Imagine this scenario: You just fixed yourself a sandwich and put it on the coffee table. Your puppy looks at the sandwich and takes a few steps toward the table. *Now* is the time to growl *"Nhaa!"* Chances are good that the puppy was thinking about taking the sandwich. Well-timed corrections will make learning quick and easy.

The next best time to correct your puppy is just as he is doing the unwanted behavior. Using our example, this means a tough *"Nhaa!"* just as the puppy's mouth is reaching for the sandwich. The worst time to correct is after the behavior has been done. Yelling at the puppy when you discover a missing sandwich will not teach him to avoid stealing sandwiches.

Canine Thinking

Puppies have active brains and the ability to think about their actions. Their ability to think never ceases to amaze me. I have witnessed many, many examples of canine behavior that have convinced me that dogs think and reason. I don't believe they have the same mental skills as humans, but I know that something is going on inside their heads. Dogs also have occasionally displayed behavior that has proven to me that they not only think but can plot out simple strategies. Some dogs also act as though they have a sense of humor. Consider these two stories:

Byron was a one-eyed black Labrador retriever. Even at age ten he loved squeaky toys, natural bones, tennis balls, and the like. He was one of the most playful old dogs I've ever known. He was also my shadow. When I worked in my office, Byron slept on the small sofa next to my desk. If I went downstairs, Byron followed me. At night he stayed up and watched TV with me. (Barbara says that was only because I'm a midnight snacker and Byron was hoping for a few late-night handouts!) Whatever the reason, where I was, Byron was. We adored each other.

Also, a day did not pass without the two of us engaging in several heavy-duty "love fests." First thing in the morning I would wake up to a giant Lab tongue, which felt like a wet ham slice, slurping my face. Byron pinned me down and kissed me until I almost couldn't breathe. Several times throughout the day I would hug Byron and kiss the daylights out of him. And several times a day he would return the favor. Nothing in particular set us off. We would just look at each other and decide it was time to kiss.

About once or twice a week Byron would come over and start licking me all over the face as he normally did. But then, as fast as lightning, he would snatch my baseball cap off my head and run away. I'd yell, "Give me my hat, you fresh dog!" and chase after him. His tail wagged ninety miles an hour as he ran. He thought this was great fun. When I'd finally catch him, I'd pry my hat from his mouth and playfully hit him on the shoulder with the hat as I'd say, "You're so fresh. You're the freshest dog I know!" Byron loved it. His entire body wagged, and he had a smile on his face and laughter in his big brown eye. No scientist in a white laboratory coat is ever going to convince me that dogs can't think and that they do not reason in some way.

One of my other dogs has convinced me of this many times over. My Australian shepherd, Drifter, was the world's greatest food thief. He trained Barbara and me *never* to leave food unattended when he was around. Drifter

This is Drifter as a puppy, destined to become the world's greatest food thief!

was not my shadow like Byron was, but he did hang out in my office quite often while I worked.

Drifter knew that I kept doggie biscuits in the briefcase that I carry to dog training lessons. On more than one occasion over the years, Drifter raided my briefcase and stole all of the biscuits inside. As a result, I was careful to keep the bag out of his reach when I was not around. (He wouldn't dare go in it when I was looking at him.)

One morning I was working on my computer and the briefcase was on my desk. The dogs were hanging out sleeping in my office while I worked. Around noontime I decided that I would take a break for lunch and then run to the post office to pick up the mail. We all came downstairs, and after I finished eating, I told Barbara that I would be right back, put my jacket on, and left the house. As I walked out the door, Drifter lifted his head from the floor, looked at me, then went back to sleep. When I got back from the post office, Barbara had a story for me.

It seems that as soon as my car door slammed and I started to pull out of the driveway, Barbara caught a gray blur out of the corner of her eye. She saw Drifter run upstairs. She quietly tiptoed up the stairs and looked for him. She found Drifter in my office with his front feet on my desk and his head buried in my briefcase, munching on biscuits. She said that he almost jumped out of his Aussie skin when she growled *"Nhaa!"* in a stern tone, catching him in the act.

Now don't get me wrong. I'm not saying that while I was working in my office Drifter was premeditating this briefcase raid. He did, however, take advantage of a great opportunity. When he saw me leave, he remembered that the briefcase was unsupervised and that this was his big chance. Certainly this requires thinking and the ability to reason—at least to a limited degree. If he could reason to a *greater* degree, he would have made sure Barbara was not around!

All dogs are great opportunists. That's important to remember when you try to teach your puppy the rules around the house. Your puppy is incapable of thinking, "I better not chew this rug now because in two hours Dad will be home and I will be corrected." A puppy will only learn to avoid doing a behavior if you correct him when he is thinking about doing the behavior or is in the process of doing it.

Puppies have great memories. A disagreeable experience in the past will have an influence on the puppy's behavior in the future. He can remember yesterday when he placed his nose on the hot oven door that it was disagreeable. Eventually he will learn to avoid doing it again.

A dog also may continue with a behavior that appears to us to have a disagreeable result. It is important to analyze the behavior closely and see what motivates the dog's actions. For example, a dog may continue to chase porcupines even after repeatedly being quilled in the nose. The dog's apparent pain may make us wonder why he does not learn to avoid this behavior. If the hunt-chase-pounce behavior is more agreeable to the dog than the quills in the nose are *dis*agreeable, he will continue to chase porcupines. Dogs will always choose what is most agreeable—from their canine point of view.

Canines have no "moral code" of right and wrong like humans do. Humans know that it is wrong to kill, steal, and lie. We know that it is right to help a friend, care for the sick, pay off a loan. Dogs don't know that it is "wrong" to urinate on your Oriental rug or to eat the cat's food. They don't know that it is "right" to sit on command and to come when called. All they know is that if something tastes good, smells good, or feels good *as they are doing it,* then it's okay to do again. If something tastes bad, smells bad, or feels bad *as they are doing it,* then it's something to avoid. This is the canine "moral code" of behavior. The only way for you to shape your puppy's behavior (i.e., train him) is to make a behavior agreeable (praise him) or disagreeable (correct him) *as he is doing the behavior.*

Practice Makes Almost-Perfect

As we have shown, canine learning is based largely on repetition. After a behavior is repeated enough times, puppies will develop habits, or conditioned responses. Assuming that those habits are positive ones—such as eliminating outside, coming when called, lying down, and staying when told—you will have what you want: a trained dog. That's because canines are creatures of habit. Once you set up a routine of various signals and conditioned responses (sit, down, stay, etc.), the puppy will do exactly what you tell him every time. Right? Wrong.

No conditioned response is infallible. Creatures with advanced brains can think. They can defy conditioning. They also can make mistakes. Think about two of your own conditioned responses. You have a habit of answering the telephone when it rings, but one day you decide not to take any calls. The telephone rings but you keep reading your book. You know what you usually do, but today you decide not to do it. You also have a habit of stopping your car at a red light. But one day you are tired or distracted and you roll through an intersection. Even the most experienced drivers sometimes make mistakes.

There will be times when even the best-trained dog will either defy conditioning or make a mistake. Handlers therefore must avoid becoming complacent or overconfident of learned behaviors. Do not rely on conditioned responses in potentially dangerous situations. For example, I would never unclip even the best-trained dog near a busy road. One mistake could result in injury or death to my dog.

Owners have to reinforce their dog's conditioned responses. Certainly the more practice and proofing you do with your puppy, the more reliable his response will be. Skilled human beings, from tennis pros to typists, need practice to stay in top form. That is because all learned skills need reinforcement.

When you feel you have achieved a well-trained adult dog, practice obedience exercises once in a while. It can be fun for both you and the dog. Plus it reinforces the good behaviors you worked so hard to achieve. When you need to call on those skills in real situations, such as calling your dog to you during a hike, you will be more confident that your dog will comply.

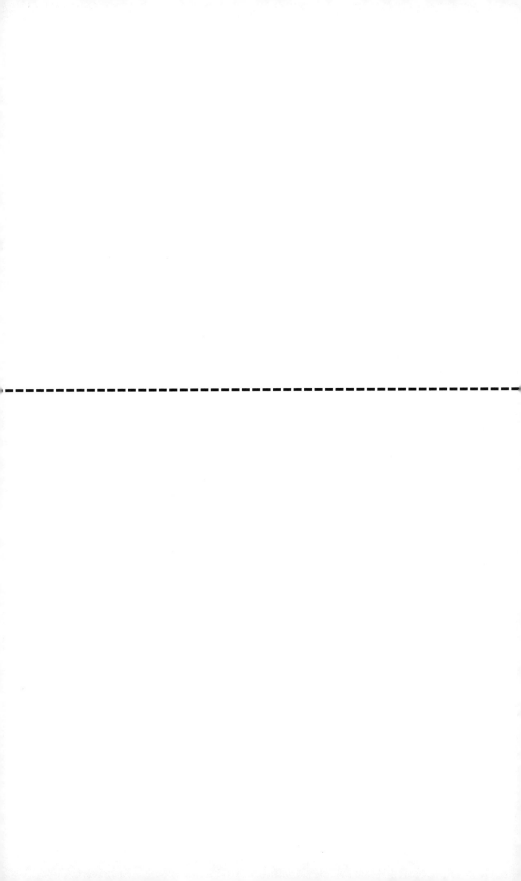

Part Two

Choosing the Right Puppy

----

*H*ave you selected your puppy yet? If not, the chapters in this section will help you find the puppy of your dreams. If you do have a puppy, the information in this section will enlighten you about puppy temperament and breed personalities. If you are ready to begin handling and training your puppy, skip ahead to the next section to get started. You can always come back to this material later—or use it when you are ready to buy another dog.

Four

Finding Puppies

Puppies are available from many sources. Some sources are better than others, but there is not just one "best" place to get a puppy. Good, healthy puppies can be found in a great many settings, from the kennels of experienced breeders to dog pounds. Unless someone chooses a puppy for you and gives it to you as a gift (always a risky thing to do), you will be the one determining where your puppy comes from.

Your own standards, values, and sensibilities will have a lot to do with that decision. For example, some people believe that because there are many thousands of unwanted dogs put to death every year, intentional dog breeding is practically a crime. Those people will only adopt a pet from an animal shelter. Others will settle for nothing less than a descendant of a breed show champion, available through a professional breeder. Still others like the idea of taking a puppy from a litter born to a neighbor's pet.

It troubles me when people act against their better judgment and actually help support—by way of the puppy's purchase price—something they don't really believe in. Your dollars speak loud and clear in the pet industry. For example, if you have strong feelings for adopting pets from animal shelters, do so! If you dislike pet stores that sell animals, stay out of them. Granted, you pick a puppy with your heart, but you drive the pet industry with your wallet. Think about what is important to you, then act and spend accordingly.

Professional Breeders

I mention this category first because professional breeders make up an enormous part of the puppy-supply business. Professional breeders typically are people who love dogs and who are devoted to one or more particular breeds. They generally are quite knowledgeable about the breed's origins, health problems, special grooming or medical requirements, and ongoing lines of well-known champions. In fact, winning championships in dog shows is an important goal for most professional breeders. In these shows, dogs are exhibited to show their perfect (or almost perfect) conformation to a breed standard. By striving for this perfection, breeders help maintain the breed within established standards for height, weight, color, and other features. No other group takes breed maintenance (and improvement) quite as seriously as professional breeders do.

There are both advantages and disadvantages to buying a puppy from a professional breeder. As discussed earlier, a purebred puppy comes with an important trait: predictability. You have a very good idea of how your

Good professional breeders have high standards of care for their dogs and puppies. Clean bedding, fresh water, and careful monitoring are just a few of the many signs indicating responsible breeding.

eight-week-old ball of fur is going to grow up. Size and—to a certain extent—personality can be predicted with a high rate of confidence. Is that good? If you don't like surprises it is. Plus, when people choose to spend hundreds of dollars for something, they want to be relatively sure of what they are buying. A purebred pet offers this reliability.

Why a professional breeder? Experience and the frequent availability of puppies are two things that a professional breeder can usually offer. Plus:

- Written guarantees (sometimes) against genetic defects or serious health problems.
- Help (hopefully) with making the puppy happy in its new home.
- High standards (ideally) when making breeding decisions between two dogs.
- Good health care (but not always) for the mother and newborn pups.

Is my pessimism showing? That's because I don't want you to think that just because they make lots of dogs reproduce that professional breeders are necessarily the ideal choice. I've heard stories of breeders mating epileptic dogs, forcing too many litters on exhausted female dogs, and making their dogs live in deplorable conditions.

Those, of course, are worst-case scenarios. Some professional breeders have impeccable standards. They screen potential puppy owners to make sure they have a safe backyard, a schedule that allows for attentive care, a household that is safe and desirable for a puppy, and a willingness to spay or neuter the pet if requested. Our two Labrador retrievers came from such a breeder. She was serious about having every one of her puppies spend their lives in safe, loving homes. I admire that.

In general, good professional breeders are probably the most reliable source for healthy, sound purebred puppies. The guarantees that some breeders offer, such as a replacement puppy if the first puppy becomes very sick or dies, can provide you with a bit of comfort when writing a check for several hundred (or several thousand) dollars to meet the purchase price.

There are some downsides to working with a professional breeder. Price is one of them. A good breeder's efforts cost money. You are paying not only for the actual medical expenses of breeding and delivering a litter but also for expertise that the breeder puts into his or her efforts. Is it worth it? That's your judgment.

Puppies from breeders typically can't be picked up the day you decide you want a dog. Often a breeder will require a deposit to hold a puppy from an upcoming litter. Then you wait until the puppies are born, wait to know if there are enough healthy puppies to go to all the people who have placed deposits, and then wait until the pups are seven or eight weeks old and can go to their new homes. Sometimes breeders have more puppies than they have deposits for. In that case, if your timing is right, you may be able to get a puppy much sooner. Also, breeders know other breeders. You may be able to get a referral to someone who has puppies available—but not always. Don't expect immediate results.

Some rare or uncommon breeds are virtually unavailable except through breeders. Seeking out one of these breeds may be a bit frustrating if you have your heart set on a particular type of dog.

A final downside to getting a puppy from a professional breeder has nothing to do with the quality of the dogs themselves. It has to do with supporting an activity that contributes to dog overpopulation. Imagine you are a terrier breeder. You love your particular breed and have dedicated years to creating beautiful terrier specimens. Many of your "creations" have become champions in the show ring, and several have won major prizes, such as Best Terrier. As a result, your puppies are sought after and command a high price. Income from puppy sales helps you to afford the expenses of competing in the shows.

In your quest to create great dogs (and win prizes), you breed several litters a year, producing between fifteen and twenty puppies a year. One or two puppies you keep, a few go to people also involved in breeding and showing, and the rest go to pet homes. Let's see, you've been at this almost twenty years. That's at least three hundred dogs you've created!

Part of me finds it hard to justify one person generating hundreds of dogs to achieve a few show champions. I'm not sure if there's a realistic solution, other than encouraging breeders to use discretion and common sense in how many litters they produce. But more litters mean more income (usually) and more chances to create a show winner. I'm convinced that many breeders' egos get tied up in their dogs and that the dozens of pet-quality "castoffs" are not a serious concern to them. They are to me. If every animal shelter and dog pound were empty, I'd have no problem with abundant dog breeding. But the shelters are not empty, and my conscience bothers me when I think about the overpopulation problem to which breeders contribute.

Backyard Breeders

I use this term to mean amateur breeders and one-time breeders. What's the difference between an amateur and a professional? Sometimes not much. Professionals were once amateurs who accumulated a lot of experience. However, amateur breeders typically are not involved in dog shows and don't produce more than a few litters in their lifetime. They may consciously dabble in dog breeding, trying the hobby on for size, or they may think they have a great pet and want a few offspring from him or her. Unfortunately, an all-too-common scenario is the family whose pet was accidentally impregnated, and there they are with a litter of puppies. That's *not* an example of backyard breeding; it's an example of irresponsible dog ownership.

A lot of people have strong feelings against backyard breeders, typically based (again) on the dog overpopulation problem. My feelings are not so clear-cut, although there are lots of negatives. One of the biggest potential negatives is puppy quality. Good professional breeders spend time and energy evaluating the dogs they are considering mating. They trace the ancestry of each dog, determining whether there are any genetic-based

Breeders who integrate puppies into their own households help make each puppy's transition to its new home a lot easier. Does your breeder do this?

problems. They have both parents examined by veterinarians for breed-related problems, such as eye and bone disorders. And they typically have homes waiting for most or all of the puppies—even before they are born.

Does the typical amateur breeder do all of this? No. Should they? Of course. Assuring puppies' physical soundness is the bottom line with any responsible breeding. That's why backyard breeders don't have a great reputation. Often they haphazardly mate dogs, often with disastrous results.

I remember one student of mine with a golden retriever pup. Someone in his town bred their golden retriever to a neighbor's golden retriever. A litter of cute puppies was born, and my student bought one. As this puppy grew, it developed crippling hip dysplasia at just six months of age. My student and his family were devastated to see their wonderful young pet in pain. Countless dollars were spent on veterinary examinations, tests, and evaluations. The dog made it to adulthood, but it lives with a serious medical condition. Had the breeder X-rayed the hips of both parents and had a veterinarian evaluate the results *before* the breeding took place, the breeding probably never would have happened. It certainly *shouldn't* have.

The amazing thing about backyard breeders is that they often get the "going rate" for their puppies. If professional breeders charge four hundred dollars for a particular breed, that's what amateur breeders often charge. The uninformed public makes this possible, essentially encouraging backyard breeders to go into business.

A big mistake that amateur breeders make is thinking that breeding dogs is cheap. It *can* be cheap if you ignore veterinary evaluations before breeding, don't bother to research the genetic history of the parents, give minimal medical care to the mother, and don't bother with veterinary checkups and vaccinations for the new pups. That's another reason why amateur breeders, as a group, do not have a good reputation.

Can amateur breeders breed responsibly? Of course. One of the nice things about getting a puppy from a responsible amateur breeder is that the mother dog and her pups probably had a lot of attentive care. The arrival of the litter was an important event for the family. It wasn't complicated by a dozen other dogs coming and going on the dog-show circuit. The puppies probably were born right in the house (instead of a separate birthing area or kennel run), and they spent their first two months of life with the mother dog's human family. They heard the sounds of a typical household, from doorbells to telephones to vacuum cleaners. The transition to your home will be a lot easier because of this. (In all fairness, I know some professional breeders who turn their entire home—

from kitchen to bedrooms—into "puppy central" when a litter arrives!)

In addition, amateur breeders may produce one litter every few years or just a single litter in their entire lifetime. In one sense they are contributing much less to canine overpopulation. However, there are many *thousands* of pet owners who end up breeding their dogs. And most of those breedings were probably not carried out responsibly. I'd love to know which group produces more dogs in a year—professional breeders or the amateurs. Between the two groups, an overwhelming number of puppies are being born every year.

Keep in mind that backyard breeders don't always breed purebred dogs. I don't necessarily think that's a bad thing. If the only dogs in the world were professionally bred, kennel-club recognized breeds, the dog world would be a less interesting place. Mutts are just as great as their purebred cousins. I've met some sweet, healthy mixed-breed dogs who wouldn't exist if it weren't for amateur breeding.

A final thought about amateur breeding that may apply to you when your puppy grows up and you are considering breeding your own dog. I've observed that many pet owners fall into a common trap when considering breeding their own dog. I call it the "My Dog Is the Greatest" syndrome. Of course you love your pet. And to many people that love means they must breed the animal and have some offspring. These are emotional feelings that should not outweigh a fair, honest assessment about creating yet another litter of puppies. Has a veterinarian confirmed that your pet is one hundred percent physically sound? Were both his parents and all four grandparents physically sound? Is his temperament sweet, willing-to-please, and friendly toward people and other dogs? Here's a good test: Would a professional breeder choose your pet for breeding purposes? Chances are good that the answer is no. If you love your dog so much, give him a great life. Fill his days with exercise, healthy food, regular grooming, and companionship. Adopt a second dog if you think he would like canine company. But don't breed him.

Pounds and Shelters

Puppies who are adopted from dog pounds and animal shelters (full orchestra, please) "are the luckiest puppies in the world!" A puppy's chance for survival is quite low when it is born in or brought to one of these settings. Granted, puppies are easier for shelter workers to place than un-wanted adult dogs, but even so, survival rates are not high for homeless pups.

For this reason, adopting a puppy from a pound or a shelter truly saves a life. If you don't take a particular puppy home, there's a good chance no one will—and the puppy will be put to sleep. Many dog owners have strong feelings about always adopting a dog from a pound or shelter, and it is really a wonderful, selfless approach to dog ownership.

There are a few downsides to getting puppies from shelters. Health is often an issue. Unwanted puppies usually are born to unwanted mother dogs who had little or no medical care. The father most probably was a wandering street dog of unknown status. Nonprofit shelters and city-run pounds rarely have adequate funds to provide top-notch medical attention to every animal brought to them. As a result, there is a greater chance for medical or genetic-based problems, only because the puppy's history (and parents' history) is so unknown. On the other hand, puppies who survive the trials of homelessness are sometimes real fighters and may possess a lot of vitality.

As mentioned in the section above on professional breeders, purebred dogs offer predictability. Puppies from pounds can be most *un*predictable! Those thick legs and big puppy feet may indicate the potential for a big adult dog—or maybe just a bassett hound in the puppy's ancestry. A mother dog who looks like a collie may in fact possess some retriever blood, and when crossed with a poodle produce puppies who look like long-haired, curly-coated Labs! You get the idea. However, only once or twice in my dog career have I met a dog whom I had absolutely no idea what breeds were combined to produce it. Not one single trait was distinctive. Usually you can get some idea but often not until the dog is an adult.

Another drawback to shelter adoptions has to do with temperament. While professional breeders sometimes do not choose breedings based on wonderful temperament, this is *never* a consideration with the random breedings that produce unwanted litters. For example, nasty mother and father dogs rarely produce sweet-natured puppies who will make loving pets. Did your puppy's parents have a good temperament? Who knows. If not, you can still turn out a well-behaved, nice pet, although you will have a tougher time than if your pup has a gentle, willing-to-please personality.

Breed Rescue Organizations

These organizations are made up of people devoted to a particular breed who try to place unwanted dogs of that breed. They often are breeders (amateur or professional) who believe that breeding new puppies is only acceptable if the homeless adolescents and adults also are placed. Those who are involved with breed rescue typically take unwanted dogs into their homes (or find foster homes) to provide the animals with a temporary place to live. The dog's health and temperament are evaluated, and if sound, the dog is made available for adoption.

The nice thing about breed rescue is that people who are truly dedicated to a breed are handling the homeless animals. The knowledge and experience they bring to the task can make a big difference in finding the right home for each dog. Their experience also helps them decide when a dog cannot be saved, either because of health problems, the harmful effects of abuse, or an aggressive temperament.

While many of the dogs that come to a breed rescue organization are adolescents or adults, puppies do come along, often when an unwanted mother dog gives birth. Sometimes the breed rescue organization knows

Professional breeders usually can put you in touch with a breed rescue organization if you like the idea of taking in an unwanted purebred dog.

that the mother and pups are purebred (because they know who gave up the dog and where the person got the dog). Sometimes they must take an educated guess that the dog is a purebred. Usually breeders of purebred dogs are involved with these rescue organizations—or can put you in touch with one.

Breed rescue organizations offer an option that is a cross between getting a puppy from an animal shelter and buying a purebred from a breeder. They are a nice alternative if you are looking for a dog of a particular breed. Keep in mind, however, that someone gave up the dog for some reason. Did the dog have a problem? Or did the owner have a problem? Often the rescue organization can answer these two important questions. And again, good rescue organizations make a sincere effort to place the right dog in the right home. For example, a shy puppy terrorized by children might go to a quiet household of retirees where he can make a fresh start. An energetic adolescent dog might do great in an active household with noisy children and teenagers. So don't be offended if the rescue group asks you details about your home and lifestyle. They are trying to give a dog a second—and perhaps last—chance for success as someone's beloved pet.

Pet Stores

When clients call me about training their puppies, I always ask them, "Where did you get your puppy?" The most common answers are a breeder, an animal welfare organization, or a pet store. I then ask how the pup is doing: "Is he healthy? Does he seem outgoing and friendly? How is housebreaking coming along?"

These three questions are my immediate concern with all puppies. However, with pet store puppies my concern is pronounced. That's because I talk to a lot of owners who have sick puppies purchased from pet stores. This observation is confirmed by the many veterinarians I talk to. They tell me that illness is prevalent in pet store puppies, partly because puppies show up at the store from so many different sources. It's like the first day of school on the bus, where the kids bring in germs from many different households. Before long, everyone has a cold.

Unfortunately for puppies, the bacteria and viruses spread in a pet store environment are not always as benign as the simple cold a child might get on the school bus. Some canine diseases, such as parvovirus and distemper, can be fatal. Others, such as digestive or respiratory infections, can cause severe sickness and make the puppy very weak. I'm not saying that puppies who come from good breeders are immune to disease. However, there is a greater risk that you will get a sick puppy if you purchase it from a pet store (or any other setting where lots of different dogs are crowded together).

Veterinarians also have a more difficult time diagnosing problems in pet store puppies. That's because the vet cannot question the breeder about disease exposures or other early problems the puppy (or its mother) may have had. As a result, veterinarians often have to run extra diagnostic tests. These tests can run up the cost of health care, and you may start the puppy-owning experience with a whopping veterinary bill.

My question about a puppy's friendliness and outgoing behavior is also a big concern with pet store puppies. That's because these puppies, in many cases, are not properly socialized. Ideally, puppies should go directly from their mother and littermate brothers and sisters into their new homes. Unfortunately, pet store puppies spend these important days or weeks sitting in a cage behind a glass window. Granted, people do come into the store, and many of them ask to hold the puppies, but this does not compensate for the love and experience an eight-week-old pup should be getting from a family. In fact, good dog breeders begin socializing their pups at three or four weeks old. You can count on it that puppies bred in a mass-production setting, such as the so-called puppy mills, do not receive this attention.

Finally, housebreaking is often a complicated issue when dealing with pet store puppies. The whole philosophy behind crate training is the fact that canines avoid soiling their living and sleeping quarters, or den. Even pups as young as eight weeks old can "hold it" during the daytime for up to four hours and at night for eight hours—if the only alternative is soiling their den area. In contrast, pet store puppies are forced to live in a cage twenty-four hours a day until they are sold. Living like this for four to six weeks is not uncommon. The puppies have no choice but to soil their cage. Although the cages are designed for excrement to fall into a compart- ment below, the puppies become accustomed to soiling their dens. The sad result is that I've met many pet store puppies who were impossible to housebreak.

Even if your pet store puppy does not come home sick, many owners have had their hearts broken a year or two down the line. Hereditary prob- lems such as hip dysplasia and retinal atrophy—to name just two—are prevalent. Responsible dog breeders are careful not to breed dogs with *any* known hereditary health problems.

People who have purchased pet store puppies sometimes defend their choice by telling me that the pet store originally got their puppy from a breeder. This may or may not be true. Even if it is true, the breeder was not a quality breeder. I've met many excellent, responsible dog breeders over the past twenty-five years. Not one of them would ever sell a puppy to a pet store. That's because it's not easy to purchase a puppy from a qualified breeder. Qualified breeders screen their prospective clients extremely well. If you do not fit the criteria of a caring, responsible dog owner, you will not get a pup from a good breeder. On the other hand, a pet store will sell a puppy to anyone who has the amount of money that the store is asking.

Bear in mind that "expensive" does not mean "quality." Although pet store puppies are almost always inferior to selectively bred dogs, pet stores charge just as much as many breeders do. It's a psychological ploy. Think about it. Imagine the average person who calls three reputable breeders. Each breeder says that their puppies sell for six hundred dollars. Then this person goes to the pet store and sees a puppy of the same breed for two hundred dollars. Their first reaction would be, "There must be something wrong with it." To prevent this dilemma, pet stores ask top dollar so that customers feel they are getting something valuable.

Another myth is that A.K.C. registration stands for quality. The American Kennel Club will accept its fee and register any purebred dog. It does not matter if the puppy was selectively bred by a top-notch dog breeder or if it came from some puppy mill where it was mass-produced. The A.K.C. is a registration service only, not a quality-control organization.

Despite the many negatives of buying a puppy from a pet store, many of them turn into great dogs despite poor breeding and a lousy initial environment. Which only proves how resilient and intelligent our canine friends are. But if I get the chance to counsel people *before* they buy a purebred puppy, I urge them to get a well-bred, properly socialized pup from a reputable breeder. Why not give yourself the best chance possible to enjoy one of life's greatest gifts—the love and companionship of a sound, healthy dog.

Five

Evaluating a Puppy

Your first difficult decision as a dog owner will be which of the cute wiggly puppies you should choose from a litter. A tough choice. If you are lucky, you will not be faced with this decision. Many qualified dog breeders make it for you. From years of experience they know which puppy, based on your family makeup and lifestyle, would be best for you.

If the breeder leaves the decision in your hands, or if you are adopting a pup from a pound or other setting where there is little professional guidance, you will have to select the puppy on your own. Here are some helpful suggestions for choosing the right dog for you.

I have found that puppies who are "middle of the road" in personality and temperament are the easiest to train. Avoid the puppies on the far ends of the social scale. In other words, don't choose the most outgoing puppy or the most reclusive puppy. The most outgoing may be the pup that is always into everything—headfirst! This pup will keep you on your toes twenty-four hours a day.

Reclusive or shy pups lack confidence. They may grow up to be dogs who are afraid of their own shadow. The worst scenario with a shy dog is the "fear biter," a dog who bites out of fear. While it is true that by doing the right things with a shy puppy you can avoid letting him develop into a fear biter, this type of dog is a lot of work. Why go through this challenge if you can avoid it?

I suggest that you choose the puppy who is interested in you without being a complete extrovert. How can you tell? First, evaluate the puppies' reactions when you enter the room. Are any of them shocked or startled by a stranger? Do any of them jump all over you the minute you arrive? Sit on the floor with the litter. A middle-of-the-road puppy will sniff you and check you out. After a short while he may climb into your lap.

When the puppy you are considering climbs into your lap, you can test his dominance level. Gently roll him belly up with his head against your chest. If he growls and fights violently, he is a dominant pup. Growl *"Nhaa!"* and gently restrain him. If he continues to resist, he is a puppy who has tendencies to lead. He will challenge you at every turn. Only experienced dog trainers will ever succeed with this guy.

If the puppy settles down rather quickly, he is an assertive individual who *is* willing to submit. You will have your work cut out for you, but with good handling and consistency this puppy can be trained. However, he may still be more work than you bargained for.

Another puppy may not growl but will mildly struggle and then stop wiggling and lick you as soon as you say *"Nhaa!"* This puppy will be much easier to train than the two types described above. If the puppy does not

Focus your attention on each individual. You'll see the rough-and-tumble behavior that puppies use to test one another.

struggle at all and just licks you, he is a submissive puppy. He will be easy to train. However, you will have to be careful never to be overcorrective with this gentle soul.

When you have assessed a few of the puppies' personalities, think about your household. Is there a lot of activity and noise from kids and their friends? A puppy who is somewhat outgoing may fit right in. Are you an

Everyone's busy eating except the puppy in the doorway. You can be sure he has an independent, outgoing personality.

Signs of dominance emerge early in puppyhood. Biting and standing over a littermate both communicate "I'm tough!" Such a puppy may or may not be right for you.

older person or the parent of a small child? A submissive, easy-to-train individual would be right for you. It's much more common to get a bad match between puppy and owner than to actually get a "bad dog." By putting some thought and common sense into your puppy selection, you have a much better chance of a long-term happy relationship with your new pet.

Sound Shyness

It's always a good idea to test puppies for sound shyness. Here's one simple way to do it. Have a friend drop a metal food pan on the floor in an adjoining room (*not* right near the puppies!). You should be sitting on the floor with the pups. Don't say anything to the puppies when the pan drops. Just watch them.

You will see one of three reactions. Some puppies will not react at all. This is good. (If you are evaluating dalmatians, make sure they are not deaf.)

Other puppies will look around and go right back to playing. There is no problem with this reaction, either. However, do be careful if you are buying this pup as a hunting dog. You should introduce him to gunfire gradually.

The third possible response is to freak out and run and hide or to shake like a leaf. This puppy will be a dog who is afraid of thunder and will be a gun-shy bird dog. The Fourth of July, with fireworks and other noise, is always a nightmare for this poor animal. A car backfiring will scare him. I recommend that you avoid this puppy. In most cases, inherent sound shyness is impossible to cure.

They All Seem the Same!

Sometimes the differences in puppies' personalities are not so dramatic that a choice is easy to make. If it's hard for you to evaluate the puppies, and the breeder or shelter workers are no help, then simply trust your intuition. Do you have a good feeling about a certain pup? Is it physically sound and emotionally stable? Can you visualize it being happy and well-adjusted with your family?

The pup's physical appearance should please you, but its personality and temperament are a lot more important. Always be sure to check out the mother and, if possible, the father dog before you select a litter or an individual pup. Puppies usually turn out just like mom and dad. If mom and dad are shy or overly exuberant, extremely aggressive or sound-shy, look for another breeder or puppy source. Problems like these you don't need.

Some dog owners have told me that "the puppy picked us!" That's okay, too, as long as you went into the selection process with a level head. If the puppy's genetic and health background checks out, if the pup's personality seems right, and if the mother and father dog are acceptable, by all means take home this little bundle. I would never deny that dogs have a sixth sense about people. If the pup picks you, enjoy your good fortune, and make every effort to be the great dog owner your new puppy believes you will be.

Part Three

Know Your Puppy

Like a good book on child development, this section will help you understand puppy development. The better you know how your puppy will grow and change, the better you will be as an owner.

Six

Puppy Development: Birth to Adulthood

As they grow up, puppies go through many developmental stages just like human children do. These developmental stages are reflected not only in the youngsters' physical appearance but also in their behavior. I've found that there are a lot of parallels between the maturity levels of puppies and children. Note that I say maturity levels and not intelligence. There are thousands of things that children learn to do that a dog will never be able to do. These include reading, writing, and speaking. But if you keep in mind that we are talking about maturity levels, you will find that the parallels between puppies and children are quite enlightening.

Child rearing takes time and effort. Some parents do a wonderful job. But regardless of the skills they possess, there is no way for parents to bypass their child's developmental stages. There is no way to get a two-year-old child to behave like a five-year-old. There is no way to get a five-year-old to behave like a twelve-year-old. And there is no way that a twelve-year-old child can have the life experiences and mature behavior of a twenty-one-year-old.

Still, good parents do not ignore their children while waiting for them to reach adulthood. These parents begin teaching their children as toddlers so that by the time they become adults, they have good habits formed.

Tiny and dependent at birth, puppies mature both physically and mentally until they reach adulthood at about two years old.

Only time and supervision on the part of the parents will turn children into mature, respectful, well-mannered adults.

This is especially true of puppies as well. The ideal time for owners to begin Puppy Preschool training is right away—when the pup is eight weeks old. Yet no type or amount of training will turn your pup into a mature, well-behaved adult dog instantly. To achieve this, time and consistent training on the part of the owner are required.

I receive phone calls on a regular basis from frustrated owners with older puppies. The usual conversation goes something like this: "I took Rover to kindergarten puppy class when he was ten weeks old. I work with him almost every day. Now he's six months old, but he still has a ton of energy. He doesn't always listen and he won't respond to commands consistently."

My answer is always the same: "Of course he has lots of energy, he's still a puppy! Responding reliably to your commands means that the dog has good habits formed. It means that when the dog hears a command he reacts with a conditioned response. Your puppy is only six months old. He has not been on earth long enough to have any strong habits or conditioned responses."

Owners *have* to live through puppyhood. There is no way to circumvent a puppy's developmental stages. Your immature young puppy won't be an adult for quite some time (until he's two years old, to be exact). So reevaluate your expectations if you think you can have a calm, perfectly behaved six-month-old dog. But don't *lower* your expectations as long as they are appropriate for the age and maturity level of your pup. The following descriptions will help you understand what to expect at each stage.

Birth to Three Weeks Old

The first stage in a puppy's life begins at birth and lasts about three weeks. During this time, all puppy behavior is instinctive. The puppies eat, sleep, and go to the bathroom. The mother dog provides for all of these needs. She nurses the puppies, providing them with nourishment with her milk.

Mother dog takes care of all her puppies' needs during the first few weeks of life.

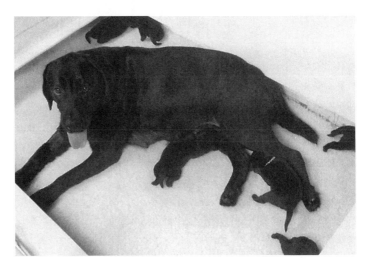

After a week or so, puppies become more active but still spend most of their time eating and sleeping.

She keeps them warm when they sleep by allowing them to snuggle up to her. She also stimulates them to eliminate by licking their rectums. Canines are incapable of learned behavior during these first three weeks of life.

About midway through this stage—somewhere between the tenth and fourteenth day—puppies open their eyes. Their sight is limited at this point, however. The same holds true for hearing. Ear canals open, but hearing is minimal.

Three Weeks to Seven Weeks Old

Around the twenty-first day, puppies start a new developmental stage. Their eyesight and hearing strengthen daily. They start to crawl around and become aware of their environment. Most significant at this stage is that puppies become capable of learning.

The period between three and seven weeks of age is a crucial learning period in a canine's life. Personality and temperament are shaped by the experiences puppies have at this time. Good breeders who expose their pups to new people as well as different sights and sounds produce more confident, outgoing individuals. During this phase breeders can also get their puppies used to being handled by gently touching the pups' feet,

These six-week-old pups have started exploring the world. They now need to play . . .

. . . but still need to eat—a lot! Mother dog still obliges.

mouths, and tails. It is imperative that puppies have gentle, positive experiences with humans during this stage.

One of the most important experiences for the puppy between the age of three and seven weeks is the interaction between the pup and his littermates and mother. Although at around four weeks puppies are capable of being weaned off their mother's milk and onto a mushy food, it is imperative that breeders allow the mother dog access to her pups until they leave for their new homes. The things that the mother dog teaches her puppies during this stage will affect training and relationships with humans throughout the dog's life.

Between the age of three weeks and seven weeks, canines learn techniques that help them to determine their position in the hierarchy of a social pack. They do this by competing for food. They may try to be first in line to nurse or first to push their way to the pan of puppy gruel provided by the breeder. They will test their vocal cords to see who growls the deepest and barks the loudest. They will try out their new puppy teeth by snapping and biting at each other. Puppies learn that when they encounter an individual who displays signs of dominance, they should submit. When they encounter submissive individuals, they can push these creatures around and dominate them. This is the give and take of pack life.

By the time these puppies are seven weeks old, a pecking order will have evolved in the litter. Experienced breeders can pretty much point out this pecking order for you. "See that big puppy with the loud bark? He was the first one to walk. He's always the first in line to eat, and he beats up all of his brothers and sisters. He is the puppy pack leader."

Fortunately for the future owner of that tough ball of fur, the puppy's mother establishes herself as the undisputed pack leader. Whenever that puppy tries his tough-guy techniques with her, she growls at him. If he ignores her growl, she grabs him in her mouth at the back of his neck and pins him. She may even snap at him, sometimes nipping him just hard enough to make him yip. The mother dog does this to intimidate her puppies. She wants to impress upon the pups that her growl means business! She wants the pups to respond immediately and stop whatever they are doing the instant she growls. Although as a carnivore she has the ability to maim or even kill a puppy in the blink of an eye, this is not her goal. She is simply teaching discipline.

I once asked a friend, who is an excellent, experienced breeder of Labrador retrievers, which sex is most often the puppy pack leader. She said that it is either the biggest male or the female with the biggest mouth! Regardless of who the puppy pack leader is, the mother dog is always the undisputed pack leader. She doles out discipline to the entire pack.

Seven Weeks to Four Months Old

Seven weeks of age is the ideal time for the puppy to leave his litter and come to live in your home. Thinking that he is the same kind of creature as you, he will view your family as his brand new pack. He will employ the same techniques that he learned in his first pack experience on his new human pack. He will do this to determine where he fits into the hierarchy of your household. This is the time for you to begin establishing yourself as your puppy's new pack leader. Success with all future obedience training depends on it!

The puppy's maturity level when joining your household at seven weeks old is comparable to that of a one-year-old human baby. Your seven-week-old puppy will be very dependent on you, much the way a one-year-old child is dependent on his parents. For example, when you take the pup

Solid food fills the bellies of these older pups, who compete for space at the food bowl.

The wide world becomes more and more fascinating to puppies as they mature.

out for a short walk in the woods, he will stay right by you. If he is a particularly bold puppy, he may stray a short distance away. By simply squatting down, clapping your hands, and making appealing sounds, you will bring even the bravest young puppy running back to you quickly. It is instinctive at this stage of their lives for puppies to stick close to pack members.

Four to Six Months: The Independence Phase

Like human children, puppies become more and more independent as they grow up. With puppies this happens very quickly. At around four months old the independence phase begins. Some behaviorists refer to this period as the flight instinct period. I call it the "terrible twos of doggiedom."

A statement I hear from puppy owners at this time is, "My puppy was so good. I used to let him out in the backyard and he never left. Now when I let him out he takes off and I find him a mile away. Why is he doing this?"

Up until four months old, it is instinctive for puppies to stick close to the den, which is your house. Then suddenly the big, scary world is not so scary. The puppy picks up a scent and off he goes. Greater supervision is *imperative* during this phase. Do not let bad and dangerous habits, such as leaving the yard, develop.

Before puppies reach four months old, they do very little destructive chewing. At four months old puppy teeth begin to fall out, and adult teeth start to come in. This is when unwanted chewing becomes more frequent. Puppies want to get into everything at this stage. You will need to watch your puppy very closely in the house. This also applies to the house training process.

I have noticed another behavior that develops at around four months old. I call it the "puppy crazies." I have heard other dog people refer to it as the "zooms." The puppy may run around in circles, over furniture, under tables, around trees, up and down the yard, etc. This may be accompanied by growling. The fur on the puppy's back may bristle up. The tail may be tucked between the legs. The puppy may shake or toss his toys. Owners seeing this behavior for the first time think their puppies are possessed! Do not despair; this is normal puppy exuberance. Unless the puppy is knocking the house down in the process of the puppy crazies, I stand back and let him do it. Actually, it's a lot of fun to watch. Your dog is having a great time. Do not try to inhibit this behavior. As puppies grow up, the occurrence of this behavior lessens.

Formal obedience training should be started at four months old. (This is after Puppy Preschool training.) Obedience training will give you control mechanisms and allow you to shape your dog's behavior. Both are necessary for you to cope effectively with the independence phase.

Six Months Old to One Year Old

I compare the maturity of six-month-old puppies to that of five- or six-year-old children. These individuals have a *lot* of energy. The more you can physically tire them out, the easier they are to live with. At this age when you growl *"Nhaa!"* you should be able to get their attention.

At six months old, puppy teeth have completely fallen out and adult teeth are in. Dogs at this stage still have a strong compulsion to chew. This is because the adult teeth are shifting and settling into the jaws. Close supervision should continue through this stage. Be sure to provide the dog with acceptable objects to chew. By one year old, the dog's adult teeth will be in their permanent positions. Chewing will slow down considerably, but unwanted chewing *may* continue if you have allowed it to develop into a bad habit.

The dog matures quickly between the ages of six months and one year. Daily obedience training sessions are imperative during this time. Dogs form habits by repeating behaviors consistently. The behaviors that you want the dog to respond to reliably as an adult must be reinforced at this stage.

One Year to Two Years Old

At one year old, a dog has the maturity level of a thirteen-year-old human. The year-old dog is calmer and easier to live with than he was when he was six months old. At last, you do not have to supervise the dog's every move.

Although dogs are considerably more mature at a year old, they still have their moments. They are teenagers! They still want to spend time playing. A case of the puppy crazies is not uncommon. Plenty of exercise and daily training sessions bring out the best behavior in the "teenage" dog.

The dog's adult personality is fully developed at about two years old. This is true of most dogs, but, like humans, individuals grow up at different rates. In fact, some breeds tend to be slower to mature than others.

At two years old, subtle behaviors that the puppy had previously displayed can become pronounced. To the dog owner with an untrained eye, some undesirable behaviors that the two-year-old dog is exhibiting seem to have appeared out of nowhere.

An example of this is the two-year-old German shepherd dog who suddenly bit the family's teenage son. The boy simply tried to remove the dog from the sofa. The bewildered owner calls me, giving me the famous line, "He never did anything like that before." After interrogating the owners, I find out that the dog frequently mouthed their arms and hands. "But he was just playing," the owners explain. I then learn that in the past the dog growled whenever they tried to clip his toenails. "That's because he doesn't like his feet touched," they say in his defense. "Did he ever bite before?" I ask. "Well, he did snap a couple of times when I tried to take his rawhide bones away. But he didn't actually bite. We stopped giving him rawhide bones, so it hasn't been a problem."

All of the signs indicating that this dog would have a biting problem as an adult were there. There are *always* subtle clues throughout puppyhood indicating potential behavioral problems in the adult dog. These behaviors are simply not as pronounced as they will be once the dog's adult personality is achieved. It is up to the owners to put a stop to undesirable puppy behaviors so that they do not have a big problem on their hands in the adult dog.

Two Years Old and Beyond

I do not believe the cliché that you can't teach an old dog new tricks. A dog does not reach a certain age at which its brain shuts down and it becomes incapable of absorbing information. However, training does become more difficult once a dog attains its adult personality. Training is extremely diffi-

Adulthood—at last!

cult (if not impossible) if the dog has achieved the status of pack leader within the family.

Although you can teach your older dog new tricks, you will have a tougher time extinguishing his bad habits. Dogs are very routine-oriented creatures. Once they develop a behavioral pattern, it becomes ingrained. So starting early with training will allow you to avoid trying to undo bad behaviors and replace them with good ones when it may be too late. With Puppy Preschool and a good formal obedience program, you are teaching good behaviors right from the start.

Part Four

Puppy Equipment

"*B*e prepared" is a good motto for puppy owners. From leashes and food bowls to safe toys and training equipment, this section covers all the essentials you need for training and responsible puppy ownership.

Seven

The Essentials

Now that you are *mentally* prepared for a puppy, are you physically prepared? Like human babies, puppies require some basic equipment so you can provide them with proper care. The equipment list is not quite so long, however—no baby monitors or strollers are needed! But you do need the puppy version of a crib or playpen—a crate. Plus you need feeding equipment and a leash and collar. This chapter describes the basic equipment you will need plus a few extras to help you be prepared.

The Kennel Crate

If I had only one piece of equipment to use with my puppy, it would be a kennel crate. The crate will help you achieve housebreaking, prevent unwanted chewing, and help control unwanted barking. These uses are described in separate sections throughout this book and will not be repeated here. Instead, this section describes types of crates and how to buy the one that's right for you and your pup.

Before considering kennel crates, I should mention that not *every* puppy

A kennel crate is the perfect home for your puppy when you can't supervise him. A few soft, old towels plus some dog toys will keep him safe, comfortable, and entertained during your absence.

needs a crate. Other structures can substitute for what the kennel crate provides, namely a secured and controlled environment. I have had clients who successfully made three-foot-high plywood "walls" to partition off a corner of a kitchen or laundry room. A few clients have had success by putting a baby gate across a small powder-room doorway. There is nothing wrong with these options if they work, but often they don't. The partitioned space is usually not small enough or puppy-proof enough to be an effective alternative. (One of Barbara's Labs literally chewed through drywall to gnaw on the wall's wooden studs. So much for her partitioned corner of the family room!)

I like crates that are made of heavy-gauge metal wire. They have a metal floor and a door at one end that swings open. Wire crates are easy to clean and airy. They're also convenient to travel with when they are the type that collapse into a flat "suitcase" shape. Some of the wire crates come with an epoxy-type coating on the wire that makes them less noisy and a bit more attractive than the metallic versions.

Some people like the molded plastic airline-style crates. If you anticipate traveling a great deal by air with your dog—and only want to buy one crate—you may want to consider this type. I find them cumbersome to handle (unless you have a small breed), not as well ventilated, and not as easy to clean. Plus, the dog has limited visibility out, while at the same time you have limited visibility in. But no matter which style you choose, the following information about purchasing the correct size applies to both types.

Most dog owners expect to buy only one crate for their dog. This means that a small puppy ends up in a very large crate—with lots of room to grow into on the way to adulthood. The ideal situation would be to have two or more crates of different sizes to accommodate your growing dog. That's not realistic for most people, so one crate is fine.

You should buy a crate that's large enough for the size your dog will be as an adult. How big is that? The adult dog should be able to stand in the crate with his head erect, turn around comfortably, and lie down without his legs, hips, or head being cramped up. Since your dog is only a puppy now, you'll have to estimate his adult size (that's hard with mixed breeds!). Breeders and veterinarians can help you make a prediction about how big your puppy will be as an adult.

Some puppies do fine in their adult-size large crates. Barbara's two Labs did. Other puppies take full advantage of the space and use one end for bathroom purposes and the other end for a dry place to sleep and play. That's counterproductive. You will learn in the chapter on house-breaking that a properly sized crate makes use of a puppy's natural instinct to keep his bed area clean. A crate that is too large may prevent this from working. If that's the case with your puppy, you will need to temporarily block off one end to make the crate smaller. (A piece of plywood, sheet metal, or rigid plastic can do the job. Be sure there are no sharp edges or open areas where the puppy could get caught or hurt.) A properly sized crate forces the puppy to sit in any mess he makes—something he instinc-tively does not want to do. Perfect! Now he has a reason to try "holding it." As you will see, that is what makes the crate so useful for housebreaking training.

When you have determined the type and size of crate you want to buy, where should you go to find one? You have several options. Pet supply stores usually sell crates, although you may need to order the particular size you need. (Smaller shops don't have room to store dozens of crates.) You may be able to save money by ordering a crate through one of the many pet-supply catalogs. If you don't already receive one in the mail, ask your veterinarian, groomer, breeder, or a friend with lots of dogs about these catalogs. Some offer better discounts than others, and I've found some great deals on crates (and other equipment) through these catalog sources.

If your budget is extremely tight, you may want to rent a crate. Some humane societies, shelters, and even breeders make crates available for short-term use. You may find, however, that you need the crate for your puppy's entire first year and that rental charges exceed the purchase price. You may get lucky and find a dog-owning friend who packed away her dog's crate years ago and is glad to lend it out to help you off to a good start. When you discover how useful and important the crate is to your puppy's training, you'll know how big a favor you owe your friend in return.

What goes in the crate besides the puppy? I like to put an old towel on the metal floor so the puppy can lie on something soft. Toys are a good idea, too, but make sure they are absolutely safe toys. An unsupervised pup can swallow pieces of vinyl, metal squeakers, chunks of rawhide, etc., when he works away on his toys. See Chapter 8, "Safe (and Fun) Toys," for a more lengthy discussion on this topic.

Your instincts will tell you to put a big soft pillow and a bowl full of water in the crate with the pup. (After all, he's "going to jail" and will need as many comforts as possible!) Resist all urges to do this. If you do it anyway, I can almost guarantee you will come home to a wet, foam-covered mess one day. It's happened to me! Your puppy should not be left alone so long that he needs an entire bowl of water to quench his thirst. (In hot weather, it's okay to put an ice cube in a small bowl in the crate. The pup may appreciate a few cool licks now and then, and if it melts and tips, no harm done.)

Your puppy doesn't need a pillow to be comfortable. You are just setting him up for some destructive chewing by providing things like pillows in the crate. Rest assured—when he's outgrown his urge to chew (between one and two years), he can have all the fluffy pillows you can afford.

Finally, I've found that winter drafts can be minimized by draping a cloth over the top, back, and sides of the crate (leaving the front uncovered). The cloth adds to the denlike feeling that the crate provides, which many dogs really seem to like. Our Lab, Bentley, loved his crate, which had a covering just on top, even as an adult. I'd long since stopped closing the door, but I didn't have the heart to break the crate down and pack it away. It was Bentley's favorite place to hang out and sleep. He felt safe and happy there, which was just fine with me.

Depending on your puppy's size, choose an appropriate food bowl and water bowl that are easy to keep clean. Heavy ceramic or metal are two good choices.

Food and Water Bowls

Most eight-week-old puppies are little creatures. They don't need a gallon-size water bowl or a half-gallon-size food bowl. In both cases they would probably climb *in* it rather than drink or eat *out* of it. Puppy-sized bowls are nice, but they will grow out of them quickly. So use your common sense. My adult dogs each have two-quart food bowls. They share a two-quart water bowl, which I fill twice a day. As puppies, they ate out of a metal pie pan. It was nice and shallow so they could reach the food easily and also was similar to the metal bowls they would use as adults.

As you shop around for these supplies, you'll see bowls made from all sorts of materials. My first preference is for bowls that can go in the dishwasher. Have you ever seen other people's dog food bowls? They can get pretty gross. A quick daily rinse and a weekly (minimum) scrub in the dishwasher (or in hot, soapy water) should keep your dog's feeding and watering bowls clean and relatively free of germs.

Leash and Collar

Puppies can grow into their crates and bowls, but they can't grow into a collar. You will need to invest a few dollars every few months for a properly fitting collar. This is especially true if you own a large breed, since the change in their neck size from the time they are eight weeks old to a full

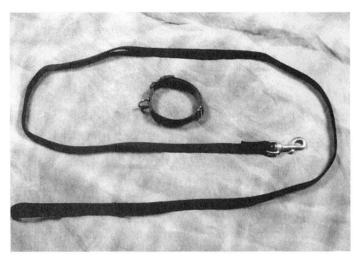

A buckle collar and a six-foot leash are necessary for Puppy Preschool training. Cloth or nylon are good choices because they are lightweight and inexpensive.

adult can be astounding. (Have you ever seen a collar to fit an adult male mastiff? It looks like a pony harness!)

Choose a buckle-style collar that's made of a soft, comfortable material such as nylon webbed cloth. The width of the collar should be narrow for small breeds and wider for large breeds. Use your common sense. No puppy needs a collar that is so wide and heavy that it intimidates him or obstructs his movement.

How long? The collar is too long if there's so much excess material that the pup can get the end of the collar in his mouth and chew it. It's too short if you can't put it on the puppy using the following guidelines: Buckle the collar on the puppy just tight enough that you can comfortably slide three or four fingers between the collar and the puppy's neck. If the collar is buckled too loosely, the puppy may be able to get his bottom jaw under the collar and either chew it or panic and feel stuck. If you buckle the collar too tight, you risk injuring your dog. And remember, puppies grow fast. Check the fit of his collar every week and be prepared to buckle it on a looser notch or buy a new collar that fits right.

The best recommendation that I can give you for the puppy's leash is to buy an inexpensive one. Unless you trust your skills at supervising the pup as carefully as possible, there's a good chance the leash will end up being chewed. Ideally that should never happen, but if it does, you'll be glad you spent just a few dollars on the leash. Splurge on a beautiful, expensive leash when the puppy is older and beyond the chewing stage.

The training exercises that I teach require a six-foot leash, so that's what I always recommend. The leash should be exactly six feet long, not those coiled leashes that expand beyond six feet when the dog pulls on it. Those leashes were a profitable invention, but they do nothing to help teach your dog not to pull on the leash and drag you down the street. I also don't like chain leashes because they are difficult to fold up in your hands when you do the training exercises. Cotton or nylon webbing are best and they're also not very expensive.

The width of the leash depends on the size of your hands and the size of your puppy. A big man with a mastiff pup needs a wider leash than a small woman with a bichon. Use your common sense to find a leash that's comfortable in your hands and an appropriate width for the size (and strength) of your dog.

A Safe Yard

Another essential you may not have thought about is a secured yard. A fenced yard is best. It keeps the puppy in and other dogs, cats, and kids out. It gives you the most control over your puppy's safety outdoors. Cable dog "runs" and narrow, fenced kennel runs are not appropriate for young

A safe yard is essential for responsible dog ownership. Make sure there are no holes in the fence for the puppy to squeeze through, because he's sure to try!

dogs. Puppies are too young to be exiled alone to a dog run. (I don't even do it with my adult dogs.) As you will see throughout this book, my belief is that if you want to own a dog, it should not be a decoration for your backyard. A dog is a living creature who should be well trained and learn to live with you as a part of your family.

Fencing around a yard should be high enough so that the dog (when an adult) cannot leap or climb over. Some breeds (especially terriers) don't think about jumping—they think about digging! Bury the fence several inches into the ground or position bricks, railroad ties, or other materials along the base of the fence to prevent Houdini-style breakouts.

I do like the type of fencing that is "invisible." A thin wire, which carries a radio signal, is buried around the property. The dog wears a collar that gives a warning noise and then a shocklike correction if he approaches and crosses the property line. Most dogs learn to stay in the yard with only a few corrections. Although the idea of an electric shock sounds harsh (it did to me at first), it's nothing compared to the pain and suffering that awaits a dog who roams. Car accidents, dog fights, poisonings, shootings, and the like happen all too frequently to roaming dogs. The traumas I saw during the years that I worked in a veterinary hospital make the shock from an electric fence system seem like a walk in the park.

Unfortunately, this type of fencing is not appropriate for young puppies. The brand I am most familiar with recommends that the dog be *at least six months old* before using this system.

Extras

What else does your puppy need? Toys, of course, which are described in the next chapter, along with things to chew on. Eventually you may want to buy a dog bed—one of those big, round stuffed pillows. Save your money until your puppy is old enough to sleep outside the crate. Their urge to chew gets strong at times, and that soft cushion may look very inviting. Have you ever seen a room after a dog bed filled with tiny Styrofoam beads has been chewed open? It's not a pretty sight! Actually, it *is* pretty—it looks like indoor snow but is about one hundred times harder to clean up. If you think your puppy needs to have a special place for naps in a room with you, fold up an old towel or use a small, washable throw rug. Remember, when you *can't* supervise the pup, he goes into the crate.

*   *   *

Most cities and towns require dog owners to license their dogs. This means puppies, too, at least by the time they are six months old. That small metal tag hanging from your dog's buckle collar may not seem too important. But the day someone leaves the gate open and Rover is out roving, you'll be glad he has identification so the dog warden can give you a call.

In addition to the license, I like my dogs to wear an identification tag with my name, address, and phone number on it. I also put the dog's name on the tag. I've returned wandering dogs to their relieved owners more than a few times—all because the ID tag told me where they belonged. The few times I picked up dogs without any ID, they go to the pound. That's the only place they are safe until the owners track them down. I feel better seeing a dog safe in a kennel run in the pound than roaming the streets and highways at risk of being injured or killed. Owners probably don't think I'm doing *them* any favors (especially when the pound charges a fee to bail the dog out), but I know I am doing the dog a favor.

Be sure to keep identification tags current. Are you moving? Order tags before you go and clip them on the day you arrive in your new home. Are you on vacation with your dog? Put a piece of masking tape over your name and address on the tag. Write your temporary location and phone number on the tape. Dogs can become lost more easily in a strange new environment. Your California phone number is not much help during your visit to relatives in St. Louis.

Should your puppy wear a flea collar? So many dogs do, but ask your veterinarian before you assume this is an essential piece of equipment. Young puppies may not tolerate the chemicals in the collars. (Be sure to read the label and package inserts before using any flea collar!) Also, the collars may give large breeds flea protection around their necks but no protection way down at their tail end. Trust your veterinarian's advice.

All dog owners become somewhat skilled in providing a bit of grooming and home health care. Things like baths, brushing, nail clipping, ear cleaning, and the like can be done at home. Some owners prefer to have a professional dog groomer handle these tasks. But even if that's the case, you may have to change a bandage, cleanse a wound, or apply medication. A few grooming and health care items will make your job of caring for your dog a bit easier. They are described in Chapter 23, "Home Grooming Tips."

Eight

Safe (and Fun) Toys

If puppies take anything seriously, it's playing. Just about *any-thing* can get their attention. If it rolls, slides, squeaks, can be tugged at, pounced on, or chewed up, puppies are interested. That means that most things around your house are fair game for that inquisitive little furball. Of course you must supervise a puppy so that your rugs and furniture are not shredded to pieces. (If you need immediate advice on that subject, skip ahead to Chapter 16, "Preventing Unwanted Chewing.") But supervision is only half of your responsibility. The other half is to provide items that *are* safe and fun to chew on. This chapter will give you guidelines on puppy toys and how to teach your puppy what does and does not belong to him!

Squeaky Toys

Barbara McKinney admits it: She's been to a puppy shower! Considering how many items that new dog owners need to take care of a puppy, puppy showers aren't such a bad idea. The thing I like about them is that they emphasize that puppies are, essentially, babies. Items appropriate for adult dogs aren't always appropriate—or safe—for canine infants.

Safe puppy toys include latex squeaky toys, tennis balls (for most breeds), nylon bones, and sterilized natural bones.

Should you have any toys waiting for your new pup when you bring him home? Of course! I like small latex toys that make a soft squeak. (Some dog toys sound like tugboat foghorns! They're sure to frighten a young puppy.) Keep in mind that "small" is a relative term. A toy that's the right size for a beagle puppy might slip down the throat of a Great Dane pup. If you have your doubts about size when choosing a toy, *think big*. You're better safe than sorry.

I like latex squeaky toys for a reason: They're almost impossible to chew up. The latex gives and stretches as the puppy bites on it. Vinyl squeaky toys are okay, as long as your pup can't chew them to pieces. I discovered very quickly that my Labs made mincemeat out of a cute, squeaky vinyl toothbrush. If one of those vinyl tidbits had gone down an airway when I wasn't home, I might have had big trouble. But Labs are known as big chewers. If your puppy likes vinyl toys and can't destroy them, they are good (and less expensive) options.

If you like buying things for your dog, squeaky toys are, frankly, a lot of fun to buy. We've had a gorilla with red toenails, a black tyrannosaurus rex, a bright pink porcupine, Foghorn Leghorn and Wile E. Coyote from the Looney Tunes collection, a Santa Claus hound, and about six "hairy beasts" with funny hats and shoes. Some friends of ours even taught their two dogs the different names for their various squeaky toys, which the dogs fetch successfully from the toy basket during a game they invented. (Rainy days don't have to be boring if you and your puppy use your imagination!)

One more word about squeaky toys. Some dogs fixate on the little plastic squeaker mounted on the toy's bottom. Drifter did. He loved squeaky toys, but his very favorite game after a vigorous game of toss-and-bite-it was to lie down and work the squeaker free. (If Drifter were a human teenager, he'd probably have my car engine disassembled on the garage floor.) That's not a very safe habit, so keep an eye on your pup. You may end up with a basket full of squeaker-less dog toys like we have in our house.

Balls

Puppies and balls seem to go together. These toys hardly need an explanatory section, but I have a reason for discussing them here. Not all balls are safe for dogs. Here's how I learned this the hard way.

Woody, the golden retriever, was one of the best baseball dogs I ever owned. He and I played our own version of canine baseball. Sometimes I'd practice my pitching, with Woody as the catcher. He could snag a fast, sly pitch incredibly well. Other times Woody was the entire outfield and I was the batter. I'd bat the ball to him, and depending on where it landed or how far he had to run to get it, invisible base runners worked their way around the plates. We both enjoyed the game immensely.

One day after a catch Woody came trotting back to me to return the ball, but where *was* the ball? Only after seeing Woody's bright blue tongue hanging out of his mouth did I realize what had happened. The ball I was using, which was wet and slobbery from repeated catches, had slipped down Woody's throat. I was horrified and foolishly did the first thing that came to mind. I reached way down his throat and was able to get two fingers around the ball and pull it out. We drove immediately to the vet to get Woody checked out. He was fine, but the vet told me that by reaching in for the ball, I could have easily pushed it farther down Woody's windpipe. A blocked windpipe means suffocation and a dead animal—not a price I would be willing to pay for a game of catch.

The ball I was using was a racquetball, one of those smooth, blue, rubber balls that are a bit smaller than tennis balls. You can imagine how easily a saliva-covered racquetball could slip down a retriever's throat during an enthusiastic catch. The same thing could happen with a squash ball and a small terrier. *Please be careful!* I now recommend tennis balls because the fuzzy surface prevents them from becoming too slippery. They're also rather big, although not big enough for a Newfoundland or a Great Dane. A dog that size needs a *big* ball to play with safely. Some of the pet supply catalogs and larger stores may carry large, hard-to-destroy balls for big dogs. Whatever size your dog, be sure the ball's surface is not too slippery—or does not become too slippery during play. I'd hate for anyone to have the scare I did with Woody.

Rawhides

A lot of dogs and puppies really like to chew on rawhide, which is a by-product from the meat-processing industry. Some rawhide is of higher quality than others. Some rawhide is thicker than others. Some is cleaned and processed more than others. Some is chopped and pressed into sticks or other shapes. Rawhide is widely available where pet supplies are sold.

The main thing I don't like about rawhide is that dogs like it so much! My Labs could chew a foot-long rawhide bone in a few hours—and would gladly do so every day of the week. That's a lot of leather sitting in their bellies and moving through their intestines.

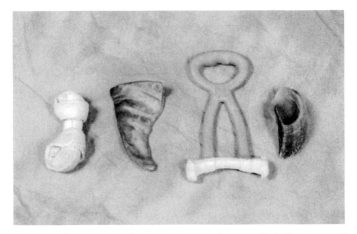

Puppies often love to chew on items such as rawhide bones, pigs' ears, and cow hooves, and to pull on rubber tug toys. These items should be used with caution.

Not all dogs are crazy about rawhide, but if yours is, you need to set a few limits. Buy high-quality rawhide (usually more expensive), which seems to need more chewing before it is used up. Buy big shapes that are twisted into bones, rings, or knots. ("Big" is relative to the size of your dog, of course.) Big rawhide shapes take a lot of chewing. It's harder to work small pieces free, and they are often easier for the dog to hold between his paws. Limit how long the dog chews the rawhide each time you give it. My dogs get no more than half an hour at a time. Then I tell them, "Give it. Thank you!" as I take the rawhide and put it away. The soggy leather dries out quickly, making the bone almost as good as new for the next chew. You'll want to let it dry out away from the dog's reach. A basement shelf, the top of the refrigerator, or a workbench in the garage are handy drying spots.

Should your pup get to chew the rawhide every day? That's up to you. Rawhides are a special treat in our house, but our friends keep several in their dog's toy basket all the time. (She's interested in chewing them only occasionally.) The answer to everyday chewing is definitely "no" if your pup won't eat her meals, has trouble moving her bowels, has excessive gas, a bloated belly, or other signs that her eating and eliminating habits are being affected. Even if your puppy *loves* rawhide, your job is to love your puppy by keeping her healthy.

A final word on rawhide bones: Always supervise your pup when you give him a rawhide, especially if he chews vigorously. When he works a piece free (or the entire bone is almost used up), pieces of wet, slimy rawhide can get caught in his throat, making him gag. If you see this happening, take the piece from him and throw it away. Do *not* dry it out for a later chew; it's too small to chew safely. The last few inches of rawhide are not worth a medical disaster.

Natural Bones

By "natural bones" I don't mean the leftover bones from your steak or chicken dinner. In fact, I never give my dogs bones from the kitchen. Most bones—especially cooked ones—will break or splinter very easily. After years of working in a vet hospital and seeing stomachs and intestines torn and punctured by kitchen bones, I never give my dogs these bones. I do

Curiosity will turn just about everything in your home into a potential chew toy. Think carefully about what objects you want your puppy to practice chewing on.

buy natural bones, however, from pet suppliers. These are sturdy, sterilized bones that are safe to give dogs. My discussion of natural bones in this section refers only to these kinds of bones.

Many dogs like natural bones because they can scrape their teeth against the bone's surface. This helps remove tartar and maintains good dental health. A great way to introduce bones to a puppy and encourage him to chew on them is to make what I call a "puppy pacifier." Take one natural bone, insert a piece of cheese (or hot dog or dog cookie) into the bone's hollow center. Give to the pup. It's fascinating! Many puppies will play with this toy for hours, puzzling over how to get at the tasty treat inside. (To avoid frustration and a smelly piece of moldy cheese, I pop the treat free after a while if the pup hasn't pulled it out himself.)

Natural bones come in a few sizes. Large breeds need the bigger sizes. Puppies of any breed usually can't wear down the bone's ends until they are adults and have stronger jaws. However, be careful. Puppies grow fast. A very small natural bone in the mouth of an adolescent bull mastiff could possibly disappear down a throat. That's not something you want to have to deal with.

Stuffed Toys

Use your common sense on this one. Are there button eyes or other loose pieces that the puppy could chew free and swallow? Does your pup like to chew the toy open and pull out all the stuffing? If your puppy can't play safely and without making a mess, it's not a good toy. But if it's safe and clean and your pup likes it, it's great!

We used to have a stuffed teddy bear (about ten inches tall) that I won for our black Lab, Byron, at our local carnival. He loved playing with it (even though he was ten years old). Barbara says that the only drawback to this toy was that it cost about twenty-three dollars in carnival tickets while I tried to aim, shoot, and toss my way to the prize.

Nylon Toys

These bones (and rings, disks, knots, balls, etc.) are made of hard nylon. You may have seen them under the brand name Nylabone. When dogs chew on a nylon bone, the nylon gets "roughed up." These rough edges are designed to help clean the teeth and stimulate the gum tissue, promoting dental health. Versions made from softer nylon are marketed especially for puppies to promote tooth and jaw development.

My dogs have given mixed reviews to nylon bones. The softer nylon makes sense for puppies, but the hard nylon, especially when it becomes very frayed, is almost sharp to the touch. Some puppies don't mind that. The multiple little nylon edges that appear never get soft during chewing the way rawhide does. The advantage of nylon bones is that they're clean, safe, and long-lasting.

Tug Toys

Tug toys come in all sorts of shapes, sizes, and materials. You'll find rubber tugs, rope tugs, fleece tugs, and so on. Are they good toys for puppies? Sort of. They're great for puppies to play with together. A lot of dogs like "testing their own strength" against someone pulling on a toy. Puppies (or dogs) doing this with each other usually does not cause trouble and can be a source of great fun.

If you have a lot of experience owning terriers, you may have strong feelings about tug toys. Terriers, who were bred to be ratters, love to pull, shake, and "kill" such toys. They sometimes get carried away and get too aggressive. That's one of the drawbacks to tug toys with *all* breeds. If the toys inspire aggression or very rough play, they should not be used.

Another drawback to tug toys is that playing tug with humans teaches dogs how strong they are and that they can pull something away from you. That's not conducive to maintaining your image as pack leader. Tug games are not a problem if your dog is sweet-natured and is not inclined to test your authority. However, puppies and adolescent dogs typically test everyone around them, so letting them engage in rough, tugging play with you is not a good idea. Use your common sense. There's a difference between a short tug game once in a while with a sweet-natured twelve-week-old pup and daily, rough tugging with an eight-month-old adolescent. If your puppy likes tug games but reaches an age where he's testing your authority, put such games to an end. They can make even a minor pack-leader problem a lot worse.

Frisbees

My yellow Lab, Bentley, thinks Frisbees are God's special gift to dogs! They are a great way to exercise an exuberant pup without exhausting yourself. And watching a Frisbee-obsessed dog leap and snag one out of the air is pure poetry. If you have seen Frisbee dogs on television, you know what I mean.

Some owners and dogs do fine with the traditional Frisbee made of firm plastic. After seeing Bentley get nicked gums and cut lips when the plastic disk hit his mouth, I came to like another version. It's a soft foam ring covered with nylon fabric. The entire disk can bend in half but still holds its shape for flying. Bentley can snag it from any position and not have a rough plastic edge cut his mouth. It's also not chew-up-able, as many of the less expensive plastic disks are. Those sometimes last only through one play session because of all the teeth marks on (and through) the plastic.

If you want to teach your puppy to play Frisbee, keep the training sessions short and fun. Roll the Frisbee a short distance as though it were a ball. If the puppy grabs it, encourage him back to you and give him lots of praise! Do this a few more times and then end it. The idea is to avoid boring your puppy with endless retrieves—that will just form a negative association to the Frisbee. I even store the Frisbee away from the other toys and just bring it out for a game. That helps keep it an exciting object.

Cow Hooves and Pigs' Ears

Blech. They splinter. They smell. Dogs love them. I don't. It's up to you if you want them around the house. Just keep safety in mind. If a hoof splinters, throw it away. If the pigs' ears get gulped down nonstop, offer just one only occasionally. If you start complaining about the smell, don't call me.

Nine

Your Voice: A Required Training Tool

Your puppy's experiences with his littermates and mother taught him about canine sounds—growls, whimpers, whines, and barks. These are natural sounds that all dogs make to help them communicate with each other. Verbal sounds are just one of the many forms of canine communication. Body postures, eye contact, and scent cues are other ways that dogs share information with each other.

Verbal forms of communication are especially important to dog owners because they are the most easily imitated for the purpose of training. I've always told people that dogs can't think and communicate like humans, but humans certainly can learn to think and communicate like a dog. Doing so makes your job of teaching your puppy the things he needs to know in life that much easier.

It's almost like teaching school in a foreign country where the children do not speak English. It will be difficult—if not impossible—to teach these children if you can't communicate in a language that the students will understand. As soon as you learn to speak their language, they will make lots of progress.

This is also true when we try to train our dogs. My approach to training is to use techniques that teach through a canine point of view. Doing so produces results quickly and efficiently—without a lot of frustration and stress. Imitating canine verbal tones is an important part of this approach.

High-Pitched Praise

Have you ever spent time with a mother dog and a litter of young puppies? If you have, you've heard mother dog whimper and watched her litter come running. Mother dog will then lick, nudge, and snuggle up to her offspring. She will flop on her side as if to say, "Dinner's served." While the pups nurse, mother dog will sometimes lick her puppies. These behaviors are all very comforting. From a very young age, a dog associates that high-pitched whimpering sound with inviting warmth and comfort.

I put this to use in my training approach, which is to train through a canine point of view. I emulate mother dog by using high-pitched sounds to praise my puppies. When I sit on the floor of my class and whimper, my students are always amazed that all of the dogs race to me to lick my face.

What Should You Say?

The words themselves don't matter, but the high-pitched tone matters a great deal. How do you know if you are doing it right? If you get your puppy's tail wagging, then you are doing it right!

Men with deep voices may have a difficult time with this at first, but with practice they will succeed.

Use this praise tone generously to encourage and reinforce good behavior in a puppy. Whenever your puppy does something right, such as going to the bathroom outdoors or picking up one of his own toys (instead of your shoe), praise him! Your praise reinforces good behavior and also helps reassure a puppy as he tries to figure out his new life in your home.

Although specific words don't matter, keep it interesting. The words you use should vary. "Good puppy, good puppy, good puppy" loses its appeal after a while. Keep your praise fun and interesting for the puppy. If the puppy is not looking at you and wagging his tail, then you're not praising effectively.

The Canine Correction: **"Nhaa!"**

Good handlers use their voice to give corrections. Hitting, kneeing, or similar techniques constitute dog abuse. Don't do it! A much more effective and natural way to correct a puppy is by growling. Say *"Nhaa!"* in a deep, *guttural* tone. When you do this, you are imitating mother dog who growled at the puppy when he misbehaved.

When mother dog growled to reprimand her puppy for nursing too roughly or chewing on her ear or leg, she was not saying to her puppy, "I'm angry," "You're bad," or "I don't like you." She was simply saying, "Stop." That is what you want to convey to your puppy when you growl *"Nhaa"*: Stop whatever you are doing! Stopping a behavior on command becomes an extremely useful skill throughout a dog's life.

Your *"Nhaa!"* must be throaty and *guttural*. Loud is not always necessary. The tone should sound like a growl; you are imitating dog language. When a dog tells another dog to stop doing whatever it is doing, it growls. It does not say "Bad dog"; it growls. I have heard trainers use the word "fooey." Think of how ridiculous this is. Have you ever heard a dog tell another dog "Fooey"? Learn to talk "dog talk" if you want to succeed in training.

Because this corrective tone is so essential to successful training, it is covered more thoroughly in the section on training steps. Read ahead to Chapter 18, "*Nhaa!*—Stopping Unwanted Behavior When You Growl," if you are ready for more information on this important topic.

Command Tones

Another important verbal tone is used for commands. You should give commands in a clear and pleasant but firm voice. You do not have to shout commands at your puppy for him to hear you or for him to learn to follow your instructions. Puppy Preschool is not boot camp—do not sound like a drill sergeant! (Actually, no dog training should be like military camp.)

However, you should not give commands in a pleading tone, either. You are telling him—in a kind way—that he must. If your tone says, "Please do it if you feel like it," you will have a difficult time convincing your puppy that you are the one in charge.

You will notice in the training section that I use short, clear, one-word commands. They are easiest for a dog to learn. The actual choice of command words is up to you, as long as your tone communicates that they are commands.

Your Puppy's Name: Use It Right!

A common mistake that many puppy owners make is to start using their pup's name in a confusing way. To use it right, you must remind yourself that a name is an attention-getting word. For example, when I need help with a project, I'll call into the next room, "Barbara! Would you please give me a hand with this?" I use Barbara's name to get her attention, and then I communicate my request.

This is true with dogs, also. First, you must teach a new puppy his name. Do this by using the name frequently when speaking to the puppy. Say your puppy's name in a clear, pleasant tone and then praise him when he looks at you. He'll soon learn his name.

When you start the exercises in Puppy Preschool training, use the pup's name prior to giving any command. The name serves to focus your pup's attention on you so that you can communicate your command. The proper sequence goes like this: You say the puppy's name. He looks up at you. You give the command. The puppy responds. If you say the pup's name *after* giving a command, the puppy may not even realize that you were speaking to him. That slows learning and reduces the odds that you will get the response that you want.

The most important rule for using your puppy's name is to *always* use it in a positive way. *Don't* correct your puppy by shouting out his name. "LOBO!" shouted in an angry tone sounds like a correction. It teaches the puppy to associate his name with your angry feelings and any other unpleasantness that may follow. Lobo will quickly learn to ignore his name if you do this. Instead, growl "*Nhaa!*" if you must correct your puppy. It's far more effective and won't undo the attentive response you want from the puppy when you say his name.

Baby Talk

I hate to take the fun out of puppy ownership. I know we get puppies to love them and baby them. And after all, your puppy *is* a baby. However, dogs interpret "baby talk" as whimpering. When you say, "Oh, Freddy, I love you, you're so sweet. You're mommy's little boy," in that cutesy, baby-talk tone, you sound just like a dog going "*EEEmmmm, EEEmmmm, EEEmmmm.*" This is exactly the sound that a submissive dog makes to a dominant pack member.

If you talk to your puppy in this tone on a regular basis, you are using "dog talk" to tell your puppy that he is your pack leader. It's okay to use baby talk sometimes—if that's your style—but some people may be inclined to use baby talk all the time. Remember, your job is to communicate through a canine point of view. Try to think—and speak—as a pack leader would.

Part Five

Starting Off Right

---

*L*et's get started. This section describes what you can do with your puppy to build a foundation for a happy and confident dog. These tips and techniques will help your puppy form positive interactions with you and the world around him.

Ten

Bonding with Your Puppy

What is bonding? It's easier to describe than define. It's that warm feeling you get when a wagging tail and happy canine face greets you at the door each evening. It's why your dog follows you from room to room and then curls up at your feet (or next to you on the sofa) when you sit down to watch TV. It's the reason your dog owns five different collars and three different leashes—when one of each would certainly do. In short, bonding is what makes owning a dog so wonderful. It's simply a feeling of connection between you and your dog.*

Our dogs become bonded with us, in part, because we feed them and provide them with a place to live. If that's all you do for your dog, however, you can't expect much of a bond to form. Food and shelter are important to a dog, but so is social interaction. By that I mean spending time with your dog, playing, hiking, training, etc. This chapter will give you some ideas about how you can start the bonding process with your new puppy. A strong bond with your dog will enhance your enjoyment of your pet a hundredfold.

---

*If you're thinking that what I'm describing sounds a lot like "love," you're right! I love my dogs and know that they love me. Scientifically speaking, what we feel is called bonding. But in my heart I know it's love, through and through.

That warm feeling you get when you hold your puppy for the first time is the start of bonding. It usually doesn't take long to realize that you belong to each other.

At Home

There are many different ways to develop a strong bond with your new puppy. The most important way is to simply spend as much time together as possible. As you go about your daily routine, your puppy will become tuned in to you and to the rhythms of your day. The more time you spend with each other, the faster that will happen. I've found that owning a puppy—especially during the first few weeks—requires a big adjustment on everyone's part. Owners have to get used to housebreaking needs and feeding schedules, while puppies have to learn about your life, too. When you and your puppy spend a lot of time in each other's company, you get familiar with each other a lot sooner. Before long you will realize that you've worked out a comfortable daily routine that includes the pup—and that the pup follows that routine pretty smoothly.

A word of caution: If your daily schedule (or life) is a chaotic mess, don't expect a puppy to make things easier. If there's no routine for the puppy to fit into, the pup will have a difficult time settling into his new life with you.

Routines are important to puppies. The more routines you can introduce into your day, such as standard feeding times and regular morning and evening walks, the better for your pup. And the better for you, too. Remember, bonding means being connected to each other. *You* may have to make some changes to accomplish this.

Be affectionate with your puppy. A gentle hug, rub, or kiss on the top of the head—just because he's there—clearly communicates that he is part of your family. Touch is important to dogs, just as it is to people. Use your dog's need for physical contact to strengthen his bond with you—and vice versa.

Another way to bond with your puppy at home is to set aside some time to play with him. Playing is one of the things puppies do best! When you join in on your puppy's fun, you help him feel bonded to you. I think of it almost like reading to a small child. By setting aside time to read to a child, you are subtly communicating to the child that he or she is important to you. The same is true for puppies. Although I don't believe they understand it in quite those terms, they do respond by bonding more strongly to you. Keep in mind that not all types of play are constructive. See Chapter 12, "Games Puppies Play," for tips on safe and constructive play.

The next suggestion will not be acceptable in every household, but it deserves mention nonetheless. Sleeping in the same room together helps your dog bond to you. Why? If your family and your puppy were a pack of wolves, you would "den" together as a pack, with the adults protecting the youngsters. Sleeping together is natural, especially to puppies. Until puppies come to live with us, they typically spend every day of their first two months of life cuddled up with their littermates and mother. That doesn't mean you need to put your ten-week-old pup in bed under the blankets with you! Putting the puppy (in his crate) in your room during the night is just fine. Doing so also will stop any crying the pup does during the night. If you have been dealing with nighttime crying, it's almost always because the puppy feels exiled from his pack. Staying together at night is natural, so if your spouse or significant other is willing to share some space in the bedroom, I recommend it.

Out and About

Bonding with your new puppy happens away from home, too. Hikes are a great way to encourage bonding. They also show your puppy that the two of you are a team. You don't need two thousand acres of wilderness to accomplish this. When your puppy is very young, your backyard will do. Then graduate to a town park or athletic field. Be sure that your pup's vaccinations are current and that you get your veterinarian's okay before bringing a young puppy to places where lots of other dogs visit.

When the pup is older, hikes in state parks, conservation areas, and beaches make great outings. The only downside is that many of these areas do not allow dogs. Do respect such rules. Other dog owners may be able to give you tips on fun spots in your area where dogs are allowed.

I like these dog hikes for several reasons. One is that they give you a

Outings with your puppy help build a positive relationship. You develop the habit of making time for your pup each day, while the puppy learns that you are the pack leader.

pack leader image in your dog's eyes. You choose the place for the hike, you know the trails, and you determine when it's time to leave. That's a powerful leadership image to a puppy. Even taking an eight-week-old pup for a stroll around your "big, scary backyard" accomplishes the same thing. The puppy must rely on you for guidance and safety. By providing that, you start to create a bond.

Another reason I like dog hikes is that you and your dog are sharing a common experience. With a little imagination, you can pretend that you are two wolves exploring new terrain. Even when your puppy is an adult, such activities are fun. Shared experiences help create bonds. In addition, the exercise is good for both of you.

Occasionally stop to rest during these hikes. Sit on a rock or the ground and just observe nature together. Pick up a leaf or twig and let your puppy sniff it. Listen to birds together. Watch a plane fly over. Stroke your pup's neck and back, telling him how much you enjoy his company. Your words won't be understood exactly, but your message will. That's bonding.

When I come home from a walk with my puppy and he is pooped out, I often will lie on the floor with him, and we'll take a nap together. The bottom line is that you do things that show your puppy that he is your buddy. Let him know that the two of you are on the same team. You're the captain of the team, but he is a valued team member.

Dog hikes are great ways to help your puppy make dog friends, too. Dogs who join their owners in various activities together often become friends themselves. My dogs have plenty of canine friends. Many of these dogs were first introduced to my dogs during a dog hike. (Neutral territory is a great setting for dog introductions. The activity of hiking together gives the dogs something to do, as opposed to looking for trouble in a fight or a scuffle.) If there are other puppies or adult dogs in your circle of acquaintants, try to organize a dog outing. Even an on-leash group walk around the block can be fun. Anything that takes you and your dog out and about together is worthwhile.

Obedience Training

Obedience training is another activity that creates bonds between owners and dogs. Good training develops communication. Owners teach while dogs learn. In doing so, they both become tuned in to each other. It's progressive, too. The more time a person devotes to training, the better he or she becomes at "reading the dog." That simply means knowing what the dog is thinking, feeling, or about to do next.

Likewise, a trained dog is highly attuned to its owner. The owner may make a small gesture or say a simple word—and the dog will respond. Sometimes that's not even necessary. My dog Drifter would wake up from a sound sleep at 4:00 A.M. when I put on my fishing vest for an early morning fishing adventure. He knew what I was up to, and he loved to join me, so off we went together. That's bonding.

Training our puppies builds relationships in the same way that parents do by spending time with their children. The father who teaches his son or daughter to hit a ball communicates that the child is important in his life. He gives the child a skill, but he also deepens the bond between them.

A Final "Must": Talk to Your Dog

Do you talk to your dog? You should. I talk to my dogs all the time. I tell them how important they are to me and that I love them dearly. Although they don't understand the language, I believe that they pick up on the feelings I'm projecting.

I've also found that talking to dogs helps them fit easier into our lives. At first your puppy won't have a clue when you say, "Let's go for a ride" or "Upstairs! It's time for bed." But soon the pup will make an association between your words and the activity to come. They will make the association even faster if you use the same phrase with the same intonation each time you say it.

My dogs know lots of phrases, and as a result I can direct them simply by talking to them. In a sense, training your dog to obey obedience commands is the same thing, but that's more formalized work. What I'm describing here is a way to direct your dog through the day simply by talking to him and getting him familiar with useful phrases.

Here are a few examples of words and phrases that my dogs and some of my friends' dogs know. The dogs learned them because they heard the words each time the activity happened and finally made an association. By looking over the list you'll get an idea of how useful talking to your dog really can be.

"Upstairs!"   "Get in the house."

"Downstairs!"   "Who's there?"

"Are you hungry for dinner?"   "There's a *dog* in the yard!"

"Do you want to go out?"   "Where's the birds?"

"Where's your squeaky toy?"*   "Joyce and Ted are here!" [or

"Let's go to bed."   whoever comes to visit

"Josh is coming to visit."   you frequently]

"Who wants a biscuit?"   "I have some cheese."†

Phrases such as these can be useful, and you will probably use them for years. Many older dogs have picked up lots of phrases during their lifetimes. To me, it's a tribute to how tuned in they are to our lives. And all it requires is that you talk to them.

---

*As I mentioned in an earlier chapter, one of our friend's dogs, Glin, knows the individual names of various squeaky toys in her toy basket. There's the Spiny Rattler, Ali the Alligator, Gigi the stuffed doll, Leggy the Octopus, and others. Playing with this dog and sending her off to search for a certain toy is a lot of fun—for all of us!

†"Cheese" is actually just one of about twenty or thirty food words that our Labrador retriever, Byron, knows. The wiring in his brain clearly is oriented toward the kitchen. Some of the words he knows especially well are "tuna fish," "ice cream," "bagel," and "banana." Of course, if you called a bagel a banana, he'd eat it anyway. So I'm not sure how useful a food vocabulary actually is.

Eleven

Socializing Your Puppy

A well-adjusted adult dog begins with a well-socialized young puppy. That's why you will hear breeders, veterinarians, and trainers encourage you to "socialize your puppy." What does that mean and how do you do it?

Start Small

Some people think that socializing a puppy means bringing an eight-week-old youngster to a family reunion, a noisy first grade classroom, and a town park full of adult dogs—all in the same week! That's overload for almost any puppy and is most definitely *not* recommended.

Good socialization means gentle introduction to the many people, places, and other animals that will be part of your pet's adult life. Your goal is to make the puppy familiar and confident with these people and places. A confident, at-ease dog is easy to control and pleasant to be with. It makes your job as the dog's handler much simpler and also enhances your enjoyment of your pet. A poorly socialized dog who shies away or bites at visitors does not make a very enjoyable companion.

Socialization is best accomplished when your dog is a puppy. Certainly

Take your puppy to new and interesting places. A well-socialized pup grows up to be a confident, well-adjusted adult.

older dogs and adolescents can learn to deal with new people and places, but the task of teaching them can be more difficult. This is especially true if the dog had strong negative experiences (such as abuse) when he was young. For example, it's hard to convince a two-year-old dog that men with beards are friendly if the dog's original owner fit that description and was abusive. Undoing such associations can be difficult. That's why giving the puppy lots of positive experiences when he's young establishes a foundation of confidence and friendliness that will last a lifetime.

The first place that socialization should begin is with the breeder or shelter where the puppies are born. If the pups are secluded for seven straight weeks in a quiet back room, the sights and sounds of your busy household are going to be a bit overwhelming. To avoid that, good breeders and shelter workers gradually expose the puppies to human stimuli

Socialization should begin while puppies are still in the litter. Good breeders expose their puppies to people and also to the sights and sounds of the backyard. This minimizes stress when the puppies move into their new homes.

(usually by the time they are about four weeks old). That means letting them hear people talking, a radio or television playing, a telephone ringing, and so on. These sounds are not so loud as to scare the pups. They're simply part of the background noise that will become part of the puppies' lives.

If the puppies are healthy, they can also meet people in their first seven weeks of life. They should have had a visit or two to a veterinarian (which usually means a car ride) and perhaps had the chance to play outside to feel the grass and smell the air.

When your puppy comes home to live with you, your job is to continue introducing these things. The most important guideline is to use common sense. *Don't* run the vacuum cleaner right next to the puppy's crate (with the puppy in it), but *do* run the vacuum cleaner, perhaps in another room or on another floor. Don't bang pots and pans in the puppy's face, but do rattle around the kitchen a bit so that cooking-related sounds become familiar. Don't put a young puppy outside alone, but do sit outside on the grass with him while he explores the yard.

People introductions also are important. Dogs who have never met children, elderly people, people of different races, people with disabilities, etc., may have a fearful response (such as snapping or biting) when they meet these people later in life. Puppies who are given the opportunity to meet a great variety of people have a lasting familiarity with the human race and are most likely to be accepting and friendly toward everyone. (If you want your dog to act aggressively toward certain groups of people, don't look for encouragement or advice from me. I believe a dog should behave like people should—with acceptance and respect for everyone. The only exception I can think of is aggression toward a burglar or other criminal sneaking into your home or trying to hurt you. Then barking and biting are A-okay in my book!)

Your lifestyle and weekly schedule may make it difficult to find time to socialize your puppy. However, I can't emphasize enough how important it is. One of our Labs, Bentley, had minimal socialization during the first few months of his life because of concerns that his vaccinations were not effective. As a result, he is much less confident around new people and strange sounds than our other dogs who were "out and about" right away. In retrospect, I would have given Bentley at least some socialization despite the risk, because we have had to spend quite a few years working with Bentley to build his confidence. He's come a long way, but he's still our shy one. (Granted, shyness may have been an inherent part of his personality anyway. But socialization at a young age would have helped minimize this undesirable trait.)

If you have trouble imagining what kinds of activities will help socialize your puppy, look over the following lists for suggestions. They are divided into "young puppy" and "older puppy" categories, since older dogs can handle more than canine infants can. Use common sense when choosing an activity. Your shy pup may need to do young puppy activities for many weeks until he handles them with confidence. Sometimes dogs adopted as older puppies, who have had little or no life experiences, need to work from the young puppy list as well. On the other hand, some young puppies are little balls of fire and can move quickly into more challenging experiences. You know your puppy best, so pace your socialization efforts to suit your dog.

A Word of Caution: Always follow your veterinarian's advice on exposing your puppy to new dogs and new places. Although newborn puppies have immunities to many diseases, those immunities "wear off" and the pups must be vaccinated to be absolutely safe. (See Chapter 22, "Health Issues.") Even simple ailments like parasitic worms can be devastating to young dogs. Your veterinarian can advise you on when your puppy can safely be exposed to other dogs. Until then, keep contact with other dogs (and especially their stools) to a minimum.

Young Puppy Suggestions

• Let the puppy explore room-to-room in your home *while you follow him*. Since housebreaking accidents are likely, make sure the pup has just eliminated outdoors before you do this.

• Go up the stairs (with you behind the pup for safety). A carpeted stairway is best to ensure a good grip. "Open" stairs (the type that you can

A puppy should meet infants and older children. Choose a time when the puppy is calm, and *always* supervise their interactions.

see through between each step) are not the best kind to start with. Puppies are reluctant to keep climbing when they are looking out into open space.

Go down the stairs, but only when your puppy is strong enough and steady enough on his feet. Walking down is harder (and scarier) than walking up, so don't rush this one.

• Have the pup in the kitchen with you while you load the dishwasher or wash some pots and pans. Better yet, attend to these activities during your pup's mealtime. Food is a great distractor. New noises that your pup hears while he eats probably won't have a negative impact on him— because the noises are associated with the positive act of eating.

• Ah, yes, the vacuum cleaner. Pull it out of the closet and put it (unplugged) in one of the rooms the puppy knows. Let him see it and sniff it. That's it. If you can stand to leave it there for a day or two, do so. When it's time to vacuum, make sure the puppy is in another room or on another floor (a helper makes this easier). Start to vacuum. The pup may come to see what all the noise is about. If he does, *ignore him*. Just let him watch and listen to what is going on. The easiest way to make a puppy fearful is to coax him too much toward something that's a bit frightening to him. Your blasé behavior while vacuuming will communicate that the noisy vacuum is nothing to be afraid of. Granted, some dogs simply don't like the loud noise of the vacuum cleaner. If your pup chooses to stay away, that's okay, too. But by introducing this household machine in a common-sense way, you can avoid the panic behavior that some dogs have when it's time to clean the house.

• Since most young puppies are quite small, they are easy to carry. That means they can be cuddled in your arms when you go on errands into town. Many merchants don't mind a puppy's presence, except of course if the merchant sells or prepares food. I know little puppies who have been carried into banks, feed stores, hardware stores, and the like. The sights and sounds of these places—not to mention the many people who will come over to say hello—will help your puppy learn about the world.

• I like puppies to meet children, but there are some important guide-lines. First, *always* supervise the interaction. Children can easily hurt a young puppy, and sharp little puppy teeth can easily hurt a small child. Second, choose children who are either infants, preschoolers, or in school. My experience with toddlers is that they are noisy and unpredictable. Their happy squealing and unsteady movements can intimidate or frighten a young dog. Certainly an older puppy who is confident around children can meet toddlers, but toddlers are not the best age group for in-troductions. (If children live in your home, see Chapter 13, "Family Mat-ters," for some additional tips.)

• If visitors to your home are willing, have them sit on the floor and allow the puppy to come over to say hello. Most puppies are curious about other creatures. If your visitor sits calmly and perhaps holds a toy, the puppy is bound to come over. The visitor should talk to the pup and may even hold him. The greater the variety of people your puppy meets, the better his social skills will be.

• Give your puppy his first bath. If he is small enough, you may want to use the kitchen sink or laundry tub. Otherwise use the bathtub. (A cold hosing-down in the backyard is no way to bathe a puppy!) Run a few inches of warm water into the tub, lift the puppy in, and be sure to provide a rubber mat for good footing. I've found that a steady stream of gentle conversation helps keep my dogs at ease. I tell them how good they are, how nice the water feels, how beautiful they will look after their bath. If they squirm too much or try to jump out of the tub, I correct them with a growl, "*Nhaa!*" Be sure to dry the puppy with a few big towels and keep him warm until he's fully air-dried. (See Chapter 23, "Home Grooming Tips," for additional information on bathing and grooming your puppy.)

• Take a car ride. Except for residents of big cities, most dog owners own cars and rely on them a great deal. When a dog is part of your life, the dog often rides in the car, too. I like to see puppies get car experience early in life. However, don't plan your ride just after the puppy has eaten a meal. Most puppies can't handle the car's motion on a full stomach and will vomit. That creates negative associations with the car, not positive ones. Also, it's best for a puppy to be confined to a crate in the car. That way he can't climb into your lap, get under your feet, or chew the seat belts while you are concentrating on the road. No amount of socialization is worth risking a car accident.

Socializing an Older Puppy

• Walks into town (or other shopping areas) are a great way to socialize your pup. The activity of a busy shopping district will allow the pup to experience new smells and sounds, not to mention new people. You can expect that a cute puppy on a leash will attract a bit of attention. I'm guilty myself of stopping to say hello to puppies and to ask their owners a few

Outdoor adventures are great ways to burn up puppy energy and also to introduce your pup to the natural world. Be sure to choose areas that are safe from cars, wild animals, hunters, and other hazards.

friendly questions. Be sure to keep the puppy's safety in mind, however. Don't let a stranger (especially a child) pick your puppy up. Not everyone can handle dogs properly—one good wiggle and your pup may be dropped or accidentally hurt. Visitors can stoop down to greet your pup, or you can pick up your puppy to show him off.

• What's a puppy party? It's my term for a canine version of a play group. If you know one or two other dog owners with puppies, schedule an hour or two together for some puppy fun. Choose a safe yard away from roadways since puppies may dash off in the excitement of their play. Now sit back and watch the games begin. You don't need to plan anything for a puppy party—puppies take care of that themselves. Wrestling, tugging, chasing, stick biting, exploring, and perhaps napping will quickly fill up the time. Few things are more fun to watch than puppies at play. For me, the stresses of the world melt away when I get a chance to watch puppies having a great time. One word of caution: If there is a real bully in the group, remove him from the pack and keep him on a leash. It's no fun if the other pups are going to be traumatized.

• Take a longer car ride. Those jaunts around town are good for your pup, but eventually you will want to make a longer excursion. A two-hour trip to visit friends or to explore a state park are good examples. First, be sure your puppy is welcome at your destination. If your pup experiences motion sickness in the car, feed him several hours before you leave or bring food and feed him when you arrive. Always bring a jug of water and a nonbreakable bowl. Stop during the trip to give your pup some water and allow him to eliminate. (Carry a roll of paper towels in the car so you can clean up stools if necessary.) *Always* clip on your puppy's leash *before* opening the car door at a rest stop. You can imagine the horrors of a loose puppy near a highway or deep woods far from home. Don't take a single chance. *Absolute safety is a must.*

• An overnight trip is a logical extension of a long car ride. Again, be sure that your pup is welcome at your destination, whether it be a friend's or relative's home or a motel. Bring your puppy's crate and bedding (whatever you use at home) plus water, a bowl, and food. I like to have an extra day's supply of food with me—I never know when circumstances may delay my return. Don't forget the leash and collar as well as any medications your puppy needs. I store essential dog supplies in a canvas sack (known as the "dog bag"), which automatically goes with us on trips. I toss in the dinner bowls, a few squeaky toys and natural bones, a supply of treats, and we're ready to go.

- Let your puppy spend an afternoon on his own at a friend's house. This gives puppies the chance to experience the world without you at their side. It's good practice for the future when you may need to rely on someone to care for your dog while you are away. Be sure to choose someone whom you absolutely trust with your pet. Do they have a safe yard? Do they have children or pets who will not hurt your pup? Do you trust their judgment? Not everyone is good at handling dogs. I have met bright, well-educated, kindly people who have no common sense with animals. I would trust these people to take out my appendix, prepare my taxes, fix my plumbing, or replace the brakes on my car—but not to watch my dog. Decide with your head, not your heart, who can be trusted with your pet.

- Have you been brushing your pup and teaching him to have his nails clipped? Now it's time for a trip to the groomer. Even if your dog is a breed that does not need regular, professional grooming, I recommend a grooming visit as part of your puppy's socialization. It's a good life experience and is essential for puppies who will be groomed professionally for the rest of their lives. Choose a groomer with a reputation for gentleness. Your veterinarian and other dog owners can give you recommendations. (You can switch later, if you wish, to Mr. Expert Dog-Show Groomer who rushes dogs through the procedure.) Be sure to tell the groomer that this is your puppy's first visit. He or she may suggest an appointment on a slow day when there's extra time for each step. Ideally, your pup should be at the shop only as long as the grooming takes, but some groomers do not offer this flexibility. Don't expect to stay with your pup during the grooming—most groomers do not like anxious owners hovering nearby while they work. When your pup is ready, greet him with lots of affection. "How beautiful he is!" and "How glad you are to see him again!" Your happy reaction to seeing him will help make a positive association with the experience.

- Visit an elementary school. If you or someone you know has an elementary student or knows one of the teachers, ask if one of the classes would like a puppy visit. Chances are the answer is yes! Don't visit a noisy kindergarten if your pup has never seen a child before, but otherwise any age group is fine. Again, you alone are responsible for your puppy's safety and comfort. Instead of letting thirty energetic kids grab for your puppy, you hold the dog. Everyone can line up to take turns petting him and saying hello. Tell about the care that a puppy requires, his need for quiet time, and what he likes to play with. When I visit elementary schools to do demonstrations, I hear lots of unusual questions and stories. You may be asked questions as well, so answer what you know. Even a responsible pet owner can educate children about responsible pet care. Your puppy is sure to be exhausted after his visit, so plan on letting him have a long nap when you get home!

• Along the same lines as visiting an elementary school is visiting a retirement or nursing home. Letting your puppy meet older people and those with disabilities is just as important as letting him meet children. Contact the social director or supervisor to obtain permission and schedule a visit. My dogs have visited a senior day care center, and I can't describe what a rewarding experience it was for all of us. Many seniors lived with dogs their entire lives, and a canine visitor is often most welcome.

• Observe a dog obedience class. This serves two purposes. One is to allow your puppy to meet some new dogs. The other is for you to check out obedience instructors. If by chance an instructor won't allow spectators, move on to someone else. Good instructors have nothing to hide and should be agreeable to prospective students evaluating their program. While observing the class, don't let your puppy jump all over the other dogs. Use the time before and after class for play. And be sure that your pup doesn't pounce on an adult dog who has no tolerance for youngsters. Your visit should be a positive experience, not a disaster.

• Walk in a wildlife sanctuary or wilderness area. If dogs are allowed, these settings will offer your pup a lot of interesting new sights and smells. Birds, rabbits, deer, squirrels, frogs, and other animals are part of the wide world that your puppy is learning about. They may not be interesting to you, but they are to your pup. Even if you don't see too many creatures during your outing, your puppy will still smell them and perhaps hear them. I guarantee it will be an enjoyable day. A word of caution: Wildlife areas may have some hazards. Depending on where you go, skunks, poisonous snakes, deer ticks (which carry Lyme disease), birds of prey, and sand fleas may spoil your outing. Use common sense and plan your outing wisely to minimize risks.

• A visit to a farm, stable, or agricultural fair is another way to let your puppy experience other animals. Keep your puppy's comfort and safety in mind. For example, keep him on a leash. Don't hold your puppy up to a cow's face, and don't let him get underfoot of horses. But do allow him to sniff around and explore things that interest him. Be sure he does not frighten or try to hurt any smaller animals, such as lambs, chickens, or rabbits.

• Visit an airplane terminal, especially if your lifestyle requires your pet to fly. Don't go on a trip the first time you visit. Just walk around the terminal and check out the setting with your pup. If possible, plan your visit to avoid holiday crowds. It's challenging enough for people to walk through an airport at those times. Adding a puppy can be a real hassle, not to mention an increased risk of mishaps.

Overcoming Fears

As you socialize your puppy, you may find that certain things frighten your dog. How should you react? The most *undesirable* thing to do is what most people instinctively do first: try to soothe and calm the pup with gentle words and pats. Why is that so bad? Because your puppy, unfortunately, cannot understand the meaning of your words. When you say, "It's okay. There's nothing to be afraid of. Good boy. It's okay," you use a sweet, soothing voice. That's a praising tone to your puppy. What you end up doing is praising your puppy's fearful behavior. That, of course, only encourages the reaction you are trying to undo.

Instead, the best reaction if you see your puppy act nervous is to say nothing. Keep your own demeanor casual and nonchalant. You want your puppy to pick up your "vibes" that there's nothing to be afraid of. With multiple experiences the puppy soon learns that whatever caused his fear is no big deal.

Again, common sense is necessary here. I would never intentionally subject my puppy to something that truly terrified him. If we came upon something that gave him a terrible fright, I would avoid it whenever possible until he was a bit older and I could introduce it slowly. An example that comes to mind is Byron's first visit to a major city when he was about six months old. While we were walking along a city street, a big motorcycle revved its engine and roared by us. I could tell it frightened Byron. Would I walk him around a Hell's Angels weekend gathering to get him used to motorcycles? Of course not. But when motorcycles passed us on the highway, I also would not praise Byron for his fears by saying, "Don't be frightened. It's okay." Instead I said nothing, which gave Byron a chance to become familiar with the sound and realize that nothing terrible happened when he heard it. Motorcycles were no longer a big deal to him.

A final thought on fears. Some dogs develop fears because of abnormal sensitivities. One of my dogs was sound sensitive. Loud noises startled Bentley easily. I believe the "wiring" of his nervous system made him this way, but he was remarkably calm and confident most of the time. That's because I responded to his fears in a way that helped minimize his fearful reactions. Bentley no longer bolted out of the kitchen when the pots and pans clanged together. He stayed close to my side but didn't panic during thunderstorms. And he even stayed in the room while we watched on video the roaring dinosaurs in *Jurassic Park*—until the velociraptors got loose and startled all the *people* in the room, too!

Twelve

Games Puppies Play

Puppies and play just seem to go together. Whether it's fetching a ball, chasing a toy, tugging a rope, or running after a bird, play is a big part of a puppy's life. The parallel to human children is especially strong in this regard. If you have ever watched a preschooler "hard at play," you will understand how strong that urge is. Kids learn about themselves and their surroundings by playing.

The same is true for puppies. Play helps young dogs explore their environment and discover what they are capable of doing. It also releases a lot of what I call "puppy energy." In fact, I've made a not-so-profound observation about puppy energy, which is the subject of the first section of this chapter.

Tired Puppies Are Good Puppies!

Proper exercise for your puppy is extremely important. Exercise also can be 50 percent of the formula for successful training. A pooped-out pup is less likely to be getting into mischief if he's taking a snooze or resting quietly after a walk. However, you must provide the proper form of exercise.

All that energy needs someplace to go! Plan to channel your puppy's exuberance with constructive play.

You do not want to put excessive stress on developing bone structures, which may create physical problems later in your dog's life. Here are some guidelines for safe ways to exercise your puppy as he grows up.

Eight Weeks to Six Months

As a rule of thumb, never push your puppy to exercise beyond the point that he would naturally choose on his own. An example of this would be taking a puppy for a walk off the leash around the local high school football field. After a period of time he would tire out. He would start to lag behind and maybe even lie down to rest. This would be a good indicator that he had had enough.

Pushing the pup too far would be to put him on a leash and jog for two miles. The pup would try to keep up with you and not be able to stop to rest if you continued to jog. This type of exercise would push the puppy beyond the point of exhaustion and would be harmful. The same holds true at this age for excessive retrieving. Throw the tennis ball a dozen or so times and then end the game until your pup catches his breath. Rest to-

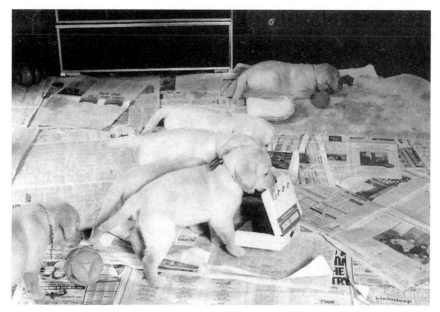

Even at six weeks, puppies explore their world through play.

gether for a while. Some puppies have such a strong retrieving instinct that they don't know when to stop. It's up to you to use good judgment and keep your pup safe and sound.

Six Months to One Year

After about six months, your puppy's endurance increases tremendously. He will appear to have an *unlimited* amount of energy. But keep in mind his bones are still growing. You can increase the amount of exercise, but you still must be careful not to overdo it. Depending on your puppy's breed and innate abilities, you can try a forty-five-minute to one-hour hike in the woods or a half-hour session of swimming and playing in a lake or pond. Daily adventures like these are great exercise at this stage in your pup's life.

The Two-Ball Retrieve

Most puppy owners enjoy a fun game of ball retrieve with their pups. Some breeds have stronger retrieving instincts than others, so bringing the ball *back* to you may not be part of your pup's game. But chasing a moving ball usually sparks a lot of fun puppy play. Here's an easy way to encourage your pup to fetch and retrieve.

First, be sure to read the section in Chapter 8, "Safe (and Fun) Toys," so that your puppy doesn't play with unsafe balls that might slip down his throat.

Let him play with the ball around your house. You can roll the ball a foot or two for a very young pup. He'll probably chase it and pounce on it, using the hunting instincts that all canines have. If he carries the ball back to you, simply praise him. After a week or so, you can start shaping his play into a more structured game of fetch.

Many years ago I discovered an easy technique to overcome a common puppy behavior: not giving up the ball. This may sound familiar. You toss the ball. The puppy chases it and runs back toward you. You reach out to take the ball, but the pup turns his head or darts away from you. If you keep up with this routine, you soon end up with a puppy who plays "keep away" with the ball instead of fetch.

To prevent this, always bring two balls to your play session. Toss one, and when the puppy catches it, encourage him back to you with your voice or by waving the second ball. If he won't drop the first ball, don't make a big issue over it. Simply toss the second ball. Most puppies then drop the first ball and go running happily after the second one. Pretty soon they learn that dropping the ball for you results in more tosses for them.

To fine-tune this game, don't toss the second ball immediately upon your pup's return. Let him mouth the ball and carry it around for a minute. The ball is his "prize," which should not be taken away too quickly. His confidence in giving up the toy will soon develop, especially since giving it up results in another fun retrieve.

The only disadvantage to this routine is that some older puppies (especially golden retrievers who can be tennis-ball obsessed) actually learn to carry two balls in their mouths at the same time. I've even seen pictures of goldens holding three tennis balls! Giant breeds like Newfoundlands and mastiffs are probably capable of this, too. Maybe you'll need a whole bucketful of tennis balls to keep these big pups busy while they learn how to play fetch.

Teaching Your Pup to Swim

Swimming is a great form of play and exercise. It's good for growing bones and muscles without putting excessive stress on hips and shoulders.

Most puppies can learn to swim with proper introduction to water. Some breeds, such as the bulldog, are not very graceful in the water. The bulldog's wide torso and short legs make swimming difficult. The pushed-in snout seems to cause breathing problems while swimming. Because of their body conformations, breeds such as the dachshund and basset hound also have difficulty in the water. If you own one of these breeds, don't become fixated on swimming. Take the cue from your pup. If he's interested, fine. If not, your pup can enjoy hikes along the shoreline just as much.

Over the years, I've met people whose adult dogs do not like to swim. This includes dogs actually bred for work in the water, like Labrador retrievers. There are two main reasons why some dogs do not like to swim. One reason is that some dogs have never been exposed to water. The other reason is that many dogs have been improperly introduced to the idea of swimming. The *biggest mistake* owners can make is to throw their puppies into the water in an attempt to teach them to swim.

Imagine being a small child and having an adult whom you trusted throw you out of a boat to teach you to swim. Your head would go under. You would gulp down mouthfuls of water. Maybe with your arms flailing and legs kicking you would swim back to the boat. You probably would survive, but you sure would not have a pleasant association with water.

Dogs are no different! *Never* undermine your puppy's trust in you by throwing him into the water. Even an experienced canine swimmer does not enjoy a sudden, abrupt heave-ho into the drink.

Of all the dogs I have known, my German shorthaired pointer, Jena, was the best swimmer. She swam circles around every Lab or golden we knew. But it took Jena dozens of exposures to the water when she was a puppy before she actually swam. And it took dozens more experiences before she swam really well. If you are lucky, you will have your dog for an average of thirteen years. So what's the rush? Of course, the sooner in your puppy's life that you expose him to water, the greater are the chances that he will learn to enjoy it. But take your time and introduce swimming properly. Here's how.

Find a gentle pond or stream. Have a seat on the bank and discreetly watch your pup. Read a book or watch a bird. Appear to ignore him. Do not attempt to encourage or coax him into the water. I've found that coaxing just makes an unsure puppy or dog suspicious. Spend half an hour allowing your pup to poke around and explore. Repeat this procedure as often as you can.

When your puppy starts to splash around on his own, praise him. Let him repeat this experience a dozen different times. When you have accomplished this, bring a tennis ball or another floating object that your pup enjoys retrieving. Throw it a few inches into the water. Encourage him to get it, but do not force him. Use only your voice to motivate him.

If your puppy is too nervous to get the object, *you* get it. After you have retrieved the ball, have your puppy do a couple of land retrieves. This will build the pup's enthusiasm and confidence. If he does retrieve the object from the water, praise him enthusiastically. Using common sense, increase the distance of the retrieves. But take your time. The increased distances should develop slowly over a period of a few weeks.

When your puppy first goes out over his head, be sure to praise him when he begins the motions of swimming. Do not be concerned if his front feet splash out of the water at first. Most puppies do this. I have never met a dog who did not stop splashing his feet after he became comfortable in the water. (Holding a big stick or other object helps them learn to keep their head more forward and their front feet underwater.) Do not overdo the number of retrieves during your pup's first swim. Two or three successful retrieves are plenty at first.

If your puppy does not like to retrieve, the best method to teach swimming is for you to go into the water with him. Do not physically bring the pup into the water with you. Wade in until you are about waist deep. With your voice and an object of attraction, invite your puppy into the water. (You should first introduce the pup to water using the same procedure recommended at the beginning of this section.) If he is not secure enough to follow you, do not force the issue. Chances are good that after a dozen or so experiences, he will follow you in. When he does, praise him lavishly! Sometimes bringing along an adult dog who likes to swim provides the extra encouragement and example that your pup needs.

A word of caution: Be careful when swimming with any dog. A dog can inadvertently scratch you with his toenails. My ninety-pound Irish setter, Jason, once tried to climb on me in water that was over my head. It took all

I had to get away from him and not drown. Although swimming with your dog is great fun, do be careful.

You may know people who were not as methodical when introducing swimming to their puppies, but whose dogs love the water anyway. These are the exceptions. The procedures outlined here may be the slow way, but they provide a dependable approach. I have never owned a dog who did not love the water. Along with the many sporting breeds I have owned—and who instinctively took to the water—I have had a bull mastiff, a poodle, and two sheepdogs who loved to swim. I taught them to love swimming by introducing them to the water in a way that was nonthreatening and fun.

Thirteen

Family Matters

You can read the title of this chapter in two ways: "family issues," or "family *does* matter." Both are correct and, in fact, accurately describe the material covered here.

I believe that the individuals in each specific family are an important component in how successfully a puppy fits into a new home. Often those individuals are human, but not always. This chapter addresses the common concerns about puppy interactions with family members of all shapes and sizes. It also provides practical tips for creating (and maintaining) peace in your home after the puppy's arrival.

Adding a Second Dog

This is one of the most common concerns I hear from puppy owners. They already have a dog and are planning to get (or already have) a new pup. What to do? Here is some useful information on helping both pets learn to get along.

Canines are pack animals and thrive on social interaction. Two dogs who get along can be a terrific combination. If you work eight hours a day away

Drifter and Crea, the needle-toothed terror. Drifter tolerated a lot of Crea's youthful brattiness but occasionally put her in her place with a growl and a snap. Not all adult dogs are so forgiving. Be sure you supervise closely until your puppy and older dog prove they can get along.

from home, the effects of your long absences will be lessened if your first dog has a canine companion to spend time with. Also, I have seen many older dogs revitalized by the presence of a new puppy in the household. Instead of spending time becoming a couch potato, that six-year-old dog often responds to a puppy by trying to stimulate him to play. My ten-year-old Lab, Byron, could even be roused from a nap by eight-month-old Crea waving a toy in his face (or dropping it on his head or pushing it against his shoulders). Puppy energy can perk up most any household.

Although having two dogs may appear to require twice as much work and expense, I've found that the virtues far outweigh the drawbacks. And it really doesn't require twice as much work or money. You have to take your dog for a walk anyway—you can walk two dogs at the same time. And you do not have to spend twice the amount of money for food, because dog food bought in larger quantities is less expensive.

I've found that bringing home a puppy who is the opposite sex of the older dog can minimize problems. For example, an adult male will usually tolerate the antics of a little female pup better than those of a young male (and vice versa). This is especially true when the pup goes through puberty. Keep in mind that sexual drives can strongly influence canine behavior, particularly aggressive behavior. For this reason, the adult dog(s) in your household should be spayed/neutered, and you should plan to do the same with the pup at the appropriate age. Even if you decide that you want to own two dogs of the same sex, they will get along better if they are spayed/neutered (discussed in Chapter 22, "Health Issues").

When Barbara and I brought our new puppy Crea home, we had three older, adult dogs (neutered males) already living in the house. On the day they met for the first time, we held the meeting outside. We also held the puppy, who was only seven weeks old, in our laps. "The boys" (our three adult dogs) all were interested in sniffing Crea and checking her out. Later that day they met indoors, but the meeting was closely supervised. We were prepared to correct the adult dogs with a tough "*Nhaa!*" or a shake at the scruff of the neck if they showed any aggression toward the puppy. Happily, the first day went smoothly. Not too many adult dogs have aggressive tendencies toward tiny seven-week-old puppies. Also, one thing working in our favor was our undisputed image as pack leaders in the household. Adding more dogs can be a disaster if you don't have control and authority over the one(s) you already own!

Barbara and I were careful to protect everyone's interests those first few weeks. The puppy was always supervised when interacting with the adult dogs, and she also was prevented from harassing the adults. As Crea got older, she was allowed to have a bit more freedom in the house—but only when we were home, of course. (The crate's importance is even greater when there are other dogs in the home.)

Crea's extra freedom meant more time to play with her "big brothers." To be honest, they were not thrilled at first with this needle-toothed little bundle of energy. A few times they growled or tried to snap if Crea got especially wild near them. But again, we were supervising, so they got corrected with a tough "*Nhaa!*" and Crea was put in her crate to settle down a bit. Over time they all became familiar with one another. Crea started learning how to behave around the house, and "the boys" decided that an energetic playmate could be fun at times.

If you are introducing a new pup to one or more adult dogs, be patient. Be vigilant in supervising them. Be firm in making everyone respect you. Enforce their respect for each other's space, especially during mealtime and naptime. (Feeding the puppy in the crate makes this a bit easier.) Finally, be willing to make an effort to promote a "pack feeling." By that I mean taking walks together, driving on errands together, and enjoying hikes or other outdoor activities together. Those kinds of activities go a long way in teaching both the puppy and adult dogs that you are all one big family. I've had many students tell me that their older dog and their year-old pup are now the best of friends. That's the sign of a happy, well-adjusted pack.

Two Puppies at the Same Time

Despite the joys of owning two dogs, I *do not* recommend that you get two puppies at the same time. This advice is especially strong for getting two puppies from the same litter. The major drawback is that the pups will bond more to each other than they will to any human family member. That's a significant problem, because in order to have a well-trained dog, it's imperative that your puppy bond most closely with you.

If you take home two littermates, they will already have developed a pack "pecking order." One puppy will always be more dominant. When littermates stay together right from birth, one puppy always seems to become shy and insecure. Also, the pups become so emotionally dependent

Double trouble? You bet. Raising two puppies at the same time is usually a bad idea.

on each other that they fall apart whenever they are separated. This greatly complicates obedience training. It's hard to train them together because they are distracted by one another. But when you try to separate them for training, they become upset and can't concentrate.

I know sibling puppies *sounds* like fun, but it rarely, if ever, works well. Supervising and training one puppy is enough work in itself—and puppyhood goes by so quickly. Put your effort into one pup and then a year or so down the road add your second pup. You'll be glad you did.

Puppies and Children

If you are bringing a puppy into a household with toddlers and young children, I have three words of advice: supervise, supervise, supervise. I get so many phone calls from frazzled parents (usually mothers) saying, "The puppy is terrorizing the kids! What should I do?" My advice before they ever got the puppy would have been, "Don't get a puppy!" But here they are with a puppy and a problem, and they need my help.

Puppies and children require a lot of work. They both must be taught to respect each other: no biting, jumping, hair pulling, food stealing, etc. That means *constant* supervision—a tough task!

Puppies and kids can learn to get along, but it takes a lot of work. Unfortunately, kids alone or a puppy alone also takes a lot of work! Putting them together will make most parents feel like they are losing their minds.

There's no easy solution, in part because puppies think of young children as littermates. They will jump on them, steal their toys, nip them, and push them around. Careful supervision can keep this to a minimum. So can lots of puppy exercise (remember, tired puppies are good puppies!). Separate play areas can help. These can be created with one or two baby gates, but you may find the puppy scaling the gate to get to the kids—that's where all the fun seems to be!

Sometimes kids create the problems. They poke at the puppy, climb on him, pull his ears or tail, and disturb him during naptime or mealtime. No puppy should be expected to put up with this kind of abuse. Responsible owners prevent their children—or other people's children—from doing this kind of behavior. Respect for others also applies to animals, so teach your kids right from the start how they are expected to behave around the new puppy. And then enforce those rules—just as you do when training the puppy to behave around the kids.

Puppies and Babies

If you actually have enough energy for a puppy and a newborn baby, drop me a note—I'd love to know how you do it! In all seriousness, the demands on you will be overwhelming. Your most important rule should be "safety first." Never put the infant on the floor where the puppy might playfully pounce on it. Never let the puppy mouth at the baby's arms or legs. Keep puppy toys picked up so you don't trip during a midnight dash into the nursery.

You *can* do a few things to integrate the puppy and the baby. Take them for walks together. The fresh air and time away from the house will be good for all of you. When housebreaking is accomplished, let the puppy be free in the house while you are holding or rocking the baby (but be careful that the puppy doesn't try to jump into your lap). Give the puppy a rawhide bone or other special chew toy while you feed the baby. While the baby naps, give the puppy some undivided attention. Even a ten-minute game of "fetch" followed by some loving rubs will make the puppy feel special.

Time is on your side. Puppies do grow up. Babies do start sleeping through the night. And parents do survive babyhood and puppyhood all at once—but it's not easy!

Puppies and the Elderly

Having an elderly person in the home is not as common as it was a generation or two ago. But many families still take in elderly members. If your family is one of them and you have a new puppy, consider these points.

Puppies are full of energy twenty-three hours a day (or so it seems). Elderly people are not. Puppies move really fast. Most elderly people cannot. Puppies are just discovering the world through taste, smell, sight, and touch. Many elderly people are set in their ways and do not appreciate an untrained newcomer investigating their possessions.

This is not to say that older people cannot enjoy a puppy's arrival in your home. Many senior citizens respond warmly to meeting a puppy. Often it evokes their own memories of puppies from many years past. But pets were treated differently a few generations ago. Dogs could wander the neighborhood more freely and were rarely obedience trained as they are today. So don't expect your eighty-six-year-old family member to have the same attitudes about owning a pet that you have.

Also, older people cannot be expected to have the same dog-handling abilities as younger adults in the household. They may be short-tempered with the pup, may lose track of time and forget to feed the pup, or may trip and fall over one of the puppy's many toys. Do a careful assessment of your elderly family member to keep everyone as safe and happy as possible. Maybe Grandpa should keep his bedroom door shut so his socks and slippers don't keep disappearing. Don't ask Grandma to feed the puppy when you've learned from previous experience that she has difficulty preparing her own meals. Don't let sweet old Aunt Susie take the puppy for a walk when an energetic lunge on the leash could bring her crashing down onto the sidewalk.

As your puppy gets older, so will your elderly family member. Be alert to changes in your family member's ability to care for—or interest in—the puppy. Happily, in a year or two your puppy will mature into a well-behaved adult dog (provided you train him!). By then you may see that a special bond has developed between your dog and his elderly friend. In fact, I hope I'm lucky enough to have a dog in my life when I'm not able to care for one on my own. That would be a really special touch to the last years of my life.

Puppies and Cats

Despite the old myths of dogs and cats not getting along, the fact is that many get along wonderfully. They play together, eat together, sleep together, and generally enjoy each other's company. While it is true that some dogs will chase or try to harm a cat, most dogs are not natural-born cat killers.

If you own a cat (or two) and decide to get a puppy, there are a few things you can do to promote harmony in your animal family. The first thing you should understand, however, is that the ultimate success or failure of your efforts has a lot to do with the personality of the cat—not the puppy.

When you first bring the puppy home, your cat will probably not be too pleased. Puppies are unpredictable, noisy, and goofy—from a cat's point of view. I've found that some cats are completely "freaked out" by the puppy's arrival. They run and hide and won't come out in the open for days or weeks. These are the cats who, at best, will probably only ever tolerate the puppy's presence. The prognosis for a close friendship is not great. But tolerance and coexistence is okay, if that's the best the cat can do.

Other cats may hiss or swat during those first few days but are curious enough about the puppy to stick around. They may run if the puppy approaches them, but a half hour later you may see them sneaking back into the room for a closer look. These kinds of cats have a good chance of developing a dog-cat friendship.

Keep in mind that puppies only know how to play like puppies. That can be a little rough for most cats. All that mouthing and growling and running can be pretty intimidating. You certainly can temper your pup's behavior around the cat. Call the cat over to you when the puppy is tired and resting after an exercise session. Growl "*Nhaa!*" at the puppy if he starts to get too excitable around the cat. Cuddle together while watching a TV show (puppies and cats both love a warm body to snuggle against). Above all, try to supervise all close interactions so that you can lay the groundwork for affections to develop.

Be aware that a cat's claws can be dangerous weapons. If truly frightened, a cat may swat with open claws, which could easily slice a nose or cut an eye. Several years ago I met a sweet springer spaniel pup who unknowingly tangled with a cat. She lost her eye as a result of an angry swat in the face.

Interestingly, some puppies learn to love their "own" cats but will chase or harass all other cats. Drifter, my Australian shepherd, was like this. He lived, briefly, in the same household as an old male tabby cat who had no interest in him. Drifter truly ignored Mittens but merrily gave chase to any cat who wandered into the yard. The difference may have been that Mittens never ran from Drifter. He stood his ground and hissed threateningly. Drifter was smart enough to understand that warning and not to approach—but I was attentive and ready to correct Drifter if he had tried to.

Keep in mind that all dogs will chase things that move quickly. Your cat may quickly figure out that by not running, there's no game of chase. Again, a lot depends on the cat's personality. However, don't force a cat to stay in place. Any animal who feels cornered can be dangerous. Let the cat work it out for herself. As with people, friendships can't be forced.

If you are really set on a happy dog-cat relationship, you may want to consider raising a puppy and a kitten together. That will give you the best prognosis for success, although you may lose your sanity when the puppy and kitten learn how much fun it is to play together! I remember one client who had three kittens and a puppy—all five months old. The puppy was an eighty-pound mastiff who jumped and ran around with the kittens like he was one of them. It sure was fun to watch, but I'm glad I didn't live there!

Time is on your side, because puppies do eventually grow into mature dogs. And obedience training will help your pup be under control around the house and yard. Cats seem to handle calm dogs the best, so don't try to rush things. A year or two from now you may walk into a room and find the two cuddled up taking a nap together. Let's hope you have film in your camera, because that will be quite a wonderful sight.

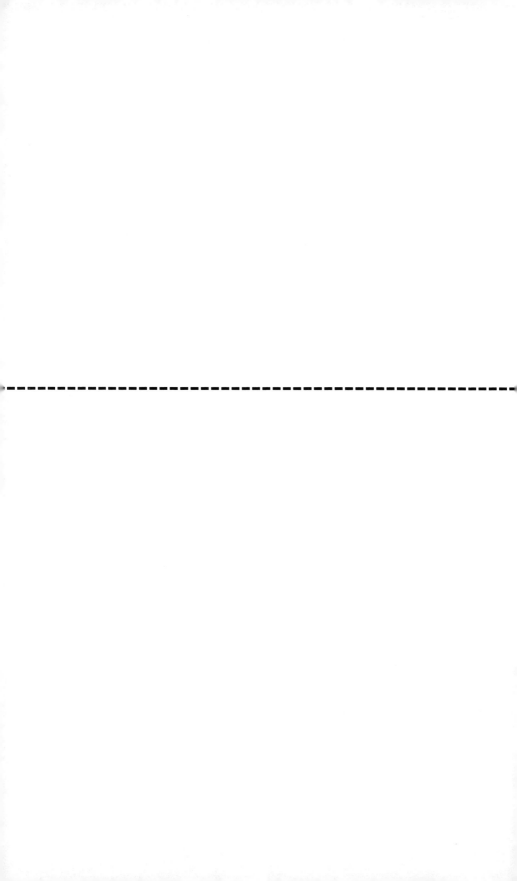

Part Six

Puppy Preschool Training

----

*N*ow it's time for the training steps. This section covers many important behaviors, such as housebreaking and preventing unwanted chewing. It also intro-
duces simple obedience commands, such as sit and lie down, which provide the
groundwork for more formal training in the months ahead. All of the exercises
are geared for very young dogs. Each exercise is described in a step-by-step
manner so that even a first-time dog owner will have success.

Fourteen

Housebreaking Your New Puppy

Few issues cause more problems in new-puppy homes than housebreaking. Here's the all-too-common scenario: A new puppy joins the family. On the day she arrives everyone holds her, plays with her, and gets her outside frequently. Then later in the day the family gets distracted with reading the newspaper, cooking dinner, doing homework, watching TV, etc. Oh no! The puppy wet on the carpet—right in front of Dad's favorite chair. "BAD DOG!" they shout and angrily clean up the mess.

When an accident happens again that evening and again the next day, tension builds around the puppy. "*You* wanted a dog!" someone says. "It was *your* turn to watch her!" the kids argue. After a week or two the family doesn't like the puppy quite as much anymore. They may decide to keep the puppy outside or in the garage or basement to avoid the messes. There the puppy barks and shreds some of the kids' toys. "She's really a *problem dog*," everyone agrees. "Maybe we should find her another home."

Ninety-nine times out of a hundred, the dog in this situation is not a "problem dog." She's an untrained dog who would have had a much happier start with her new family if someone took the time to teach housebreaking. Stained rugs and smelly piles in your home *are* miserable to deal with. They make it hard to adore that little bundle of fur. At times they make it hard to even *want* a dog in the house. Do yourself and your puppy

"Why am I out here?" At first, puppies don't understand that your trips outside are for elimination. With a consistent housebreaking routine, they soon learn what to do.

a favor: Take housebreaking seriously. You'll be happier. Your family will be happier. And your puppy will get off to a much better start in finding a secure place in your home and your heart.

The key to housebreaking success is a well-planned housebreaking system. Housebreaking is just one of the many things you will train your dog to do during his lifetime. But like any training, haphazard instruction creates frustration, slow learning, and, often, haphazard results. Treat housebreaking with the same degree of attention and commitment that you will give to an obedience exercise.

As with any training, patience, consistency, and a sound training program are essential for success. However, the best part about this exercise (unlike some others) is that results come very quickly. Your efforts start to pay off in a very short time.

The system outlined in this chapter will show you how to train your puppy quickly and efficiently to eliminate outdoors. If you strictly adhere to this system, it is quite possible that your pup will never have an accident in the house.

Before You Start

First off, decide *where* outside you want your dog to go to the bathroom. Some people feel that anywhere outside is fine. That's okay, as long as it is on your property (or property that you have permission to use for this purpose). Other people want their dog to go to one specific area in their yard every time. That's a good idea if you have flower or vegetable gardens, children's play areas, picnic areas, and the like. Aesthetics aside, urine can burn some plants, and solid waste is unsanitary, especially around garden crops and children. So think about how your yard is used and plan the puppy's "spot" carefully.

If you do want your puppy, by the time he's an adult, to go to a particular area of your yard, it is imperative that you bring your puppy to that spot *every time* he needs to eliminate. By doing this you are establishing a pattern for the puppy. If you are consistent, he will eventually follow the pattern on his own.

Be sure to clean up the area on a regular basis. Dogs do not like stepping in defecation. If the area gets too messy, the dog will avoid going there despite all your training. (Plus your yard will look awful and your neighbors will complain!) A garden shovel and a supply of trash bags at your back door will help you stay on top of the problem.

If you have not yet brought your new puppy home, plan his "bathroom spot" now. Be sure that is the *first place* you take him after bringing him home. Often people are so excited about getting their puppy home that they bring him directly from the car into the house. After a car ride and the excitement of seeing new people and a new environment, the puppy needs to eliminate. And where is the first place he does the deed? On the kitchen floor or the living room rug! That's not a great start for establishing a housebreaking pattern. Remember, puppies are creatures of habit. If you start him going in one area, he will more readily eliminate in that area the next time you take him there. So set the precedent of going *outside* from day one. This is not the whole answer to housebreaking your puppy, but it certainly will help you step off on the right foot—without stepping in poop!

Setting the Pattern

Before you can help your puppy learn to eliminate outdoors, you must learn when your puppy has to go to the bathroom—and how long at this young age he can be expected to control his bladder and bowels. The puppy's needs (not yours) set the initial pattern for housebreaking training. Puppies have to relieve themselves after they eat or take a drink of water. They also have to go after waking from a nap and after vigorous play. How soon after? Depending on the individual, anywhere from one minute to ten minutes after any of these activities.

When you take your puppy outside to eliminate, you too must go outside with your puppy—every time. (That's why housebreaking a puppy in the dead of winter is no fun.) It is not good enough to let the puppy into a fenced yard for ten minutes and assume that "he must have done his thing." A puppy has no understanding yet of why he's outside. He may become interested in exploring your yard and spend ten minutes chewing on a stick or looking at a bird. If it's cold or raining outside, he may sit by the door and never venture away from the house. When you bring him back indoors, *then* he will go to the bathroom! That's not what you want. Your job is to stay with him (despite the weather), see him eliminate, and then praise him immediately after he finishes.

Spend no more than ten minutes outdoors with your puppy during each trip to the yard. Initially, each trip outside should be all business. You are teaching the puppy to associate "outdoors" with emptying his bladder and bowels. If the puppy does not eliminate within ten minutes, bring him back into the house and put him in his kennel crate (see the section about crates, below). *You are not crating him as punishment for failing to eliminate outside.* You are putting him in the crate because that's the one place you can be sure he will not have an accident. If instead of crating, you let the puppy roam freely in the house, he probably will eliminate somewhere in your home. That's exactly what you are trying to prevent! So be strict with this rule: Failure to eliminate outdoors means the puppy goes into the crate—but not for long. Here's the next step.

After the puppy has spent about fifteen minutes in the crate, take him back outdoors for another try. Chances are that his urge to go will have increased and he will eliminate in the yard. Great! That is exactly what you

Your kennel crate is an important housebreaking tool. Gently lead the puppy into his crate. Make sure he has a few safe toys and some old towels for bedding. And be sure to observe the crate safety rules described in this chapter.

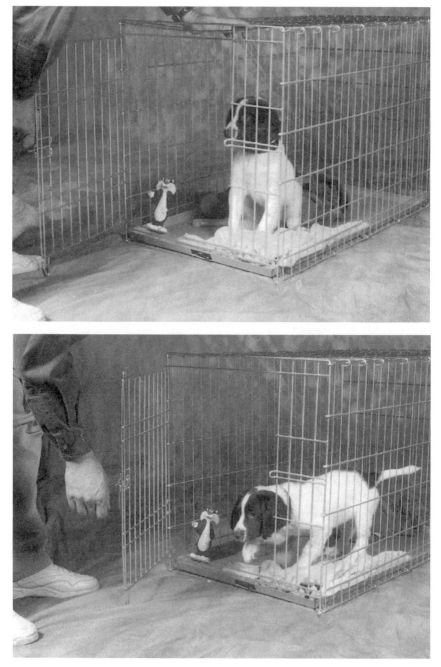

Your puppy does not have to barge out of the crate as soon as you open the door. Tell him "Wait," and shut the door quickly if he tries to run out. When he's waiting patiently, say "Okay!" and encourage him to you.

want the puppy to do. Praise him warmly. Now your puppy can have some freedom in the house. Why? Since he just emptied out, the puppy is unlikely to eliminate again soon. Take advantage of this. Play with your puppy, let him explore the kitchen while you prepare dinner, let him cuddle up next to you for a nap, or feed him a meal. Freedom in your home to play, nap, eat, and explore is good for puppies, and it allows you and your family to interact with and enjoy your canine youngster. It also helps establish the housebreaking concept: "Indoors" is associated with *not* eliminating—even while playing or exploring around—while "outdoors" is associated with emptying out. But remember! At this stage in a puppy's life, freedom means *supervised freedom*. You cannot prevent an accident or give a timely correction if you are not watching your puppy. If you need further convincing, see Chapter 16, "Preventing Unwanted Chewing."

Some Tricks of the Trade

When you begin housebreaking training, it's a good idea to keep the puppy on a leash, at least initially. If you are using a designated area in your yard, the leash will help you keep the puppy in that area. (But never drag him to the spot. See Chapter 17, "Introducing the Leash and Collar," if you are having problems using the leash.) Many puppies who never learn to eliminate while on a leash become inhibited from doing so. I'm not sure why this occurs, but I've seen it happen frequently. This can create problems in the future. There probably will be times when you and your dog are traveling together, taking a walk in a new area, or exploring a beach or park with "dogs must be leashed" rules. It will be imperative that your dog stay on a leash and be able to eliminate.

Here's another great option that many owners come to appreciate: Teach your puppy to eliminate on command. Is that really possible? Sure. You simply associate a verbal phrase with elimination—and use that phrase every time you take the puppy out to go. Eventually the puppy associates the phrase with eliminating and will try to go when you ask him to. Human nature being what it is, people come up with some pretty amusing phrases to encourage their dogs to go. A few normal ones that have reached our ears include "Hurry up," "Go on," and "Go to the bathroom." Then there's "Take a poopy," "Let's have a tinkle," and "Go poopy for Poppy." (An appreciation of bathroom humor is essential here!) Say whatever you are comfortable with—and whatever you can risk your neighbors overhearing. Say the phrase as you walk your pup around his designated bathroom area. Remember to give him lots of praise when he does what you've asked.

By observing your puppy's actions (see below), you can determine when he will need to go outside. It is *your* job to get him there! If your puppy has an accident indoors because you failed to take him out at the appropriate time, it's your fault, not the puppy's. All that an untrained puppy knows is that he has an urge to go, so he does. You must create a pattern where the urge to go is satisfied *outdoors*.

Accidents

No one's perfect. Not your puppy. Not you. There may be a time when the puppy goes unexpectedly or when you became too distracted to notice his activities. If you walk into a room and find an accident, say nothing. It's too late to correct your puppy for the mistake. Dragging him over and showing him the mess will do no good. Clean it up and be more vigilant next time.

If you catch your puppy *in the act* of having an accident, correct him with a growl. "*Nhaa!*" Do not hit him with a newspaper or rub his nose in the mess. These are forms of dog abuse. They confuse the puppy, teach nothing, and undermine his trust in you. Simply growl, which communicates "Stop what you are doing immediately!" (See Chapter 18, "*Nhaa!*—Stopping Unwanted Behavior When You Growl.") Then pick up the puppy and bring him outside to the spot where he should have gone. If he finishes eliminating outside, praise him warmly.

The ideal time to growl "*Nhaa!*" at your puppy is when he is *getting ready* to urinate or defecate in the house. How will you know? Depending on the dog, the clues may include sniffing the floor, walking quickly, moving onto a carpeted area, and, of course, squatting. The next best time is as he is in the process of eliminating. The worst time is after he has eliminated! Watch him closely so that you can time corrections properly.

Kennel Crates and Housebreaking

When you cannot watch your puppy closely, you must have a structured environment that will serve as your puppy's den. A kennel crate is an ideal tool for this purpose. Canines instinctively do not soil areas where they sleep and rest. The crate puts this instinct to good use. A puppy confined to a crate will try to control his bladder and bowels. This helps the puppy learn to "hold it" indoors. When the puppy is released from the crate and taken immediately outside—where he can eliminate—he soon learns the housebreaking pattern you are trying to teach. Hold it indoors; eliminate outdoors.

If a crate (or similar structured environment) is not used, the puppy is free to roam around a large area of the house (or, God forbid, the entire house). The puppy can go to one area to eliminate and then move to a clean, dry place for a nap or play. He will have no reason to try to "hold it," and housebreaking may never be accomplished.

Warning: Puppies never should be crated for more than four hours at a time during the daytime. Before six months of age, a puppy has not yet developed full bladder control. It is counterproductive to successful housebreaking to confine a puppy for so long that he just cannot hold it and is forced to eliminate in the crate. If this happens repeatedly, the urge to keep his den clean will start to break down. Then you may have big problems teaching housebreaking. (This is one of many reasons I don't recommend purchasing a pet store puppy. These puppies typically spend their entire lives in a crate, soiling it as needed and losing the urge to keep it clean.)

Kennel Crate Guidelines

For short periods of up to four hours, you can crate your puppy safely. A puppy can hold it for that length of time and will try hard to do so in an attempt to keep his den area clean. As soon as you open the crate door, clip on the puppy's leash and immediately take him outside. If you have a fenced yard, you may not see the need for a leash. I recommend that you use it, at least for the first few weeks. The short walk from the crate to the back door will present lots of opportunities to squat and go (especially if the puppy's bladder is very full). The leash keeps the puppy moving and helps prevent accidents on the way outside.

During the late evening hours, puppy metabolisms slow down. Their need to eliminate is much less than during the daytime. As a result, you can double the time in which you crate your pup overnight. Even young puppies usually can make it from 11:00 at night until 7:00 in the morning. However, the first week that a seven- or eight-week-old puppy is in your home, a nighttime bathroom run may be necessary. Here's how to handle it.

If the puppy cries in the crate at night, he may be telling you that he needs to go. Don't ignore him. Part of gaining your puppy's trust is teaching him that you will take care of his needs. Treat nighttime outings in a businesslike manner. Bundle up. Clip on the leash. Walk outside and let the puppy go. Then back into the crate and back to sleep. If you talk to the puppy, play with him, cuddle him, etc., you will teach the puppy how *wonderful* it is to wake up at 3:00 A.M. for all that love and attention. Don't make the mistake of giving your pup that message. Take care of business and then everyone back to bed.

Sometimes owners call me and say, "He was only in his crate two hours when I was out shopping, but while I was gone he messed in the crate." The problem almost always turns out to be the crate's size. If the crate is so large that the pup can go to one end to eliminate and then return to the other end to be clean, he may not be compelled to hold it. Your puppy should have just enough room to walk into the crate with his head erect, turn around, and lie down comfortably.

"But my little puppy will soon grow into a big dog! What size crate should I buy?" Invest in a crate that you can use until your puppy is about one year old. Although he will be reliably housebroken long before that, you will consider the crate a godsend when your puppy goes through the normal chewing phase at four months old to about one year.

If your puppy has accidents in a too-large crate, you can use a piece of plywood, stiff plastic, or other material as a partition to reduce the size of the crate. The partition can be removed as the puppy grows. Be sure to use caution in building a partition, however. Puppies will test your handiwork by crawling through small openings, chewing interesting edges, and licking unusual substances. Whatever could possibly create a hazard probably will, so safety concerns are of utmost importance. If you don't have confidence in your partition-building skills—and you really need a smaller crate—rent or borrow one until your puppy grows into yours.

Crate Safety

Sometimes people are apprehensive about using a crate as a training tool. "Is it cruel? What if he doesn't like it?" When used properly, a crate is not cruel. And most dogs do like their crate—again, if it is used correctly. However, confining a puppy to a crate for longer than four hours at a time is cruel. If your schedule dictates that you must confine your puppy longer than four hours, hire a pet sitter to come to your house to let him out. If you can't afford a pet sitter, ask a friend or relative to help. If nobody can help you and you cannot come up with an alternative plan, do not get a puppy! Simply loving puppies and wanting one does not make you a good owner if your schedule does not provide you with the time to raise and train one correctly.

Make sure that your puppy has the opportunity to empty out before he goes to sleep for the night. Until housebreaking is achieved, give no water for the three hours before bedtime. (Put an ice cube in his bowl in warm weather so he can cool down with a few licks.) Even throughout the day, water should be regulated. Do not put down a full bowl and allow your puppy to drink, drink, drink. Every hour or so offer your puppy a dozen laps of water. Do not leave water in the crate. Puppies have a tendency to tip the bowl over, and you will come home to a soggy mess. In hot weather (if your puppy is not left in an air-conditioned room), give him a couple of ice cubes to chew on. This will allow him to ingest a small amount of water and stay cool.

The best place to keep the crate at night when you go to bed is in your bedroom. It is natural for canines to den together. Puppies who are not allowed to den with their owners will often wake up in the middle of the night and feel as though they have been abandoned by their pack. They will begin to bark or cry and often urinate in the crate. I can't count the number of times over the years that I've received calls from distressed owners telling me this tale. Without exception, the problem stops when they move the crate into their bedroom at night. Also, there is no better place for a well-trained adult dog to be at night if ever a criminal breaks into your home. If for some reason you are adamant that you do not want a dog in your bedroom, those first few nights (or weeks) of puppyhood may be more difficult. However, many people do succeed without bringing the pup into their bedroom at night. Just be prepared for some middle-of-the-night crying!

Telling You "I Need to Go Out"

After a few weeks of following this housebreaking system, your puppy will form a habit of always eliminating outdoors. Keep in mind that a housebreaking *habit* is not achieved after one or two days of success. A habit, as it relates to dogs and puppies, is an ingrained behavior. Only when eliminating outdoors becomes a habit will your puppy start to "tell you" that he has to go out.

How will he tell you? Some puppies sit by the door or scratch at the door. Others bark at you or spin in circles. Overt signals such as these are relatively easy to pick up on. Other puppies give very subtle clues, such as whimpering. Watch your puppy closely while he is free in the house so you don't miss your cue to open the door and get the puppy outside. If you find that accidents are starting to happen again, go back to using the crate more frequently to limit freedom in the house. And even with puppies who have a good housebreaking habit, freedom in the house still means supervised freedom—until the chewing stage is over.

Owners often want to know how quickly a housebreaking habit will form. It depends on a few things. The first is the puppy himself. Some pups achieve bladder and bowel control quicker than others. Also, some puppies understand and respond to training (of all kinds) faster than others. A second factor is how consistent you have been. If you follow the system carefully and supervise the puppy closely, the habit of going outdoors should form quickly. If you are lax and allow accidents to happen, a housebreaking habit will take more time. No formula can give you an exact timetable, but consistency on your part will make a big difference in how quickly you achieve success.

Fifteen

Canine Separation Anxiety

The best approach to understanding any dog behavior and/or training issue is to look at the world through a canine point of view. It has been the basis of my thirty-plus years of success with dogs. So let's take a look at separation from the pack from your puppy's perspective.

The first thing you should understand about canine separation anxiety is that *all* dogs experience it. No dog likes to be left alone. Dogs are by nature pack animals, and they feel anxious when separated from their pack. When canines are anxious or mildly stressed, they behave in ways that release stress. This behavior is normal.

However, some dogs that are separated from pack members come unglued. They become so stressed that they destroy things. They urinate and defecate, chew furniture, scratch doors, crash through windows, etc. The bad news is that this happens with thousands of dogs. The good news is that it can be avoided.

A puppy's reaction to separation from the pack typically does not start off as dramatic as that. Extreme behavior in a dog usually evolves over days, weeks, and months of improper handling on the part of the owner.

As I have said, the anxious feeling that a dog has when separated from the pack does not have to evolve into destructive behavior. If you handle your puppy correctly from the time he joins your family, he will learn to deal appropriately with the stress of being left home alone. What is appropriate behavior? Appropriate behavior is taking a nap and chewing on dog toys. It is *not* losing control, barking nonstop, or trashing your house.

To achieve this, let's take a look at things from the canine point of view. Consider how your puppy views the world. To help you do this, I'm going to make you the new puppy, born to a mother dog who is well cared for in a family home or a well-managed kennel.

Pack Life!

You—an adorable little puppy—have spent the first eight weeks of your life 24/7 with members of your pack. You were *always* with your littermate brothers and sisters and your mother. Maybe even dear old dad was around from time to time. You might have occasionally interacted with a canine aunt or uncle. It was a world of dogs!

Some tall, two-legged dogs (humans, that is) would also visit every day. They would pick you up, play with you, and coo at you in friendly, soothing tones. You were never completely alone.

As the weeks moved on, mother dog would leave the pack each day for short periods of time. However, she was never gone too long, and you still had your siblings for company. When she did return, mother dog was happy to see you. She always provided licks, motherly nudges, and *food*. You knew that Mom accepted and loved you, in whatever way canines understand acceptance and love (I wish I truly knew!). Through her actions she let you know that you were part of the pack.

As you got a little older, the tall, two-legged dogs started showing up with your food. It was kind of a mushy gruel, but pretty tasty. They too were always so happy to see you.

Even when you left the den (puppy pen) to go out on adventures, you were with Mom and the two-legged dogs.

Life was pretty grand. You were happy and content.

Joining a New Pack

Then one day you leave the pack. You're picked up and carried away by tall, two-legged dogs that you may have met once or twice. Or maybe you never met them before. But they are kind to you. They talk to you in friendly tones and pet and snuggle with you.

The next thing you know, you find yourself exploring a brand-new territory. Being curious by nature, you find this adventure kind of interesting. There are lots of new smells, sights, and sounds. They're interesting, but a little scary, too. You find yourself sticking pretty close to your new companions.

What a day! You play, play, and play some more. You're picked up and put down multiple times. You're brought inside and outside. Little, two-legged dogs play with you. They are squealing and rolling objects for you to chase.

These new two-legged dogs serve you food several times a day. You don't even have to compete with your brothers and sisters for it. Basically, it's the same mushy gruel that you used to get, but now it's all yours!

By the end of this wonderful and exciting day, you are so tired that you pass out from exhaustion on a nice soft place.

Where Did Everyone Go?

The next thing you know, you wake up and no one is around. The room is dark. There are no brothers or sisters snuggled with you. No mother dog. No tall, two-legged dogs. Where is everyone? And you're trapped! Confined to a place that you can't get out of.

You start to yip. A distressed-puppy where-the-heck-is-everyone? yip. After yipping a while, now you need to urinate. So you go as far away from your soft sleeping spot as you can get and pee. Your stomach is feeling a little queasy. Maybe pooping will help.

You feel a little better now. However, now you're really wide awake— and where the heck is everyone? *Yip! Yip! Yip! Yip! Yip!*

After a while the big female two-legged dog shows up, cooing to you in a soothing tone, "What's the matter, puppy? It's okay."

You feel relief at last! Somebody is around. You feel much happier. And then all of a sudden the two-legged dog is snarling. "Bad puppy! Bad. Look at this mess! Bad."

You have no idea what went wrong. You were glad to see her, and she seemed glad to see you. Now you are being snarled at for no reason that you can understand. Your ears go down, and you instinctively go belly up.

You're picked up and are taken outside, where you urinate again. The two-legged dog is very happy that you do. She coos at you. Maybe everything is all right? Maybe now we can play?

However, the two-legged dog brings you back inside, puts you back into the isolated space, and disappears. After a few minutes when no one reappears, you try the distressed yipping. Oh, that works! Here she comes again.

"Be quiet. Go to sleep. Bad puppy," she snarls.

Cower. Belly up. Don't look at her.

She leaves again. Should you yip? You want to, but what if this time she attacks? So you flop on your soft sleeping area. You are feeling extremely disoriented and confused. Why are you being exiled from the pack? What went wrong?

When you begin to chew on the corner of the soft sleeping area, you feel better. Ah, this works! It feels good to chew something. Hey, look at all this fun stuff in here. This stuff is fun to pull out. You wonder what it is.

After around a half hour of pulling fun stuff out of the sleeping area and spreading it around the room, you do one more long pee and then you fall asleep again. They next thing you know, sunlight is shining in through the window. Time to get up.

Yip. Yip. Yip. Yip. After a few minutes of yipping, you hear sounds coming your way. In burst the three little two-legged dogs. "Puppy, puppy, puppy!" they squeal. They are happy to see you. But then they stop dead in their tracks. Now a more alarmed squeal. "Mom, come quick! Look what this dumb puppy did. He destroyed part of his dog bed. And he peed on the kitchen floor. Yuck!"

In charges the big female two-legged dog. "Oh, no," she snarls. "What did you do? Bad, bad puppy." The next thing you know you are being dragged by the back of your neck and having your face shoved into your soft sleeping area. "Snarl, Snarl, Snarl" is all you hear. You cower and roll belly up. With your body language you are saying, "Please don't kill me." Finally it stops.

The next thing you know, you are outside with a couple of the little two-legged dogs. Hey, these guys like to play. Run, squeal, run, squeal. Nip a leg. Bite a foot. This is fun. Jump up, nip a hand. The littlest of the two-legged dogs doesn't seem too happy. She is whimpering.

Out charges the big female two-legged dog. You immediately go belly up. Self-preservation! You are starting to suspect that maybe this female two-legged dog doesn't like you all that much.

However, the rest of the day goes pretty well. Lots of in and out. Lots of play. Lots of attention. It feels like you are being accepted into a new pack! Unfortunately, at the end of the day, after passing out and then waking up with the pack missing, you experience a repeat of the night before. *Yip. Yip. Yip!* And then the big male two-legged dog comes in and snarls.

The next thing you know, you are being smacked on the backside with a rolled-up "paper something." It doesn't hurt all that much, but you are extremely frightened. Again you cower and roll belly up. "Please don't kill me." Your bladder lets go and you urinate. Finally the big male two-legged dog leaves, snarling as he goes.

You don't move or make a sound. You feel overwhelmed with fear and confusion. You can't understand why this new pack resents you.

After a while you start to roam around your confined area out of boredom. Hmm, wood. This looks appealing to chew on. Chewing certainly helps relieve how stressed you feel about being exiled from the pack. Maybe they will accept you tomorrow.

After a long and lonely second night of isolation—spent pacing, chewing, urinating, defecating, trying to dig your way out, with a little yipping thrown in—the sun comes up.

Sadly, you are greeted by the pack in much the same way that you were the previous morning. You're very confused. They will share food with you. They will allow you to explore away from the den with them and will even socially interact with you. But then they will abandon you for periods of time, and reunions always result in them attacking you.

It is very confusing. You want to be accepted, but you are having a hard time trusting them. You suspect that you will soon either be completely abandoned by them or driven from the pack.

Today is different from the previous two days. Today, immediately after being given some food and going outside the den to explore, you are placed in the isolation area. You can hear the entire pack leave. This must be it. They are gone for good. You yip and howl in distress. You dig as hard as you can at the spot where the pack left. You do this for hours until you fall asleep from exhaustion.

When you wake up, you are still alone. They are gone, and you are trapped. There is some food and water that the pack left behind, so you eat and drink. You go as far away from where you eat, sleep, and play to urinate and defecate.

After a little more digging to escape and find the pack, you try more distress howling and yipping. Nothing works. You go back to the wood that you chewed the night before. Chewing helps. But the wood tastes weird—it's bitter. That's okay, there's lots of wood here. You try a new area of wood that tastes fine. Chew, chew, chew. Chewing definitely helps.

The Pack Does Return. Yippee!

The first to return is the big two-legged female. She is not happy. She comes at you snarling. You roll belly up, but it does not help. She is hovering over you, snarling. You run to the corner of the room, and she comes after you. Again you are belly up. The next thing that you know, you are outside alone. The big two-legged female has left you.

It is a scary world, and you have never been out here alone before. You don't wander far from the den.

Eventually, the small two-legged dogs return. Then the big male returns. The pack is reunited. You receive mixed signals from the pack. Food is shared with you. The pack interacts with you some. The big male seems aloof. You are careful to avoid him.

Your evening turns out to be very similar to the previous evenings. You are isolated. You yip and howl. You chew to feel better. The big male two-legged dog shows up, and you are attacked.

You can sense that it is only a matter of time before the pack abandons you completely or drives you from the territory. Each time the pack leaves, you feel more anxious and desperate.

As Time Goes By

Let's take a break from being a puppy and consider the all-too-familiar scenario we just experienced. Dogs are routine-oriented creatures. If owners do not change their handling routine and training approach, the dog's behavior will not change. The new-puppy description above is typical of how dogs with out-of-control separation anxiety were first handled. I may have taken a little poetic license telling this tale in order to make my point, but I think it's clear what's happening to the puppy—and where this family's experience with their new dog is headed.

Puppies that are treated this way feel more and more insecure as days, weeks, and months pass. With this sort of handling, they do not magically become more secure, confident, and able to behave appropriately when left alone.

With steady repetition of the scenario I described, one day the puppy's worst fears are realized. Typically, the puppy is about seven or eight months old. The puppy is put into the car and driven to an animal shelter where, as he feared, he is truly abandoned by his pack.

How to Avoid This Nightmare

As I have already said, all dogs experience separation anxiety. No dog is ever going to be happy about being left behind and separated from his pack. Dogs instinctively fear abandonment. I believe it's because in the wild, wolves—our dog's ancestors—cannot survive alone for long. Being with a pack is crucial to a canine's life.

When we leave the house to go to work, school, and all the other places we go, dogs have no idea where we are going, and when they are puppies they are not sure if we will ever return. Chewing, digging, barking, and howling are behaviors that dogs resort to when they feel stressed. Stressed dogs also urinate and defecate more often.

In most cases of extreme separation anxiety, in which the dog becomes highly destructive, the problem developed during the first year of the dog's life. The scenario described earlier shows how it started.

A young dog that is left alone in an unstructured environment is given repeated opportunities to destroy household items. Of course, dogs have no concept of the value of material things. To a dog, a sofa has no more worth that a tree stump. A rug has no more value than a patch of grass.

With repetition throughout the first year of the dog's life, this stress-reducing, destructive behavior becomes a habit. This habit is triggered and repeatedly reinforced every time the dog is left home alone. The owner exacerbates the entire syndrome if the dog is punished when the owner returns home.

A dog interprets this punishment by the owner as an "attack" by a returning pack member. Valued individuals are never attacked when the pack returns! As a matter of fact, the opposite happens: Valued pack members are greeted with joy.

An attack-style greeting leaves the dog feeling confused and insecure. The next time the dog is left alone, he will feel even more anxious.

Do It Right Instead

When you have to leave your puppy alone for a period of time, do not make a big deal out of it.

When Sophie was a puppy, I would put her into her kennel crate and say, "See ya. I'll be back. You're in charge," and I would leave. In the crate was a toy or two that Sophie could safely chew on if she felt the need to chew.

Initially, I left Sophie several times throughout the day for short periods. Eventually I expanded the time she was left for up to four hours. Except for overnight, I never left her crated longer than four hours.

As I discussed in Chapter 14 on house training, dogs should not be crated during the daytime for more than four hours at a stretch. If you can't get home from work to let your puppy out to urinate and defecate, experience a little exercise, and interact socially, then you need to make some type of arrangement to achieve this. Elicit the help of a friend, relative, or neighbor. Hire a professional pet sitter or look into doggie day care. If you keep your puppy alone and confined for longer periods of time, you will in all likelihood create negative backlash. If you cannot change your schedule to meet the needs of a puppy, maybe having one at this point in your life is not a good idea.

Whenever I went out, I left Sophie in her structured environment. A structured environment might mean a kennel crate or simply a sectioned-off area with no enticing objects to destroy. The bottom line is to establish a safe, confined area where your puppy's only options are curling up and going to sleep or chewing on an appropriate doggie toy.

If you manage your puppy's surroundings, he will start to repeat appropriate behavior when left alone for brief periods of time. He won't *like* being alone, of course, but he can chew on a doggie toy for stress relief and comfort—not your woodwork, sofa, or leather shoes.

Whenever I returned from my excursions away from Sophie, I always greeted her joyously. "Hello, puppy! How was your afternoon? I missed you! What a good girl you were! Let's go outside and take a walk together."

I also always gave her a small food treat when I returned. In the wild, the pack leader shares some of the kill with valued pack members. Where did Sophie think I might have gone? Hunting, of course! I believe that giving your puppy a treat when you return helps him feel valued. It helps him form an understanding of why you sometimes leave. And it builds the puppy's confidence, based on his natural canine instincts about pack life, that you will always return.

Training Through a Canine Point of View Makes Everyone Happy

There's a bonus to this approach: You come home to a safe puppy and an intact house. How great is that? You feel happy that all is well—and there's the little fellow, wagging his tail and waiting for you.

Now if you were the puppy, how would that make you feel? Pretty darn wonderful, I think. You're greeted warmly, you're talked to, you're petted, and you're taken out for bathroom relief and a little adventure with your pack member. It happens like this day after day. Life with *this* pack is going to be great.

A Tail of Two Crates

During Sophie's first year I used two kennel crates. One crate was kept in the family room. Since we spent a lot of time in this room reading and watching TV, Sophie spent a lot of time in this room playing and exploring. The room was separated from the rest of the house by baby gates, and it was easy to supervise a feisty Lab puppy in one room. When we left during the day for short periods of time, Sophie was crated in this room with the TV left on.

The second crate was set up in the bedroom next to my side of the bed. After Sophie was let out to urinate and defecate for the last time in the evening, I put her in the crate.

At first she whimpered a little. Keep in mind that up until her first night with me, Sophie had spent her nights literally curled up with littermates. Sleeping alone was a new experience to her.

When Sophie whimpered, I leaned over and gently but firmly reassured her. "It's okay. Go to sleep." And she did. A few hours later she awoke and began to cry. I threw on a robe, took her outside, and she urinated. Good girl!

Although she would have liked to play, I put her back in the crate. (It was 3:20 A.M.) She whimpered a little. I lightly tapped on the top of the crate and said, "Go back to sleep." She did.

This pattern went on for about a week. Now, I know that getting up in the middle of the night to take out a puppy is a hassle. But it's part of the price one pays for the joys of puppy raising and the important achievement of housebreaking. Don't forget that with human babies we sometimes get up in the middle of the night for months!

By the beginning of the second week, Sophie's bladder was getting stronger and she was making it pretty well through the night. If she woke up distressed, I simply leaned over and let her know I was there.

Can I Bring Him in the Bed with Me?

Sometimes owners call me for a phone consultation and, very sheepishly, announce that they felt sorry for their new puppy when he cried at night. They admit, "I let him sleep in our bed. He curled right up and went to sleep."

They are always shocked when I say, "Good. Sleeping with pack members is a very natural thing."

Are there problems with allowing your puppy to sleep with you? Potentially there are. You are setting a behavioral precedent that you may decide to change later on. If you don't want a hundred-pound rottweiler stretched out sharing your bed for the next fourteen years, you may not want to introduce your puppy to the comforts of your bed. But if you don't mind, I sure don't. However . . .

Sharing the Pack Leader's Nest Is a Privilege, Not a Right

I don't have a problem with a dog sleeping in bed with his owner. But the dog has to remember *at all times* that bed sleeping is a dog's privilege, not his right.

I have received countless calls, letters, and e-mails over the years telling me about dogs that growl at their owners for trying to move them over a little bit. Or dogs that would not allow the owner to get back into the bed after the owner got up to use the bathroom. These surly characters should lose their bed privileges, pronto!

Only dogs that are submissive to their owners earn bed privileges.

Other Potential Problems

If your new bed-sleeping puppy is urinating or defecating on the bed, you must use the crate. It is very unusual for this to happen, but it sometimes does. Puppies do not like to soil their sleeping area. Nevertheless, I've seen puppies, particularly toy breeds, that go to the far end of the bed to urinate or defecate. Do not allow this behavior to be repeated. If your puppy does this, use the crate.

Some puppies get off the bed in the middle of the night to relieve themselves. I'm a very light sleeper. I would sense any movement by a puppy on the bed. Heavy sleepers might not. If you are finding messy "gifts" the next morning, puppy bed sleeping is not for you. Try again when housebreaking is perfected.

Nighttime chewing could also be a problem. Do not let your puppy get into the habit of chewing bed quilts, pillows, sheets, etc. If this happens, again the solution is to use the crate.

If your puppy sleeps through the night uneventfully and you don't mind sharing your bed with a dog (and dog fur), then I can't see anything wrong with sleeping with your dog. Curl up together, imagine that you are sharing a cave in the woods, and have wolf dreams. I've done it a few times.

Physical Exercise

For years I have been advocating the value of exercising dogs. As I've said many times, a tired puppy is a good puppy. Dogs that are tired are mentally content creatures. Physical exercise is as important to developing a great dog as training and socialization. I call this formula the Canine Triangle, and it's a surefire way to raise a great dog.

Having your puppy pooped out before you leave him alone helps the puppy deal better with your absence. He's not going to spend much time feeling anxious if he's sleeping. As much as possible, always try to find a way to exercise your puppy before you leave him.

Ten Ways to Help Make Your Puppy Feel Like a Valued Pack Member

1. Provide your puppy with a structured environment such as a kennel crate or a sectioned-off area with no enticing objects to destroy.

2. Make sure that your puppy has an appropriate dog toy or two in the crate to chew if he feels the need to do so.

3. Start by leaving your puppy in a structured environment several times throughout the day for short periods of time.

4. When you leave, keep the departure low-key. Put your puppy in the structured environment, say, "I'll be back," and then leave.

5. Never leave your puppy during the first year of his life for longer than four hours.

6. If your dog somehow slips up and destroys something or has a housebreaking accident, never reprimand him when you return home. Never, under any circumstances, try to correct your puppy after the fact. Late corrections do nothing except create fear, distrust, and insecurity.

7. Greet your puppy joyously when you return. Canines have instinctive greeting rituals. Valued pack members are greeted enthusiastically when the pack is reunited.

8. When you return, share a food treat with your puppy. Your puppy assumes that you have left the pack to hunt. Pack leaders share the kill with valued pack members and puppies. Let your puppy know that you, the mighty pack leader, successfully captured that box of doggie treats!

9. At night have your puppy sleep in his crate, in your bedroom right next to your bed.

10. If it works for you, consider allowing your puppy the privilege of sharing the pack leader's sleeping nest (your bed).

Sixteen

Preventing Unwanted Chewing

Chewing is one of the most prominent, frustrating, and potentially destructive aspects of puppy development. The term "chewing" means chewing on *objects*. It is quite different from mouthing, which means chewing on you or other people. Controlling mouthing is equally important for different reasons. It is covered in Chapter 18, "*Nhaa!*— Stopping Unwanted Behavior When You Growl."

The urge to chew is natural in dogs. It appears during the puppy's independence phase, or what I refer to as "the terrible twos of doggiedom"—at around four months of age (see Chapter 6, "Puppy Development"). *All* puppies go through a chewing period. However, depending on the puppy's breed, health, activity level, and personality, chewing may be more or less pronounced in the individual animal.

The best game plan is to expect your puppy to be a strong chewer. Being prepared will help you prevent big, expensive problems—such as chewed rugs, gnarled furniture, ripped-up upholstery, destroyed shoes and clothing, damaged woodwork, and holes in household walls. Sound awful? It is, but I've seen it all happen. Destructive chewing can be *very* destructive. But it also can be prevented with the guidelines described in this chapter.

The greatest hazard with destructive chewing—aside from the damage done to your home and property—is that chewing can become a lifelong

Dogs don't know the difference between old, unwanted items (such as worn-out shoes) and new, expensive versions of the same thing. To avoid chewing problems later, don't give your puppy anything but dog toys.

habit. Puppies who are free to chew on things usually do, day after day after day. Allowing destructive chewing to continue will create a *habit* of destructive chewing.

Very few chronic chewers stop on their own. Patterns established in puppyhood often last a lifetime. And even if a chronic chewer stops chewing on a daily basis, he will likely revert to destructive chewing when faced with stresses such as loneliness, a move to a new home, or a change in household members. Your job during puppyhood is to prevent chewing from becoming destructive, chronic chewing. Then you can enjoy the next twelve to fifteen years of your dog's life without this miserable problem hanging over your head.

Puppy Teeth

Anyone who has played with a young dog knows what puppy teeth, or milk teeth, feel like—sharp little pins! Although the teeth can scratch or prick your skin, they are not yet the dangerous weapons found in the mouth of an adult dog. (Nevertheless, puppies must be taught at a very young age that biting at you is *unacceptable*. Be sure to deal with mouthing right from day one.)

*   *   *

At four months old puppies lose their milk teeth. These little teeth have extremely shallow roots, so the adult teeth simply push the puppy teeth out of the jaw. Owners often never find the milk teeth because the puppy swallows them when they come out. Some owners do find the teeth and may even save them. (I'm guilty of this! Drifter's little box of puppy teeth is in one of my office drawers. Maybe the Doggie Tooth Fairy will exchange them for quarters or silver dollars someday.)

By six months old the puppy's adult teeth have emerged through the gums, and the milk teeth are replaced. (Sometimes the puppy teeth remain in the jaw for a short time next to the adult teeth. Have your veterinarian check the puppy's mouth if you are concerned that the milk teeth are not dropping out properly.) Canine adult teeth have very long, strong roots. When they erupt in the jaw, they are beautifully white. With proper care, these teeth will last the rest of your dog's life.

Although the adult teeth have emerged through the gums by the time the puppy is six months old, the teeth are still settling into the jaw. This process is complete at around a year old. As a result of this settling process, puppies tend to chew until their first year—not just during the short period when the adult teeth are actually coming in.

The Urge to Chew

I have found that puppies have the greatest urge to chew when they are between seven and nine months old. *Chewing is normal behavior in canines.* For this reason, we do not want to prevent the puppy from chewing. Trying to prevent chewing is like trying to prevent other natural behaviors, such as barking. We don't want the dog *never* to do these behaviors; we just want them channeled so the behaviors do not cause problems.

To prevent unwanted chewing, you must condition the puppy to chew appropriate items. Furniture and shoes are not appropriate items—ever. Giving the puppy an old slipper or throw pillow to play with (and chew on) are big mistakes, because puppies and dogs do not discriminate between "old" and "new." Your good slippers are just like your old slippers as far as the puppy is concerned. Toys for the puppy must be clearly and distinctly his own. Rawhide bones, squeaky toys, hard "natural" bones, and the like are items that the puppy should chew on.

All puppies have an urge to chew. Even after adult teeth appear in their mouths, puppies like to work their teeth and gums against almost any firm surface.

Supervise, Supervise, Supervise

How do you get your puppy to chew only his own toys? First, you must provide him with dog toys that are acceptable to chew. (See Chapter 8, "Safe [and Fun] Toys.") Then you must supervise, supervise, supervise! When you are home with your puppy, watch him closely. Make sure that when he lies down to chew on something, the object in his mouth is one of his own toys. If it is not, you must be watching the puppy so that you can correct the problem *as it is happening.* Scolding a puppy when you find a chewed-up pillow an hour—or even ten minutes—after the chewing took place is pointless. The puppy may look intimidated or sad during your scolding, but he has no understanding that your anger now has anything to do with his actions an hour ago. An effective correction (one that will help the puppy learn not to do it again) must be timed properly. That means *as the unwanted behavior is about to happen or is in the process of happening.*

I correct puppies for chewing inappropriate items in the same manner that I correct a housebreaking accident. I growl. *"Nhaa!"* I will only escalate my aggression toward the pup if he does not stop chewing when I growl.

Then I will give a shake at the scruff of the neck and growl louder. (See Chapter 18, "*Nhaa!*—Stopping Unwanted Behavior When You Growl.") Ideally, this correction is given when my intuition tells me the puppy is *about* to begin chewing something. My growl at that point is saying, "Don't even *start* to chew that item!" The next best time to give a correction is just as the pup begins to chew something. After the item has been chewed and you find a soggy, frayed corner of the living room rug, it's too late. Clean up the mess, repair the damage, and promise yourself that you will supervise better next time.

Some people tell me that instead of correcting the puppy, they simply want to take away the unwanted object and give the puppy one of his own toys. Switching the objects *after* a correction is okay, but there are a few important guidelines.

First, always give the verbal correction ("*Nhaa!*"). It's important that the puppy have a disagreeable experience when he chews on forbidden objects. This disagreeable experience (your growl) actually speeds up learning. It makes the puppy want to avoid the behavior that caused his disagreeable experience. After you correct your puppy, remove him from

Appropriate chew items help puppies learn what they can and cannot chew. By teaching the rules early in life, you will avoid having a dog who is a chronic, destructive chewer.

the immediate area if possible. Wait about thirty seconds and then provide the puppy with one of his own dog toys. Waiting is important. If you switch objects immediately, the puppy will learn that he can get a rawhide or other great toy simply by chewing something of yours. Don't laugh! Puppies are smart, and I've really seen this happen. You do not want the puppy to think of the toy as a reward for chewing the unwanted item.

Chewing When You're Not Home

Watching your puppy like a hawk is an important rule—but it's only possible when you are there to do it. When you can't watch your puppy, use the kennel crate. This is the puppy's den, the place where he can safely rest when you are not home. (Remember that your puppy should not be confined to a crate during the day more than four hours at a time.) A properly used crate is a great tool to help you shape acceptable chewing behavior in a puppy. When the puppy is in the crate, appropriate dog toys should be in the crate with him.

The structured environment of the crate not only prevents destructive chewing, it also teaches your puppy how to behave when you are not home. A puppy in a crate has only two options: curl up and go to sleep or chew on his own toys. Remember, repetition creates habits. Throughout the first year of your puppy's life, you must crate him every time you cannot supervise him. If you are consistent with this, your puppy will form a wonderful habit of going to sleep or chewing on his own toys when you are not home.

Of course, it works the other way, too. If every time you leave your puppy unsupervised throughout the chewing phase—and he chews something inappropriate—he will form a habit of destructive chewing when left alone. This habit can last well into adulthood. In more than twenty years of dog training, I've found this to be true without exception. I have yet to meet a dog who had been supervised closely throughout puppyhood and crated when left alone and then *suddenly* became a destructive chewer as an adult dog. It just doesn't happen. Chronic, destructive chewing is a bad habit that forms during the puppy's first year. Do the right thing through the first year and I can almost guarantee that you will have an adult dog whom you can leave all day without a problem.

Introducing Freedom in the House

Chewing typically lasts until the puppy is about a year old. For this reason, it is imperative that you use a kennel crate or similar structured environment until your dog outgrows this phase. Does that mean that on the dog's first birthday you open the crate door and go off to work for the day? No! As with other training, you have to introduce new behaviors in small steps. Too much too fast is a good formula for failure.

Here's a typical scenario for introducing a year-old dog to freedom in the house. First, I evaluate the dog's personality and behavior. Is he still grabbing at things when I'm around? At a year old, Drifter would pick up a coaster from the coffee table or have his head in the bathroom trash the minute I turned my back. He was not ready for even five minutes of unsupervised freedom! Other dogs are ready at a year and others (unfortunately) not until they are almost two.

By the time Drifter was fifteen months old, his grabbing behaviors had diminished greatly. Maturity no longer seemed to be so far off. That was my cue that I could start to introduce unsupervised freedom. For the first few days I would leave him free in the house while I walked to the end of the driveway to get the mail. If he did not touch anything in those few minutes, I gave him lots of praise. I'm not sure he understood exactly what the praise was for, but I wanted to do everything possible to encourage and reinforce good behavior. If he did get into trouble, I cleaned up or fixed the mess and decided to wait a few more weeks before trying unsupervised freedom again. When my few minutes out of the house were successful, I gradually increased the time I was away.

Again, don't do too much too fast. Spend a week at one level, such as the time it takes to drive the kids to school or to pick up some bread or milk at the corner store. Increase the time only as you have success. One mistake on the dog's part means that you must immediately back down to shorter times or even start all over again. Why? If the dog makes a mistake the second day and then maybe again on the third, you are *repeating unwanted behavior.* Do not give the dog the opportunity to do this! If I could explain to my dog in clear English, "You let me down. Don't do that tomorrow," I would not need this system. But I can't, so putting restrictions on what behaviors he can do is my only option. It's your job to prevent unwanted behaviors from being repeated.

I build slowly toward a full day of unsupervised freedom in the house.

At first I add only ten or fifteen minutes to practice at a new level. Later I usually can jump in one-hour increments. The dog's increasing maturity helps make my job progressively easier. Remember, time is on your side. Your puppy one day *will* be a mature, adult dog who is completely trustworthy when home alone—as long as you make the effort to shape that trustworthy behavior.

A Puppy-Proof House

The job of supervising a puppy is not an easy one. Life in an average household is busy and at times extremely hectic. Although supervision is your most important way to prevent destructive chewing, you can create a second line of defense. This is called a puppy-proof house.

Rule number one for a puppy-proof house is to pick up after yourself and your young children. (Older children and teens should be picking up their own items. If they don't, a puppy who is a destructive chewer will quickly teach them to!) Shoes left in the middle of the bedroom, stuffed animals on the stairs, a leather belt draped on a chair, a baseball glove on the floor by the back door—these are all enticing objects for an inquisitive puppy with the urge to chew. If you put things away—even if they are tossed onto a shelf or thrown in a basket that's off the floor—they are not within puppy range. Look at it this way: Each object you put away is one less item that you need to keep your eye on when the puppy is loose. Limiting clutter will make your job of supervision much easier.

Rule number two is to close doors, especially closet doors. An unlatched door is an invitation to a curious puppy to see what's on the other side. If your designer leather pumps or expensive briefcase are there, they are vulnerable to attack. I also close doors to rooms that are unused or filled with many valuable items, such as antiques or important papers. My office door in my home stays closed much of the time. I don't want manuscript papers chewed or walked on.

An alternative to a closed door is a baby gate. Baby gates limit access to rooms without doors or to rooms that you want open (for ventilation, for example). I use baby gates to keep a puppy in the kitchen with me while I wash dishes. I put a baby gate at the bottom of the stairs so the puppy doesn't sneak upstairs and wander around unsupervised. I put a baby gate across the front porch opening so that while I read outside, my puppy can be with me without wandering away. Baby gates are simple, inexpensive tools that will make your job of puppy supervision a lot easier.

Rule number three is to look for puppy-level dangers. Hazards in the home are abundant, as any parent of a two-year-old toddler can tell you. Electrical cords, toxic chemicals, sharp objects, and the like are all potential dangers to a puppy. Do you want to look at your house through a puppy point of view? Crawl around each room on your hands and knees. You'll see lots of things that were not visible from your normal viewpoint. Those electrical cords dangling under an end table might entice the puppy to chew them, causing serious electrical burns or death. The cords could tangle around him, pulling the lamp over. An ironing board could easily be bumped during play, sending a heavy iron onto a puppy's head. A pile of old rags soaked with cleaning chemicals could get chewed on, poisoning a dog. The potential hazards are endless! It's your job to anticipate trouble and prevent it from ever happening. Believe me, if anyone can find trouble, puppies can. Think long and hard about your home. How safe is it?

The dangers described above are multiplied when no one is home to supervise a wandering-gypsy pup. Small problems can quickly become disasters when a puppy is free in the house without anyone at home. Uncontrolled bleeding can weaken or kill a dog. A swallowed sock (or worse, a pair of pantyhose) can gag a puppy or block up his intestine. The puppy's collar can get caught on something, causing him to strangle. Do these sound like scare tactics? They are! But they are also real possibilities. Even if you don't want to confine your puppy when no one is home to protect your valuable home and items in it, you must do it to protect your puppy's life. Baby gates, closed doors, and a kennel crate will not only confine the pup and protect your possessions, they will protect the puppy himself.

Seventeen

Introducing the Leash and Collar

For the next ten to fifteen years of his life, your dog probably will wear a dog collar. Attached to that collar probably will be a rabies tag, a license tag, and, I hope, an identification tag with your address and telephone number. Frequently attached to that collar will be a leash. For most dogs the leash and collar are basic equipment for their entire lives. For this reason, it is important that your puppy has a positive introduction to both.

A Puppy Collar

Fitting and introducing a collar to your puppy is a relatively easy process. First, buy a lightweight, nylon buckle collar that fits properly. Be sure that it's not too tight or too loose. How can you tell? It should be just loose enough so that you can slide your hand under the collar. However, it should not be so loose that the collar can slip over your pup's head without being unbuckled. Many pet supply shops will let you bring your puppy into the store for a fitting. Or you can simply measure around your puppy's neck with a cloth tape measure to determine the proper length.

Your puppy's worried expression over a leash and collar won't last long if you introduce them properly. Plus, many puppies quickly associate the leash with a walk or other fun outing.

Be sure that the collar you choose does not have so much excess material that the puppy could get the end in his mouth and chew it. Also, use common sense in selecting an appropriate width. A short but wide collar would be inappropriate for a tiny Yorkshire terrier, and a long skinny collar would probably not be very comfortable around the neck of a Saint Bernard pup. If the collar is lightweight, the right length, and a suitable width, it will be accepted more readily by your puppy.

Now put the collar on the puppy. If your puppy is a wiggler, you may want to have someone hold him while you buckle it on. Some puppies do not react at all to the feel of a collar. If that describes your puppy, praise him! Most puppies do react, however, because the collar feels foreign. Puppies may scratch at it with a rear foot. (If your puppy does this, be careful that he doesn't get his foot stuck in the collar. I've seen it happen!) Puppies may roll on the collar or even rub their neck on the ground. This behavior generally lasts a couple of minutes. Puppies may do it off and on that first day before they adjust to the feel of the collar. In the rare event that a puppy is truly upset, you can distract him by getting on the floor and playing with him. Squeeze a squeaky toy or roll a tennis ball to redirect his attention. I've never met a puppy who could not learn to wear a collar when it was properly fitted and introduced carefully.

I have found that it's best to leave the collar on all the time so the puppy gets used to wearing it. Safety comes first, however. If there is *any* chance that it might get stuck on anything, such as hardware on a kennel crate, remove the collar when you are not supervising the pup.

At this stage, do not put ID tags on your puppy's collar. Young puppies have the uncanny knack of getting the tags stuck on something—or they end up with the tags in their mouths. I suggest waiting until the pup is about six months old before putting tags on the collar. (This is assuming, of course, that the puppy is not roaming free around your neighborhood—which he certainly should not be doing.) Use the time before then to order ID tags so they are ready to wear when the pup is old enough.

Introducing the Leash

If, after a couple of days, your puppy is no longer paying attention to his new collar, you can begin introducing him to a leash. I suggest a *six-foot cloth leash*. Cloth leashes are lightweight, washable, and inexpensive to buy. They're also inexpensive to replace if your puppy happens to chew one up when you're not looking! If you like the idea of a nice leather leash, save your money until your puppy is a bit older and has acquired a little training.

Some people like those expandable leashes that go six feet and beyond. I don't like them for several reasons. One, they allow (and actually encourage) the dog to pull on the leash, which is essentially an out-of-control behavior. (All dogs can learn to walk comfortably on a loose leash. It's a training exercise I call Controlled Walking, which is described thoroughly in my training book, *Dog Talk: Training Your Dog Through a Canine Point of View.*) Two, expandable leashes are cumbersome to handle and are not a good training tool. They prevent handlers from carrying out the techniques properly. And three, I've seen a lot of dim-witted dog owners "let the leash out" at completely inappropriate times, such as on a crowded sidewalk or in a busy airport. (Dog ownership and common sense don't always go together!) If you like the idea of an expandable leash for your particular needs, that's okay. Just wait to use it until your puppy is a trained adult.

Puppies sometimes are reluctant to move when first wearing a leash. Encourage the puppy forward with an interesting object. *Never* pull the puppy along.

To introduce a six-foot leash to your pup, simply attach it to his buckle collar and let him drag it around the house or yard while you are watching. Be sure to supervise closely so the leash doesn't get stuck around furniture, bushes, etc. Also, don't let your puppy lie down and chew the leash. Keep an eye on him! If your puppy seems inhibited and doesn't want to walk along dragging the leash, encourage him by throwing a ball or simply run around and prompt him to chase you. It's okay to play games where your puppy chases you, but never chase your puppy. Chasing puppies can undermine your come-on-command training. Be sure to discourage nipping and mouthing if your pup tries these behaviors when he chases you.

Repeat this practice session every day for at least ten minutes at a time. Again, watch your puppy closely. Don't let him flop down and chew the leash in half.

After about a week of daily practice, your puppy should be comfortable dragging the leash behind him. He's now ready for the next step. Pick up the end of the leash and follow the puppy around. Go where he wants to go, providing it's not toward a danger, such as a road. Try to keep the leash as loose as possible at all times. Follow the puppy around the house and yard for several minutes at a time. Don't worry if the puppy pulls a bit at this point, but do discourage chewing on the leash. When the leash is in your hand, it becomes an extension of you. (See the section below on how to put a stop to leash chewing.)

Repeat this procedure for about a week or until the puppy appears unconcerned with the feel of being attached to a leash. Remember, keep the leash loose as much as possible.

When the puppy starts pulling you around most of the time, that's the sign that you are ready for the next step. Now *you* pick the direction. Have an object of attraction ready in one hand. A squeaky toy, a ball, or a piece of doggie biscuit usually will do the job. Hold the leash in one hand and the object of attraction in the other. Step off in any direction. If your puppy follows along willingly, praise him! Verbally encourage him. This is exactly what you want him to do.

If your puppy "puts his brakes on" and does not want to follow you, here's what to do: Wave the object around directly in front of your pup's nose to attract his attention. Step off again, but be sure not to pull on the leash. Just keep showing him the object as you move along together. Sometimes a more interesting object, such as a rawhide or tidbit of food, will make a difference. I'll even stoop down on the ground (with the leash still in my hand) to encourage the puppy to move along.

It's okay to give gentle jerks and releases as you induce the puppy with the object, but *do not* pull on the leash. Pulling causes dogs of any age to resist and even to pull in the opposite direction. The end result is dragging your pup. Dragging a puppy on the leash is one of the worst things you can do! I have met several dogs who hate the leash because their owners created a disagreeable association with it. They dragged the dogs along in an attempt to get them to walk.

Here's the hard part. Praise your puppy only when he starts to move. Be careful that you do not unintentionally reinforce his resistance. A lot of owners make this mistake. They encourage the resistant puppy to move by talking to him in sweet, soothing tones. "Come on, puppy! Let's go! That's a good puppy! You can do it!" These tones are actually praise. If the puppy won't move and is firmly planted in place, you are actually praising this behavior! The best thing is to say nothing until he moves, then begin to praise. Certainly do not growl "*Nhaa!*" in an attempt to correct a resistant puppy. The puppy probably is resisting because he is intimidated by the new situation. Growling would only intimidate him more. *So say nothing.* Only when he moves in the direction you want him to go should you begin to praise.

Repeat this exercise with your puppy for about ten minutes every day. With just a little practice, your puppy will become familiar and confident walking on the leash.

Biting on the Leash

I discourage biting on the leash at all stages of training, including Puppy Preschool. That's because the leash is simply an extension of you. Biting on the leash while you are on the other end is the same as mouthing your hand or arm. The puppy is testing you.

I curb leash-biting by growling "*Nhaa!*" at the pup. If the puppy does not stop mouthing the leash when I growl, I'll abruptly jerk the leash upward out of the pup's mouth as I growl "*Nhaa!*" again. Be astute. The ideal time to growl is when the puppy is *about* to put the leash in his mouth. If you time the correction properly, you will be saying to the puppy, "Don't mouth the leash." If you correct the pup after he already has the leash in his mouth, all your correction says is, "Stop mouthing the leash." That's not as effective as preventing the behavior in the first place. Good timing with the correction is important—it greatly speeds up the learning process.

Leash-biting should be discouraged right from the start. Immediately growl *"Nhaa!"* if the puppy grabs at the leash. Abruptly jerk it up and out of his mouth and growl again if the puppy ignores your first correction.

If your puppy is a persistent leash-biter, you should actually bait the pup into biting at the leash. This will give you the opportunity for numerous corrections, which are necessary to eliminate this unwanted behavior. Wave the leash in front of the puppy's face. When he looks interested and seems like he is ready to grab it, growl "*Nhaa!*" If he gets it in his mouth before your correction stops him, abruptly jerk it out as described above. Repeat this procedure several times. (You may even want to do it as a "warm-up" before your daily leash-walking sessions.) Most puppies actually turn their heads away from the leash after a minute or two of this routine. That's because each time your puppy tried to bite the leash, you made it into a disagreeable experience.

Introducing a Training Collar

When your puppy begins his formal education at four months old, chances are good that he will need a training collar. I recommend that you introduce a training collar to the puppy when he is around fourteen weeks (three and a half months) old. Then when he begins school he will be familiar with it.

A training collar is simply a chain made of small, round, metal links with a large metal ring at each end. The chain is dropped through one of the rings to form the collar.

A training collar is also sometimes referred to as a choke collar. However, the name "choke collar" is a misnomer. A training collar will choke your puppy *only if it is misused.* Allowing your puppy to pull you down the street—with the collar tightened around his neck—is an example of misuse. Purposely pulling your puppy off the ground with this type of collar also will choke him. Neither puppies nor adult dogs should ever be choked in this way. It's dangerous and unnecessary in an effective training program. The proper way to use the training collar is to jerk and release. When you jerk and release a training collar, the dog feels the correction across the muscular back of his neck. The back of a dog's neck and his chest are the strongest part of his body. No harm or pain is inflicted when a training collar is used properly.

During Puppy Preschool, you do not need to concern yourself with how to correct your puppy with the training collar. At this point in your dog's life, simply becoming familiar with the collar is all that is necessary.

Fitting the collar properly is important. You will need to choose both the length and width (link size). No matter what size your pup, the links should be either "medium" or "heavy" gauge. Avoid the extremes of "fine" or "extra heavy." Fine links are too sharp against a dog's neck, and extra heavy links don't release smoothly when you try to jerk and release. Small-to-medium-sized puppies should use a medium-gauge training collar, and medium- to large-sized puppies should use a heavy-gauge training collar. Don't let a pet-store clerk talk you into anything else. Also, make sure that the two metal rings don't have any clips, hooks, or tags on them. These get in the way of using the collar correctly.

The length of the collar is also important. When the collar is slipped over your puppy's head and you pull up on the ring that the leash attaches to, you should have no more than two to three inches of excess chain. Too much chain will prevent you from using the collar properly during formal training.

To introduce your puppy to a training collar, slip it over his head and just let him wear it around the house while you are at home supervising. (You can leave his buckle collar on if you wish.) The metal links will probably sound and feel strange to him. He may shake his head, scratch at his neck, or roll around on the floor. Or he may ignore the collar completely. If he seems especially worried, distract him with a biscuit or toy.

Let the puppy wear the training collar for twenty or thirty minutes each day. After a few days, reach down and put your finger through the ring that the leash would attach to. Lift the ring up and down a few times, but do not pull the collar tight. Your goal is simply to make the "zipping" noise that is associated with a proper jerk-and-release correction. (Again, corrections on a training collar are not part of Puppy Preschool.) We just want the puppy to become familiar with the sounds of his training collar so that he's a confident student during formal training.

A final caution: Always supervise your pup while he's wearing a training collar, and *never* put him in his crate with the collar on. Puppies are such active and curious creatures that one of the rings could easily get caught on a part of the crate. When the puppy is out of the crate, the collar could get caught on a window handle, tree branch, or other unforeseen object. Then you have a struggling, frightened puppy who could actually strangle himself. This precaution is true for adult dogs as well. Never leave a dog unsupervised while he's wearing a training collar. It's just not worth the risk.

Eighteen

"Nhaa!"—Stopping Unwanted Behavior When You Growl

The primary form of communication in canines is body language. Dogs use their ears, tail, head, and body to share information with other dogs. The message may be "I'm tough" or "Let's play." But dogs do communicate verbally as well. A variety of barks, growls, whimpers, and howls all have specific meaning to a dog.

One verbal tone is essential for all dog owners. It's a tone that will help you communicate clearly with your dog. What is it? It's *Nhaa*—the growl!

Mother dogs use the growl to teach their puppies to stop whatever they are doing. For example, when puppies nurse too vigorously or chew on Mom's ears or legs, she will growl. This is a warning to the puppies. If they ignore the warning, mother dog will escalate her aggression toward the puppies by snapping at them. That usually gets their attention! I have even seen mother dogs grab an especially bold pup by the scruff of the neck and give a firm but gentle shake and then roll him over, belly up. On occasion, I've seen mother dogs nip their puppies hard enough to cause them to yipe.

All of these behaviors are done to develop respect. Mother dog expects her puppies to stop in their tracks when she growls. She demands—and

Mother dogs put up with a lot from their puppies. If the puppies get too wild or try biting her, she may growl or even snap at them. This teaches the puppies that she is in charge.

gets—that respect by increasing her aggression when the puppies fail to listen. Mother dogs usually do not have to be aggressive with their pups day in and day out. A few aggressive snaps often teach bold pups that the growl really means business. Then the growl is all the mother dog needs to use. The pups learn that mother dog is capable of being tougher if she needs to—so they might as well pay attention right away.

One other way a mother dog develops respect is by being consistent. In fact, it's been my observation that mother dogs are the most consistent creatures on the face of the earth! They will growl *every time* their puppies do something they don't like until eventually the pups learn to avoid that behavior.

Your Turn to Growl

When your puppy comes home to live with you at seven or eight weeks old, it is important that you step right in where mother dog left off. To imitate mother dog's growl, I use a guttural sound. It is low in tone and comes from deep in my throat: "*Nhaa!*" Most puppies instantly understand what this means, and they stop whatever they are doing. Like mother dog, consistency is the key. You should growl every time your puppy does an unwanted behavior.

Chances are great that your puppy will not learn to avoid a particular behavior with one growl. Clients sometimes ask me how many times they will need to growl before their puppy learns to avoid a behavior. My standard answer is ten to ten thousand times! That's because it's difficult to predict learning. How fast your puppy learns something depends on so many things—his temperament, the behavior you want him to learn, his maturity level, and so on. However, there is one guarantee: The more consistent you are, the quicker the puppy will learn.

Several years ago I did a private consultation with a woman and her extremely feisty eleven-week-old Airedale. This puppy was very mouthy. He was constantly chewing on her hands and arms. The woman was trying to correct this behavior by swatting at the puppy's muzzle and saying "*No bite.*" The puppy just got nasty when she did this. He would snarl and snap at her in response.

When I picked him up he immediately started mouthing my hand. I growled "*Nhaa!*" He stopped mouthing instantly and licked my hand. I praised him and gently started to touch his front foot. As soon as I touched his foot, he began chewing at my hand again. "*Nhaa!*" I growled. He immediately stopped mouthing and licked my hand. His owner was astounded.

I handed the puppy over to her and as soon as he began to mouth her hand, she growled "*Nhaa!*" He stopped mouthing and licked her hand. She could not believe it. The consultation went very well and when I left, my client was confident that she was on the right track. I didn't hear from her for several weeks and then one day she called me on the phone. She had a couple of questions about her puppy, which I answered. Then I asked her about the mouthing. "Is he getting better with it?"

"Definitely," she replied, "he rarely does it anymore."

"Great!" I said. "And how about your growl? Is he still responsive to it?"

"Yes," she said, "But I wanted to ask you about that. I think he thinks his name is *Nhaa!* Is it normal that I growl as much as I do?"

To all puppy owners: Yes! Do not be concerned if you find yourself

When mother dog growls, puppies learn to submit. Puppy owners should pick up right where mother dog left off, teaching the puppy that *"Nhaa!"* really means business.

growling a lot the first few months that you live with your puppy. It's quite natural. In fact, if you were a female wolf with a litter of pups, you and the other adults in the pack would be growling and snapping at puppies at various times during the day. As you have probably discovered, puppies try all sorts of behaviors. They'll repeat the ones that are agreeable to them and eventually stop the ones that are disagreeable.

Keep in mind that growling is communication. Your goal is to make unwanted behaviors (like chewing the rug or mouthing your hand) disagreeable to your pup. The better you become at growling in a timely and consistent way, the faster your puppy will learn. Remember, *every time* you want your puppy to stop what he is doing, communicate with him by using dog talk: *"Nhaa!"*

Mouthing

Mouthing is the term used when a puppy chews on your hands, arms, or other body parts. Inexperienced dog owners sometimes interpret this behavior as playing. Others think this behavior has to do with teething. Both interpretations are wrong. Although puppies do chew things while they are teething, chewing items and mouthing people are two totally different behaviors. (To deal with chewing, see Chapter 16, "Preventing Unwanted Chewing.")

Mouthing behavior in puppies is not a sign that a pup has a bad temperament or a "mean streak." All puppies mouth to a greater or lesser degree. The experienced dog owner understands this behavior for what it is: It's simply a form of testing. This is your puppy's way of finding out where in the hierarchy of the pack he stands with you and other members of your family.

Dealing with mouthing is a very cut-and-dry process. If you allow a puppy to mouth you, he will view you as an individual of lower standing in the pack. He will expect you to follow direction from him and will never become a truly obedient dog. On the other hand, if you consistently correct your puppy whenever he mouths you, he will think of you as a dominant pack member. He will want to follow direction from you.

Although mouthing does not necessarily mean that your puppy will grow up to become a vicious dog, many puppies who get away with mouthing do get nasty when they become adults. This is because they grow up thinking that they are the pack leader and can bite whenever they want to. In other words, among canines, pack leaders growl at and bite underlings—not the other way around. An adult dog in your home who thinks he is pack leader may resist being removed from the bed or the sofa by growling and snapping. Dogs who think they are boss will bite when their subordinate owners try to move them or take something from them.

One of my guidelines with puppies is that I don't allow them to do anything as a puppy that I don't want them to do as an adult. A lot of people tell me how cute it is when their little puppy chews on their hand or fingers. Then a few weeks later they tell me the puppy is getting too tough, always mouthing and sometimes biting. Then I hear that their eight-month-old adolescent is snapping at them. The worst-case end-result is when I hear that the dog has seriously bitten a family member or the mail carrier or a neighbor's child. That dog never learned that putting teeth onto human skin is absolutely unacceptable behavior. The time to teach this most effectively is during Puppy Preschool when the pup's still trying to find his place in the pack. The longer you wait to deal with a mouthing pup, the greater your potential for getting a snapping or biting older dog.

So keep in mind how significant mouthing really is. Along with never achieving the goal of an obedient dog, you may potentially create a monster by tolerating mouthing. Nip it in the muzzle (excuse the pun) and you will be doing yourself and your dog a big favor.

Are Growling and Biting Really Necessary?

Although discipline is not the most pleasant aspect of raising and training a puppy, in some ways it is the most essential. If your dog does not respect you, he will *never* be obedient. And the time to gain respect is when puppies are young. But is all that growling and biting really necessary?

Keep in mind that your puppy's temperament will have a lot to do with how much growling goes on in your household. Some puppies are "live wires" and are into everything every chance they get. They try to chew on the furniture, jump on the kids, torment the cat, grab things from the laundry basket, explore interesting closets, etc., etc., etc! This kind of adventurous puppy is often headstrong and will keep trying unwanted behaviors many times before your corrections start to make a difference.

Close supervision and a lot of tough, consistent growling are absolutely essential to gain control over a puppy like this.

Other puppies are marshmallows. They are content to lie near their owners, chew on their own toys, and not bother with the kids or the cat. One or two growls for an unwanted behavior may be all it takes to teach this kind of puppy to avoid doing something. But be advised—not too many puppies fit this description! Those that do often are quite young. After a few weeks in your home, their confidence will build and you may have a more adventurous sort. So be prepared. Probably the most reliable thing you can say about puppies is that they can be unpredictable!

Keep in mind that the techniques I have described here should be used on puppies between eight weeks and four months old. By the time your puppy begins formal obedience training at four months old, he should understand that *"Nhaa!"* means to stop immediately. Owners who have accomplished this goal will have a much easier time training their dogs. It goes without saying that training will be frustrating if your attempts to practice obedience exercises are inhibited because your puppy thinks he is the pack leader.

Nineteen

Handling Your Puppy

Have you ever held a puppy and had him wiggle and squirm until you let him go? Do you try to hold your own puppy to brush his fur, clip his nails, or check his teeth—only to have him flip around in resistance? Although many puppies like being held and petted, they often do not like being physically controlled. Puppies have to be taught how to respond to brushing, nail clipping, and the like. I give this the general term "handling."

Handling is one of the most important things that owners can do with their puppies. In fact, conditioning the puppy to be handled should begin the first week the puppy comes into your home. It's essential that the puppy (and later, the adult dog) accept your hands as you gently control or manipulate any part of his body.

By the time puppies are adults, they should allow their owners and their veterinarian to touch and examine them without growling, snapping, or biting. You should be able to do *anything* from the following list to your dog without a struggle: brush your dog's coat, clean his ears, inspect his teeth, give him a bath, administer drugs or medications (or first aid), clip his toenails, check his body for fleas, put on and take off a collar, remove a tick. The list could go on and on. The point should be clear. Your dog must be able to tolerate whatever you must do to keep him healthy, clean, and well trained.

*   *   *

This discussion, unfortunately, requires commentary about dog abuse. A dog should *never* be expected to tolerate hitting, kicking, or any harmful, aggressive acts. You should never use any of these acts on a dog (except, of course, in self-defense if you are literally being attacked). Abuse can certainly intimidate a dog, but it destroys all trust and bonding with your pet. If you or members of your family cannot control your abusive actions, do the dog a favor and find him another home. Every dog owner has the responsibility of *protecting* his or her pets from harm—not inflicting it or standing by while someone else inflicts it. So when I talk about handling in this book, I mean gentle, caring handling. Anything else is dog abuse, and it has no place in any situation.

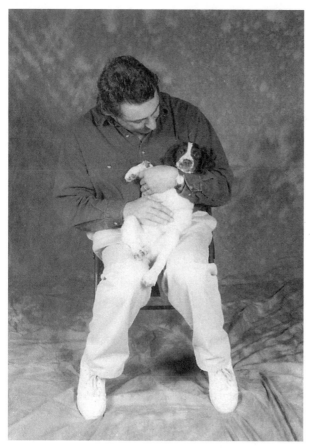

Teaching your puppy to accept gentle handling is an important part of Puppy Preschool.

Starting Belly-Up

If you do not teach dogs to be handled early in their lives, visits to the veterinarian or groomer and home examinations by you can become a real trauma. I remember one owner who avoided taking her golden retriever to the veterinarian for an annual heartworm check and medication, all because it was a huge struggle. Sure enough, the unprotected dog became infected with heartworm, and the poor animal had to suffer through weeks of intensive therapy, almost losing his life. It would have been so easy to avoid this upsetting experience if the dog had been taught to accept being handled.

Here's how to start. At least once a day, sit on a comfortable chair and put your puppy on your lap. Gently roll him onto his back, belly up. His head should be resting on your chest with his tail near your knees. If he wiggles and fights because he does not like being in this position, hold him firmly in place and growl, "*Nhaa!*" Remember, the phrase "But he doesn't like it" is not part of your vocabulary in this instance! You know this is for his own good.

If your growl stops the puppy's resistance, that's great. Relax your hold on him and praise him in a calm, soothing tone: "What a good boy. You're learning to be handled today. That's really very good!" As long as the puppy stays relaxed in your lap, keep up the gentle praise. It will reinforce to your puppy that he's doing the right thing by submitting to your handling.

If he ignores your growl and keeps squirming around, you will need to make your correction a bit tougher. In a sense, you are playing the role of mother dog. Mother dog would escalate her aggression if her puppies ignored her growl. That's what you should do, too. Try an angry, growly snap toward the puppy's muzzle. If that doesn't do the job, reread Chapter 18, "*Nhaa!*—Stopping Unwanted Behavior When You Growl."

When the puppy finally settles down after your correction, be sure to praise him. Again, your praise will help reinforce that he's now doing the right thing. When you are ready to end the practice session, which at first should be no more than about fifteen seconds, *you* let the puppy up. Don't let him up while he's having a wingding. That will only teach him that fighting you and squirming around successfully gets him free. Let him up while he's submitting and relaxed. Then give him lots of praise for a job well done.

When the puppy is relaxed in your lap, begin handling by gently touching your puppy's paw and toes. Keep in mind that dogs are very protective of their feet and will distrust you if you hurt them.

If getting the puppy to relax in your lap for about fifteen seconds is all you can accomplish for a few days, that's fine. That's a big step for some pups, especially if they have dominant puppy personalities. Just this act of making him submit in a belly-up position is a way of communicating that you are pack leader. Achieving it with some pups is no small thing.

Teaching the Puppy to Accept Being Handled

When your puppy is lying relaxed in your lap, you can begin actual handling. Start by holding one of the puppy's front paws in your hands and with deliberate action, gently touch each toe. If the puppy pulls his foot away, growl "*Nhaa!*" As he lets you handle his foot, praise him.

Keep in mind that dogs are instinctively nervous about having their feet handled. For good reason, canines are very protective of their feet, which allow them to walk, run, and hunt. It is important that your puppy learn that his feet are safe in your hands. Eventually he will need his toenails trimmed. This is a major hassle with dogs who are not used to having their feet touched. Dogs also sometimes cut a pad or get a thorn stuck in their feet. If your dog learns that you will handle his feet in a gentle manner, you can effectively treat him in such situations.

After you handle his feet, lift your puppy's lips and look at his teeth. Gently open his mouth and glance down his throat. You don't have to keep his mouth open for a long time—just long enough to look in. Place your index finger in his mouth and run it along the roof of his mouth. Remember to growl "*Nhaa!*" if the puppy tries to chew on or bite your hand.

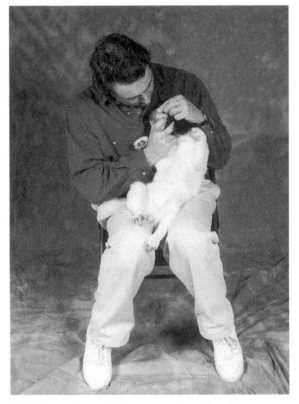

A brief mouth exam is important. It teaches the puppy to accept care of his teeth and gums and to allow you to remove objects from his mouth when necessary.

This mouth-handling sounds like a strange procedure, but I've found that it is an important one. When I worked as a veterinary technician many years ago, I recall several occasions when dogs came to the animal hospital with a piece of broken stick wedged across the roofs of their mouths. The dogs would shake their heads and paw at their faces to try to remove it, but to no avail. Removing the stick would be a simple procedure of opening the dog's mouth and reaching in with a pair of forceps—or even a finger—and popping the stick free. However, this was impossible with dogs who would not let you handle their mouths. These individuals would snap and bite when you reached toward their mouths. As a result, the veterinarian would have to put these dogs under general anesthesia so that an incredibly simple procedure would be performed. This made a big, expensive ordeal out of something that should have been quick and easy.

Handle other parts of your puppy's body while the puppy is still in your lap. Touch his tail. Run your hand along his belly. Lift his limbs and look in his "armpits" and along his thighs (favorite hiding places for ticks and fleas). Check every part of your dog. The day will soon come when you will need to inspect or handle him for health or hygiene reasons. Teaching him now to accept your handling will make that job much easier.

Knowing Your Dog's Body

There is another benefit to this handling procedure: You become familiar with your dog's anatomy. I remember one client at the veterinary hospital where I once worked. She called us in a panic, saying that her dog had mouth cancer. She rushed in and had us examine the dog. What did we find? A large "freckle" of pigment on the dog's tongue that clearly had been there his entire life. There were no signs of mouth cancer or ill health. What had panicked this owner was actually her unfamiliarity with her dog's body. It reinforced to me how important it is to know what's normal on your pet.

Knowing your dog's body greatly improves your chances of taking care of medical problems early on. When something abnormal appears, you notice it quickly and can act accordingly. Just as in people, early treatment of small problems often prevents them from becoming big, serious problems requiring extensive treatment. For example, a small lump under the

Hooray! A successful handling session is completed. Actually, I call this a stress yawn, which dogs seem to do to release tension. Your puppy doesn't have to *like* handling practice, he just has to accept it.

skin can be removed by your veterinarian with a scalpel and a few stitches. The dog may only have to spend a few hours at the hospital. On the other hand, a grapefruit-sized tumor that no one noticed until it was enormous may require complicated surgery, an extended hospital stay, and a long recovery.

One of my own dogs benefited enormously from my attentiveness and from early medical intervention. Byron's pinkish, bloodshot left eye did not respond to eye drops for conjunctivitis, a minor eye infection. The day he began blinking that eye more than normal and turning away from sunlight was the day he went straight back to the vet's office for another exam. The bad news was that a tumor was forming inside his eye, which was tough to take. But the good news was that removing the diseased eye would mean a healthy dog. No spreading of the cancer, no ruptured tumor, no premature death. Byron was middle-aged when that happened, and he lived to be a sweet, healthy old fellow who was one of the joys of my life.

Knowing what looks normal on your dog is incredibly important. In the future, if something does not look right, you will know it immediately and will be able to tend to the problem without delay. I like to remind dog owners that it is our responsibility to provide complete "social security" to our dogs. Full health insurance—which begins with teaching a puppy to accept your handling—is part of that package.

Twenty

Introducing Basic Obedience Commands: Part I

My obedience training courses have a minimum age requirement. Puppies must be *at least four months old* to be enrolled.
Why? If you are living with a puppy right now, you probably know the answer. Puppies under four months are still babies—infants, actually. They
are just learning to live away from their mother, learning their name, learning about their new family, learning to eliminate outdoors, learning to
wear a leash and collar, and so on. Plus, they don't have much of an attention span. But by the time puppies are four months old, they are usually
settled into their new lives. They are still youngsters, but they start being
able to pay better attention to training.

My minimum age requirement applies to formal obedience training
classes. It does *not* apply to the puppy training you can do before then. In
fact, there's a lot you can do between eight weeks and four months that
will give you and your puppy a head start on obedience training.

All of the steps described in this chapter are gentle introductions to basic
commands for puppies under four months. We are not asking the puppy
to achieve adult-level obedience. Not only would that be unrealistic, it
probably would be harmful. Puppies are not miniature adult dogs; they are
immature, inexperienced youngsters who must be treated accordingly.

A Formula for Effective Training

Before you try introducing any obedience commands to your puppy, you should understand a few basics about training a dog. My approach to training involves three phases. Phase one is getting the dog to do a desired behavior and attaching a command to that behavior. The second phase is forming an association in the dog's mind between the behavior and the command. This simply means to practice the exercise, letting the dog hear the command every time you cause him to do the behavior. The third phase is testing the dog. This means giving the dog the command and evaluating how he responds. If the dog responds correctly during the testing phase, you praise him enthusiastically. If he does not respond the way he is supposed to, you correct him.

In Puppy Preschool I don't use the testing phase. Puppies under four months are simply too inexperienced to test their response to an obedience command. They haven't been on earth long enough to have learned an exercise well enough to be tested! In Puppy Preschool I simply show my puppy what I want him to do and practice a lot. My goal is to form a good, strong association between the command and the behavior. As my puppy grows older there is plenty of time later on to test him.

Inducive vs. Compulsive Training

Now it's time to start with phase one: getting my puppy to do a behavior and attaching a command to that behavior. I use two forms of training when I want to cause a dog to do a behavior (although only one of them is part of the Puppy Preschool program). One form is called inducive training. It involves luring, or inducing, the dog to do something, such as to sit or lie down. When training with inducive techniques, I use a desirable object, which I call an object of attraction, to lure my dog to do the behavior. The object of attraction can be a dog biscuit, a tennis ball, a squeaky toy, a nylon bone, or anything that the dog likes. (Hot dogs or sirloin steak are okay if that's all that works!)

Here's how the inducive method works. I first get my dog's attention with the object of attraction. Then I move the object to a strategic position. If the dog is interested in the object, he'll follow the object into a sitting,

These photos show the difference between inducive and compulsive training methods. Inducive techniques involve luring the puppy into position with an object of attraction. Compulsive techniques require gently putting the puppy into the desired position.

standing, or lying-down position. I even can induce the dog to come to me with the object. At the same time I'm inducing the dog into the desired position, I say the appropriate command. With enough repetition (i.e., practice) the dog will form a strong association between doing the behavior and hearing the command. That's what phase two is all about—practicing enough times so that an association forms in the dog's mind between your command and his behavior.

I use inducive training in my obedience course for older puppies and adult dogs. I like it because it tends to speed up the learning process. Many dogs form associations to commands rather quickly when trained with objects of attraction. Inducive training also seems to make dogs respond to commands in a more animated manner.

The other form of training I use is called compulsive training, which is part of formal obedience training as well as of Puppy Preschool. This approach involves compelling the dog to do a behavior by physically manipulating the dog's body into the desired position. Compulsive training is always done in a gentle manner. You do not need to be rough with your dog in order to compel him to do something.

Although dogs do not seem to learn as quickly as they do with inducive methods, compulsive training has important advantages. Compulsive training teaches your puppy that you are in charge. Every time you physically compel your puppy to do a behavior, you are also psychologically saying, "I'm pack leader. If I want to make you sit or lift your legs so you lie down, I can do so." This is an incredibly important lesson for puppies (and all dogs) to learn. For more on this subject, see Chapter 19, "Handling Your Puppy."

Here is an example of inducive and compulsive training methods. Let's say my puppy is on the sofa and I want to get him off. I could wave a dog biscuit in front of his nose. When he showed interest in the biscuit, I could say "Off" as I lured him off the sofa. This would be an inducive method. Or, I could grab hold of his collar and gently pull or lift him off the sofa as I said "Off." This would be a compulsive method. Although the dog probably would learn the command "Off" faster with the inducive approach, he would understand that I was in charge if I employed the compulsive technique.

The majority of puppy training programs that I've seen use only inducive training methods for young puppies. Perhaps because they are dealing with puppies, these trainers think that all training should be "fun and games." I disagree. I *do* believe that all forms of puppy training should be carried out in a gentle way to make it pleasant for the dog. However, the time frame from eight weeks to four months old is the ideal time to teach your puppy that you are pack leader. It's important to handle your puppy as much as possible during this stage. In addition, it's likely that your puppy will try to mouth your hands as you compel him to do a behavior. Compelling him to do things will provide you with an opportunity to correct mouthing.

I've seen many older puppies who have gone through kindergarten puppy training programs that were based solely on inducive methods. At four months old these puppies had a good association with commands, but they had no respect for their owners. I always tell my students that if your dog does not respect you he will never be obedient—regardless of how clearly he understands a command. In order to be an obedient adult, dogs must understand not only what we want them to do, but also that they have to do it. This does not mean that it's wrong to use an inducive training technique with a puppy. But I do recommend that you gain your puppy's respect at an early age by using gentle compulsive methods. That's why I emphasize compulsive methods during Puppy Preschool. Then when your puppy reaches four months of age and starts regular obedience training, he will already be letting you handle him and be ready for all of the advantages that inducive training can provide.

Let's Begin Training

What follows are step-by-step instructions for introducing basic obedience commands to your puppy. Take your time. Introduce the exercises in a quiet room where there are few or no distractions (such as other people or pets, a TV or radio playing, toys, or food). Choose a time when your puppy is rested but has had some playtime or exercise. Make sure the puppy has recently been out to eliminate. Make sure your training time is not right around mealtime when the pup may be distracted by hunger. And make sure that you are in a relaxed, patient mood. An uptight owner who is quick to lose his or her temper with a novice obedience student has no business trying to teach anything! When you, the puppy, and the setting are prepared, it's time to begin.

Sit on Command

The objective of this exercise is to get your puppy to sit as you associate the command "Sit" with the act of sitting. In Puppy Preschool you are simply *showing* the puppy what it is you want him to do. There's plenty of time during formal training (when he's older) for you to test his response to "see if he'll do it." An untrained puppy *won't* do it! In fact, you will be teaching him to ignore the command "Sit" (or any command, for that matter) if you don't show him exactly what to do *as you are saying the command*. Remember, Puppy Preschool is about teaching and showing a puppy how to respond. There's no testing or correcting at this stage.

A methodical, consistent approach to teaching Sit on Command will help your puppy learn quickly. Here's what to do.

- Place your right hand through your puppy's buckle collar with your palm facing up. Lightly grasp the collar.
- Place your left hand, palm down, on your puppy's shoulders.
- As you gently pull up and back on your puppy's collar, slide your left hand down his back, tucking him into a sitting position.
- As you compel your puppy to sit, say his name and give the command "Sit." Here is a cardinal rule with all training: *Give one command and one command only.* Even if it takes you a few seconds to tuck the pup into a sit, do not repeat the command.
- Praise your puppy as soon as he sits.

This is easy. Although compelling your puppy to sit may not feel like earth-shattering progress, it's a great first step toward training. When your puppy starts obedience school in a few months, you will be amazed at how reliably he responds to the "Sit" command. To get good results, however, you must consistently *show* the puppy what to do throughout this Puppy Preschool phase.

People often tell me that their dog already knows "sit" when he's just ten or twelve weeks old. There's an interesting explanation for this. If you get your puppy's attention at this age, particularly if you are holding a dog treat, and say, "Sit. Sit. Sit," puppies sit. You could say just about anything else for that matter. "Apples. Apples. Apples," produces the same result. For some reason, most puppies sit when they have a word repeatedly thrown at them.

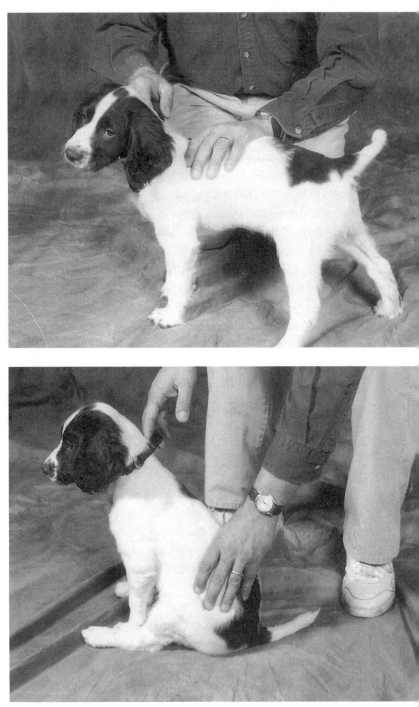

Sit on Command is easy for most pups. Grasp the puppy's collar with one hand, slide your other hand along his back, and gently pull up on the collar as you push down on his backside. Be sure to say the puppy's name and give the command "Sit" as you do this.

Unfortunately, this approach to "training" leads to an unreliable response. I've seen that most puppies "trained" this way always require numerous commands before they will do the behavior. Also, many of these puppies respond only if the doggie biscuit is in hand. Other puppies end up responding to the repeated commands only some of the time. That's not what we are looking for in a trained dog. Our goal is a reliable response each and every time one command is given to the pup. That's why the cardinal rule of saying the command just once is so important. You want a trained adult dog who will respond to you with one command. That's the pattern you must set right from the beginning during Puppy Preschool. If you find yourself repeating commands, tape a big sign to your refrigerator door and say it to yourself each day: "Give one command and one command only!"

Down on Command

Lying down on command is an important obedience exercise that's great to begin during Puppy Preschool. Why? Teaching it early on is vastly easier than teaching it to an older puppy or adult dog. That's because lying down is a highly submissive position from a dog's point of view. A dog who has any resistance to accepting you as his pack leader will be resistant to this exercise. Young puppies typically don't have that resistance—or they don't have it as strongly as they would when they mature. So take advantage of the innocence of youth and make Down on Command a big part of your Puppy Preschool training.

As with Sit on Command, a methodical, consistent approach works best and helps your puppy learn faster. Here's what to do:

• Compel your dog to sit at your left side using the Sit on Command training technique described above. (In case you were wondering, there's nothing magical about the left side. That's just how dog training has evolved over the years. Plus, it gives an instructor the ability to direct the handler's hands and body motions accurately.)
• With your dog sitting at your left side, hook the thumb of your left hand through the top of your puppy's collar at the back of his neck. Your

Down on Command requires precise handling. While the puppy is sitting, hook your thumb under the collar and spread your fingers along the pup's back, pulling back gently. Lift the pup's front legs and lower the puppy to the ground. Say the puppy's name and give the command "Down" as you do so.

open palm of that same hand should be positioned on your puppy's back with your fingers pointing toward his tail.

• Pull back on the collar with your thumb, using just enough pressure to keep the puppy's backside glued to the ground. That's the job of your left hand—to keep the puppy's back end on the ground. If the puppy keeps standing up, stretch your open palm and fingers farther down his spine and use a bit more pressure.

• With your right hand, lift your puppy's front legs off the ground—but do not try to grab both front legs in your right hand. That's too cumbersome. Instead, reach *behind* both of the puppy's front legs with your right hand. Let the leg closer to you rest on your right arm, while you take hold of the farther front leg. Grasp the leg gently from behind and lift up with your hand and arm. This will raise both of the pup's front legs a few inches off the ground. (It's also easier if you take hold of your puppy's leg more toward his foot rather than higher up toward his "armpit.") This sounds complicated, but it's not. (See photo.)

• When you have both front legs off the ground, say your puppy's name followed by the command "Down." As you give the command, lower your pup's body to the ground and remove your hands.

• Your puppy does not have to go down straight onto his chest. You may have to roll him toward one side at first to get him to go down. That's fine. Be sure to lower him down gently, however.

• As soon as your puppy is in the down position, praise him lavishly! He can pop up quickly if he does not want to stay down—this is not a Stay exercise.

Some puppies may resist being handled when you try this. If your pup *never* likes being handled, reread Chapter 19, "Handling Your Puppy," and work on general handling before you practice this specific exercise. If your puppy usually accepts being handled but resists this exercise in particular—by mouthing or growling—you are probably dealing with a dominant little pup. (Remember, lying down is a very submissive position.)

It's important that you not tolerate or give in to this growling or biting. Your job is to be a more dominant creature in your pack, and the Down on Command exercise will give you a great opportunity to communicate that to your pup. So when he mouths or growls, growl back: "*Nhaa!*" If he persists, growl louder and review Chapter 18, "*Nhaa!*"—Stopping Unwanted Behavior When You Growl." And then practice lots of Down on Command exercises each day. They are an effective but gentle way to communicate to a young puppy that you are in charge.

When your dominant little friend starts to accept going down, really lay on the praise. Make being in a down position a wonderful thing! That will certainly help him understand that he is doing the right thing.

Remember, don't worry about testing during this stage. In other words, don't say "Down" and wait to see what happens. Your job is to show the puppy what to do and to associate the command. His job is simply to allow you to show him. In fact, the same philosophy holds true for all obedience exercises in Puppy Preschool. You are *teaching* your puppy. So when you say the command, *show* him what to do—every single time.

A Few Training Tips

It is important that your timing is right when teaching both Sit and Down on Command. Here's an example of bad timing: You command "Sit" from across the room, then a second or two later walk over and compel your puppy to sit. Good timing means that the command and the behavior happen together. You want your puppy to make an association between your command and his behavior. So therefore you want your pup to hear the command "Sit" *as* you sit him and the command "Down" *as* you lower his body to the ground. Any passage of time in between will slow down learning.

Practice several sit and down exercises throughout the day rather than all at one time. Anytime you happen to be near your puppy, you can bend over and compel him to sit or lie down. Remember, you are helping your puppy to form an association. Puppies naturally explore and learn things about their world throughout the entire day. Take advantage of this by practicing a bit in the morning, a few times in the afternoon, and then again in the evening. That makes more sense—especially when working with puppies—than a long fifteen-minute training. It should be fun and painless—not drudgery.

Don't undermine the learning process by repeating the commands "Sit" or "Down" and not showing the puppy what to do. Show him *every time!* In fact, make it a rule to have your hands in position on your puppy before you even give a command. That way you always will be prepared to do it right.

Some puppies fight or bite when you try to carry out training techniques. Be prepared to growl *"Nhaa!"* or even to bite the pup if he mouths your hands, growls, or bites. Remember, part of Puppy Preschool is teaching your puppy to accept being handled.

Your puppy does not have to show any response to the commands at this stage. His job is simply to allow you to compel him to sit and lie down. The only thing he could do wrong would be to bite, fight, and resist, which some dominant puppies may try to do. If your puppy does this, growl *"Nhaa!"* as a correction. Then follow through with the sit or down (whichever you were doing) so that you don't teach the pup that biting or resisting helps him to get his own way. Remember, part of Puppy Preschool training is teaching the puppy to take direction from you, not the other way around.

Behavior Chains

At this stage of training, your puppy must be in a sitting position to do the Down on Command exercise. However, don't always do the Down on Command exercise immediately after you do the Sit exercise. If you do, when you get to the testing stages of these exercises later in your puppy's life, you will have created a behavior chain. A behavior chain is a set of behaviors that happen after only one command. For example, you will say "Sit" and your puppy will sit and then anticipate your next command before you even give it—and automatically lie down.

In order to avoid creating a behavior chain, you should sometimes exclusively sit your puppy. At other times use both the Sit on Command exercise followed by the Down on Command exercise. Periodically, you will find your puppy already in the sitting position, and you can exclusively down him. By "mixing and matching" the exercises in this manner, you will avoid training your puppy to anticipate a command.

Why is anticipating a command not a good thing? Because we are training our puppies (and dogs) to listen to our commands and then comply. Deciding on their own what behavior to do is not the same as listening to you and following your direction. Granted, the behaviors the dogs choose may not be unwanted or bad behaviors (such as lying down when you say "Sit" instead of just sitting). But the end result is a dog who does not respond as you asked him to or a dog who responds correctly only part of the time. Your goal is a dog who clearly understands what you ask and then does exactly that.

This does not mean that you must train with a military boot-camp mentality, where your commands become harsh or unfriendly. It just means that you are showing your puppy what each command means and then are following through so he does just what you've asked and nothing else. The end result will be a beautifully trained dog who knows just what to do when you give a command—and who earns your praise for doing the right thing each and every time.

Choosing Your Command Words

When I train my dogs I use standard obedience commands such as "Sit," "Down," "Stay," etc. However, it is irrelevant which word or sound you associate with any particular behavior. In other words, if you said "Peaches" every time you compelled your puppy to sit, eventually your puppy would learn to sit when he heard this command. Whichever words you choose, your puppy will learn them fastest if they are short, one-syllable words instead of multisyllabic. For example, "Drifter, Sit" is much easier for a puppy to absorb than "Drifter, I would appreciate if sometime in the next few minutes you would sit." So if you decide to be creative with your own unique commands, keep them short.

Although the word you use as a command is insignificant, it is imperative that you use the same word every time. Don't say "Down" one day, then "Lie down" the next, and "Go down" the third day. Choose one version and stick with it. To speed up learning, have everyone in your household use the same command words as well. When each person practices with the puppy, the puppy will hear those words over and over, further strengthening his association between the commands and his behavior.

It is also important that each command you give have only one meaning to your dog. The most misused command in this way is the command "Down." People will command their dog "Down" and expect him to lie down. Then in the next breath they are commanding "Down" when their dog jumps up on them. They may also use the same "Down" to tell the dog to get off the sofa or a kitchen counter. If a command has three or four different meanings, your dog will never clearly understand how to react when hearing it! In this particular example, I use "Down" to mean lie down, "Off" to get off the sofa, and the versatile "*Nhaa!*" to mean stop jumping up and get away from the kitchen counter.

Strictly speaking, "*Nhaa!*" also has just one meaning: Stop what you are doing immediately! However, it can be used in many different circumstances. When your dog mouths you, growl "*Nhaa!*" When he jumps up on you, say "*Nhaa!*" When he is chewing on inappropriate items, correct him with "*Nhaa!*" It's a useful and multipurpose word, but it always has one meaning: Stop what you are doing—now!

Staying in Place

You can begin to train your puppy to stay in place during the Puppy Preschool phase. One of the stay exercises I like to begin during this period is Sit-Stay. Sit-Stay means to stay in a sitting position until released. I release my dogs from a stay exercise by using a specific release word, which is "Okay!" You can use this release word or any other short-syllable word. Over the years I've had students use "Go!" or "Freedom!" I remember one student who even used the word "Release" as her dog's release command. Choose one that you like. But remember, like any other command this word must have one specific meaning.

Teaching a puppy to stay in place takes a bit of patience. Place the puppy into a sitting position, but be prepared to immediately growl *"Nhaa!"* and to sit him again if he tries to get up.

You will find that having your dog stay in a sitting position is a very practical exercise. Here are some examples of its uses. Beginning at the Puppy Preschool phase, I make my puppies sit and stay at the doorway whenever I let them out into the yard. As adult dogs they wait until released before going outside. This prevents the dogs from shooting outside every time a door is left open. I do the same thing with my dogs when getting in and out of the car. I don't want my dogs bounding over my lap when I open the driver-side door to get out, and I don't want them leaping all over my mail or groceries when I open the door to get in. Sit-Stay lets me get organized first, and then, when I'm ready for them, cues the dogs that they can move.

Sit-Stay is also a useful exercise for controlling unwanted behaviors. My Australian shepherd, Drifter, was a herding dog. Due to my nonfarming lifestyle, Drifter did not get to herd sheep or cattle as part of his normal routine (although he participated in a few herding events, and he passed a herding instinct test with flying colors). Because of this, Drifter found other outlets for his herding instincts. He came to think of people on bicycles and rollerskates as "city sheep." I *know* that he would have loved to chase them down the street, nipping at their heels. But when we were taking a walk, I controled Drifter when he saw a biker or skater coming at us. I simply commanded him to sit and stay. Drifter couldn't run after anyone and cause trouble when sitting comfortably at my side. After the biker or skater rolled by, I released Drifter with "Okay!" followed by lots of praise for doing the right thing. Sit-Stay has provided me with a constructive, nonviolent, and easy way to prevent problem behavior.

When Drifter and I would greet a friend in town, I would tell Drifter to sit and stay. By doing this I had a dog who was under control and not bounding around at the end of the leash while I tried to visit with my friend. Plus, Drifter got more attention because he was calm and approachable. Everybody wins.

Several of the obedience exercises your puppy will learn during formal obedience training, such as greeting people without jumping and coming on command, will require that he sits and stays reliably. So this is an important exercise to start young. It's the basis for a lot of good behavior.

Our objective with Puppy Preschool Sit-Stay is to keep your puppy staying in place without moving for *two complete minutes*. Not moving does not mean that he has to be a statue. He can move his head and wag his tail. However, he may not lie down or stand up. He also may not wiggle all over the place. He must remain in one spot sitting calmly.

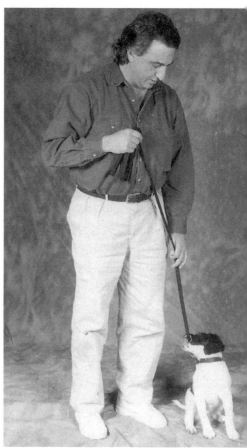

Keep your eyes on your puppy even after you stand up. He *should* stay in place, but he may keep getting up or trying other unwanted behaviors, such as leash-biting. Again, be ready to growl *"Nhaa!"* to correct him.

This is how the Sit-Stay is taught:

• Start by clipping your pup's leash to his buckle collar. Then sit your puppy at your left side, using the Sit on Command technique described earlier in this chapter.

• While you are still bent over with your hands on your puppy, give your puppy the command "Stay." (I recommend *not* using your pup's name when giving the "Stay" command. The pup's name is an attention-getting word that, in formal obedience training, cues the pup that he is going to be asked to do something, such as lie down or come. Here we are asking him to remain still—*not* to move or to anticipate movement. I have found that simply saying "Stay" helps him figure that out a lot faster.)

• After telling your puppy "Stay," remove your hands and stand erect next to him. Watch your puppy closely as you do this. If your puppy stands up or lies down, growl "*Nhaa!*" and use your hands to gently replace him into a sitting position. Remind him again to "Stay."

• Continue to do this until your puppy remains sitting calmly at your left side. Remember, he can wag his tail and move his head. He does not have to be a statue, but do not allow him to stand up or lie down.

• While you are keeping the puppy staying at your side, gather his leash up in your right hand. Your left hand should be grasping the leash in a palm-down position, roughly halfway between your right hand and the leash's metal clip.

• If your puppy starts to get up again, again tell him "*Nhaa!*" The best time to correct your puppy is when you think he's *thinking* about getting up. The next best time is when your puppy starts to get up. And the worst time is when you look down and he's gone. Watch your pup closely!

• Start practicing for short periods of time. The first practice session should be fifteen seconds long. If you had success with fifteen seconds, the second practice session should be thirty seconds long. Increase each successful session by fifteen seconds until your puppy will stay without moving for two full minutes.

• At the end of the designated time, use your release word ("Okay!") as you take a step forward. (Stepping forward gets your pup to move, helping him to learn what the release word means.) Do not release your puppy with praise, because in formal training you should be able to praise him *while* he stays—as a verbal reward for doing the right thing. At this stage, however, praise would be too much of a distraction to a puppy who is just learning what "Stay" is all about.

- *After* you release your puppy, praise him lavishly. What a good job he did!

If your puppy does well with the Sit-Stay exercise, you may increase the time beyond two minutes. However, do not make the mistake that many novice trainers make and try to increase the distance away from your puppy. Stay right next to him where you can correct him and re-sit him as soon as he starts to move. *Timing your corrections properly is essential to help your puppy understand what you want from him.* Practice at least three Sit-Stays a day with your pup.

Twenty-One

Introducing Basic Obedience Commands: Part II

In the previous chapter we introduced the puppy to three basic obedience exercises, Sit on Command, Down on Command, and Sit-Stay. This chapter adds a few more basics to your Puppy Preschool training.

Don't overwhelm yourself or your puppy by trying to start on all the exercises at once. Stick with the first three exercises for a few weeks and then start to add these. Most puppy owners find that it takes a while to work a short session of obedience practice into their daily routines. Just housebreaking and supervising an active puppy are enough to keep most owners busy!

Do keep in mind, however, that by starting to make your puppy practice obedience exercises, you are establishing yourself as the puppy's leader. At the same time, the puppy starts to "learn how to learn." That is, he becomes attuned to working with you and learns how to take a direction from you. So one or two minutes of practice is better than none at all. Waiting to begin any sort of obedience practice until the puppy "grows up a bit" only wastes valuable learning time and lets unwanted behaviors develop, making your job harder down the road.

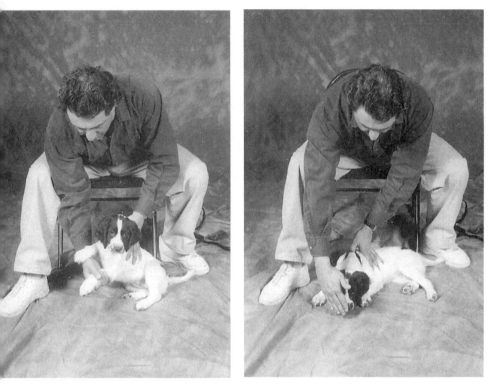

Down-Stay is one of the most useful behaviors a dog can learn. Gently lower your pup to the ground, give the "Stay" command, provide a chew toy, and then *watch your puppy*. Every time he gets up, you must growl *"Nhaa!"* and then put him back. Before long he'll understand what you want.

Down-Stay

Down-Stay means for your puppy to stay in place in a lying-down position until, like Sit-Stay, he is released with a specific command from you. You will find Down-Stay to be an extremely useful exercise throughout your dog's entire life. The dog who masters Down-Stay can go anywhere and always be under control. A dog who has learned Down-Stay never has to be locked in the bedroom or put down in the basement when guests come by for a visit. A dog who is doing a Down-Stay cannot beg at the dinner table during mealtime. You will find many, many times when Down-Stay proves to be a truly wonderful obedience exercise.

Down-Stay is an important control exercise that can be introduced during Puppy Preschool training. Here's how to teach it.

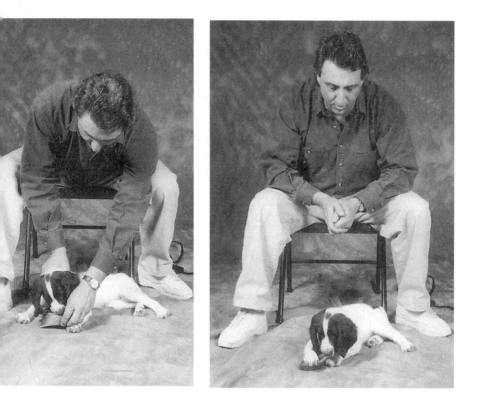

• At least once a day bring your puppy in front of your favorite chair. Your puppy should be wearing his buckle collar with the six-foot leash attached. Also have your puppy's favorite chew toy with you.

• Make your puppy lie down, using the technique described in Chapter 20 for Down on Command. When your puppy is lying down, tell him "Stay," simultaneously placing your open palm briefly in front of his face. This is the hand signal for stay. (It's not possible to use the hand signal with the Sit-Stay exercise because both of your hands are busy holding the leash.) Give your puppy his toy to chew and have a seat in your chair.

• If your puppy gets up, growl "*Nhaa!*" and quickly but gently push him back into the down position. Again tell him "Stay." Continue to do this as many times as necessary until he remains down.

• In your mind draw an imaginary circle around your puppy. Your puppy may shift position within the confines of the imaginary circle. However, if he rolls or does G.I. Joe crawls to get outside the circle, growl "*Nhaa!*" and put him back inside the circle.

• Do not sit on the floor with your puppy when you practice Down-Stay. If you are on his level, which is a submissive position, he will test you more. Instead, sit in a chair so that you are above him. You should not be more than a foot away from your pup.

• The ideal time for you to correct him with the growl "*Nhaa!*" is when you feel he is *about* to move. So watch him closely. The next best time is just as he is getting up. The worst time is when you look down and he is gone! Keep an eye on him.

• Do not restrain your puppy on a tight leash during this exercise. Your goal is not to hold him down but to teach him how to stay down on his own. However, do position the leash near your foot where you can step on it quickly if he attempts to bolt out of the imaginary circle. But don't let him chew up the leash! If he starts chewing the leash, growl "*Nhaa!*" and remove the leash from his mouth. Give him his chew toy again.

• After your puppy has remained staying in the down position for your designated practice time, stand up so that he is at your left side. Use your release word, "Okay!" and encourage him up. Give him lots of praise for a job well done.

Do not release your puppy while you are sitting in the chair. If you do, your puppy will lie there expecting that at any second you will release him. Teach him that he may not get up until you are standing next to him and he hears the release word. Periodically stand up next to him and do *not* release him. Tell him "Stay" and have a seat again. This will teach him that just because you stand, it does not mean it's time to get up. *Always* make him wait for the release word.

Practice Down-Stay with your puppy at least once a day for thirty seconds each time. Do this for one week. Each week increase the designated practice time by thirty seconds. Your goal in Puppy Preschool is a puppy who can lie down and stay for *three full minutes*. As with Sit-Stay, do not increase the designated time until you have been successful with a shorter time—even if it takes longer than one week. There's no need to rush to keep up with a particular time schedule. Puppies learn at different speeds, and a good trainer adapts to his or her pup for maximum success.

When your puppy is four months old and you begin formal training, you can greatly increase the designated Down-Stay time. My adult dogs can easily do a half-hour Down-Stay. However, during Puppy Preschool, three minutes is great.

Down-Stay and Pack Leadership

Besides being a major control exercise, the Down-Stay is a very effective and natural way to convince your puppy that you are pack leader. I told this story in my book *Dog Talk: Training Your Dog Through a Canine Point of View*, but I feel it is worth repeating.

Several years ago, for a short period of time, I trained dogs and taught obedience classes at a boarding and breeding kennel in Connecticut. The people who owned the kennel bred collies. They usually bred a litter once a year. Their breeding objective was to produce show dogs. As many breeders do, they sold their non-show-quality puppies to families as pets. Often they would keep for themselves the puppy they believed to be the "pick of the litter." If this puppy turned out as they hoped, they would use him or her to show and to breed.

While I was working at this kennel, the breeders had a litter of nine pups. At eight weeks old, six of the puppies were sold. Three remained for several more weeks while the breeders tried to determine which of the three (if any) they wanted to keep.

Several times a day the breeders would let these three puppies, who were now about eleven weeks old, and the mother dog into a small fenced yard to get fresh air and to play. One day a woman who worked at the kennel and I were standing at a window watching the three pups wrestle and play-fight with each other. Mother dog was keeping cool by lying in the shade under a small tree. After a few minutes of their game, the puppies got bored and decided that it would be more fun to gang up on Mom.

First, the puppies started some little "shark attacks." They would run in at mother dog and nip at her legs, ears, and tail. When she snarled they would scamper away, regroup, build confidence, and charge at her again. This went on for a few minutes. Mother dog just stared at them, and when they got close to her, she would show her teeth and growl in a low tone. They were cautious but obviously not too intimidated.

Suddenly like a flash, mother dog shot out after each puppy. She stood over each of them and growled ferociously. Each of the pups rolled belly-up in a submissive position when she did this. For the next twenty minutes, mother dog walked a slow circle around her pups. Each time a puppy attempted to get up, Mom was standing over him growling. It was an incredible scene—I wish I'd had a video recorder!

While watching this display of canine behavior, my first reaction was, She's teaching the pups Down-Stay, the same way I do with the dogs in my classes. Then it occurred to me. Mother dog could care less about unruly behavior when guests visit or about begging at the supper table. This was simply her natural, canine way of saying, "I'm pack leader. When I growl, respect me!"

When you practice Down-Stay with your puppy, you are not only teaching him a tremendously useful obedience exercise, you are convincing him, through a canine point of view, that you are pack leader.

Come on Command

Almost every dog owner I know wants their dog to come when called. But many owners never achieve that goal—at least not to the degree they would like. But getting a dog to come when called is not all that hard. It's just that owners make a lot of mistakes when they try to get their dogs to come. And few actually take the time to *teach* their dogs to come—they somehow imagine that the dogs will just figure out what they want.

If you get your puppy started correctly during Puppy Preschool, you will have taken a big step toward successful Coming on Command. At four months old when your pup begins formal Come on Command training, you will be well on your way to having a dog that comes reliably whenever you call him.

During the Puppy Preschool stage, what you do *not* do (in regard to Come on Command) is as important as what you do. You can avoid creating a lot of problems in later training by strictly following these guidelines. Here are the most important rules of what *not* to do when setting the foundation for a reliable Come on Command.

Rule Number One: Do not make coming to you a disagreeable experience for your puppy. It is imperative that you teach your puppy that coming to you is a *wonderful* experience. In fact, never correct your puppy for *any* reason when he comes to you, no matter how angry you are about his misdeeds. One of the biggest mistakes new dog owners make is to call the puppy to them and then discipline him. Here's an example. The owner looks down and notices that the puppy has one of the children's shoes. The owner then calls the puppy. "Rover, Come!" The puppy comes to the owner and the owner says in a harsh tone, "Bad puppy! Don't you chew this shoe!" The association that the puppy makes is that coming to his owner is a disagreeable experience. Keep in mind that canines avoid disagreeable experiences. By repeating this behavior a certain number of times, you soon will have a puppy who *avoids* coming to you.

It is your job to condition your puppy that coming to you always results in an *agreeable* experience. As a matter of fact, I want you to condition your puppy to believe that coming to you is the greatest thing that can happen to him! Hugs, kisses, praise, and petting should be given out whenever he comes to you.

You may be wondering how you ever correct a puppy for an unwanted behavior. In situations such as the one I described above with the child's shoe, the best time to correct the puppy is just as he is approaching the shoe and is about to pick it up. The next best time is just as he puts his mouth on the shoe. It's too late to correct when the pup's prancing around the house with the shoe in his mouth. At that point all you want to do is to get the shoe back. You have two options to accomplish this. One is to call the puppy to you in a pleasant tone of voice. When he reaches you, praise him warmly for coming to you. Calmly take the shoe from his mouth and after a few seconds give him one of his dog toys. Your second choice is to calmly go to the puppy and gently take the shoe from him.

Rule Number Two: Do *not* go charging after your puppy as you scream at him for doing something wrong (or for not coming when you called him). If you do this, you will trigger his flight instinct and he will run from you. Many puppies even turn this into a game. It only takes a couple of times before you have created a puppy who snatches things he is not supposed to have—and then expects you to chase him around the house. That's fun and games to most puppies! Once he has the forbidden item, forget about correction. (That's tough to do, I know.) If you want to time corrections properly, "tighten up the ship" in your household by supervising your puppy more closely.

Body Language and Verbal Tone: What Messages Are You Giving?

Whenever you call your puppy to you, it is important that you use the proper verbal tone and body language. An important rule is to always squat down on your puppy's level. If you stand erect, your body posture is dominant, which can be intimidating. Most puppies will not come toward a dominant body posture. Squatting down makes you look more inviting from the puppy's perspective and makes the pup come to you more readily.

A harsh verbal tone is also bad news. It will trigger either a flight-instinct response, which means your pup will run from you, or a submissive response, in which your puppy rolls over belly-up. Neither of these responses is what we are looking for. The response we want is for your puppy to come running to you eagerly. So make sure that your voice is inviting whenever you call your pup. A high-pitched, enthusiastic tone works best. It often is what's needed to inspire the right response.

Also have an object of attraction in your hand whenever you call your puppy. A squeaky toy, a tennis ball, or a doggie biscuit may help induce your puppy to you. In some cases, this object of attraction will be the difference between your puppy coming and not coming to you.

To encourage your puppy to come when called, your body language and verbal tone must be inviting and non-threatening. Kneel down, hold an object of attraction, and call your pup using a friendly, enthusiastic voice.

How to Avoid Practicing Not Coming

When used in the context of dog training, the words "repeat" and "practice" are interchangeable. Whenever you repeat a behavior, you are practicing. When you spend ten minutes practicing with your dog, you are repeating behaviors. Dogs form habits by repeating behaviors consistently. You want to be sure that every time you call your puppy, he comes running to you.

It is imperative that you do not repeat or practice *not* coming. What does that mean? "Practicing not coming" means using the command "Come" in situations where your puppy does not respond properly. For example, if you regularly use the command "Come" and your puppy runs from you or just stands there sniffing a bush, you are teaching him to ignore the "Come" command. That's *not* a lesson you want him to learn.

In order to form a conditioned response to your command "Come," you must tip the scales in one direction. By this I mean that every time your puppy hears the command "Come," he must come to you. Saying "Come! Come! Come!" while you get no response from your pup balances the scales evenly between coming and not coming. Tip those scales so that "Come!" gets the right response every time.

Don't despair: An occasional improper response on the part of your puppy will not be the undoing of his Come on Command training. However, you must learn from experience when to use the "Come" command. Here's an example of what I mean. Let's say that on Monday morning you put on your jacket to go out somewhere. You want to put your puppy in his crate for a few hours while you are gone. So you squat down on your puppy's level with his favorite object of attraction in your hand. In a pleasant, exuberant tone of voice, you call, "Puppy, Come!" But noooo, he's figured out that you are leaving. So instead of coming to you, he runs and hides behind the sofa.

If you repeat this scenario on Tuesday, Wednesday, Thursday, and again on Friday, you are practicing not coming. Before long you will have a puppy who is conditioned to respond to your "Come" command by hiding behind the sofa!

Instead, when you have that experience on Monday, do something on Tuesday to prevent it. Before you put on your jacket, pick up your puppy, give him a hug, and put him in his crate. Be sure that he has a few safe toys so that he can play or sleep until you return home.

If your puppy's episodes of not coming when called are happening outside, do not take your puppy off the leash until he is trained to come reliably. Remember, dogs form habits by repeating behaviors consistently. Practicing not coming is the biggest mistake people make with their dogs in conjunction with Come on Command.

Training Your Puppy to Come

Don't forget that coming when called doesn't just happen. Dogs who come reliably have been *trained* to respond this way. I've never met a dog who just figured it out and came right away whenever he was called. Formal obedience training includes a series of step-by-step procedures for teaching a reliable Come on Command. But you certainly can get started with some simple steps during Puppy Preschool. Be sure not to practice *not* coming. It will undo all your hard work with these training procedures. Here's what to do.

• Bring your puppy on his leash to a big open field along with his favorite object of attraction and a dozen small doggie treats. Make sure that the field is not close to any busy roads. If you live in the city, find a park. A football or softball field is great.

• Bring your puppy into the middle of the field and unclip his leash. Chances are great that puppies between the age of eight weeks and four months old will not wander more than a few yards away from you, in a strange place. However, when your puppy does get a few yards away from you, call his name. In a pleasant, excited, and exuberant tone, use the "Come" command, and immediately after you call "Come," run *away* from the pup. As you run away from him praise and encourage him to come to you.

This exercise will trigger your puppy's chase reflex, and he's going to come running after you. As you start to run, watch him over your shoulder. When you see him running after you, turn toward him and squat down on his level. Wave the object of attraction around and induce him to you. When he reaches you, praise him enthusiastically! Hug and kiss him, and perhaps give him a small doggie treat. Make him think he just did the *greatest* thing he has ever done in his entire puppy life.

• Repeat this exercise six or eight times every day until your puppy is ready to start school at four months old. With a good foundation in Puppy Preschool and then some formal training, he'll be running to you like a pro every time you call. That's the kind of dog most people only dream about owning!

Most young puppies will come running when you call them in a nonthreatening way. You can even run *away* from the pup for a short distance to trigger his urge to chase you. Be sure to offer lots of praise when he arrives!

Greeting People Without Jumping

Puppy Preschool is a great time to start shaping a behavior that will be an important "social skill" for the rest of your dog's life. I call it Greeting People Without Jumping. Dogs jump on people they greet for one reason: They want attention! This is precisely why training methods such as kneeing the dog in the chest do not work. Kneeing the dog is a form of attention. The dog is getting exactly what he craves. Dogs—especially puppies—will settle for negative attention over no attention at all.

Not only is kneeing dogs ineffective, it is also dangerous, especially to puppies. If you knee a dog *hard* enough, you may discourage him from jumping on you, but you may also cause a severe injury. Over the years, veterinarians have shown me X rays of several injured dogs. These dogs were hurt by people trying to discourage unwanted jumping. The X rays revealed injuries ranging from broken jaws to fractured shoulders.

No training method should cause injury or pain! Avoid any physically abusive training methods that attempt to eliminate unwanted jumping. Such techniques are ineffective at best and harmful to the dog at worst.

The best way to start teaching your puppy to greet people without jumping is to capitalize on your pup's motivation. Attention is what the puppy wants. He must become conditioned to seek attention from a sitting position. In formal obedience training, I capitalize on the dog's ability to sit

Puppies are some of the friendliest creatures on earth. Their urge to say hello often involves jumping up, a behavior that should be discouraged right away.

and stay while he is being greeted. Young puppies are not ready for that step, but they are ready to be *shown* that greetings happen only while they are sitting.

Most people aren't even aware that they are encouraging their puppy to jump up for attention. How many times have you picked up a little puppy to say hello and held him close to your face for a greeting? I admit that there's nothing cuter than a cuddly pup giving out puppy kisses. But that cuddly pup may one day be a 160-pound Saint Bernard or an energetic, 80-pound golden retriever. That's not what you want jumping up at your face to say hello.

The answer to shaping good greeting behavior right from the beginning is to get down on your pup's level to say hello. Bend down quickly and

Before the puppy has a chance to jump, quickly bend over and push his backside into a sitting position. Greeting him in this manner teaches the pup that he'll get attention without having to leap all over people. You even can kneel down, if you wish, for a face-to-face greeting!

push the puppy's backside into a sitting position when you greet him. Do this *before* the pup jumps on you. Sitting on the floor with him is fine if that's what you want to do. If not, remain standing but bent over, holding the puppy in a sitting position while you rub his chest, stroke his head, kiss his face, or whatever sort of greeting you like. Your goal is to show the puppy that his urge for attention will be fulfilled even while his feet remain on the floor.

If your puppy beats you to the punch and jumps on you, tell him "*Nhaa!*" and quickly sit him. Keep in mind that telling the puppy "*Nhaa!*" after he already has his front feet on you does *not* teach the pup to avoid jumping. It simply tells him to stop jumping once he has already begun. Instead, you want the puppy conditioned not to jump in the first place. It is your responsibility to react quickly and push his backside down *before* he jumps on you.

This exercise will be more or less difficult depending on your puppy's breed and his particular personality. Owners of bouncy poodles and energetic springer spaniels typically face bigger potential jumping problems than owners of short-legged basset hounds and heavyweight Newfoundlands. But it need not be a problem at all if you start showing your puppy early on how greetings are supposed to happen—with his feet and backside on the floor. Then when you start using Sit-Stay for this purpose in formal obedience training, your puppy will already have an idea of what you expect from him.

A final thought: Learn to acknowledge your puppy whenever you arrive home. All dogs have a strong instinct to greet a newcomer to their den, or home. Even when you walk to the end of the driveway to get the mail and then return inside, your puppy will probably come to greet you. Take advantage of each of those moments to sit your pup and reinforce this exercise. Not only will you make quick progress with good greeting behavior, you will be reinforcing the bond between you and your pup by frequently acknowledging each other as members of the same pack, or family.

Quiet on Command

Barking is a normal and natural behavior in dogs. In fact, it is mentally healthy for dogs to bark. Barking releases frustration. In addition, it is a form of canine communication and, in adult dogs, a territorial warning device. But barking can be annoying and can become a bad habit. To avoid this, I teach my dogs to be quiet on command. This means for the dog to stop barking immediately in response to my signal.

Introducing the concept of Quiet on Command can begin during puppyhood. Your puppy's barking behavior will determine whether this is something you need to work on. Most young puppies are not problem barkers, but as they start to mature they may develop this noisy habit. Some puppies "complain" by barking, such as when they are confined to a crate or want you to play with them. Teaching these puppies to be quiet on command can be a very useful exercise.

Two different techniques can be used. Either (or both) are acceptable, depending on the situation. If your puppy barks while in the crate, this is a good time to teach him this exercise. First, be sure that he is not telling you that he has to go outside to relieve himself. If he is just barking to complain or make noise, bang on the top of the crate with your hand or something that will make a loud noise. Give the command "Quiet!" in a firm voice. The noise startles the puppy into silence, and your verbal command becomes associated with his action of getting quiet. Repeat this procedure whenever your puppy barks. Eventually you won't need to bang on the crate at all. Your verbal command will do the job of silencing your pup.

If you are lazy about quieting your puppy or try to ignore the puppy's barking, *you* are letting a bad habit develop. If you let your puppy out of the crate when he barks, you are rewarding the barking behavior and he will bark even more. If you stop using the crate because the puppy barks and "doesn't like the crate," the puppy is telling *you* what to do. This is not at all conducive to teaching good obedience or to establishing your image as the pack leader.

Another method for teaching this exercise is to gently hold the puppy's muzzle closed for a few seconds as you give the command "Quiet." Do *not* squeeze the pup's muzzle tightly as you do this. If you do, you will either scare or hurt the puppy. He will flap his head back and forth and make whimpering sounds. You should simply hold the pup's mouth closed to show what the command "Quiet" means. Eventually you will not need to hold the puppy's muzzle. The command "Quiet" will be all that is needed to quiet your pup.

The following analogy will help you understand why this works. Imagine if you were visiting China and did not speak the language. If someone asked you to be quiet and you did not understand what they wanted, you would probably continue to talk. But if every time you spoke, the person gently put a hand over your mouth and said "Quiet" in Chinese, before long you would know what was wanted. The same holds true with dogs. Dogs do not understand language. They simply form associations with sounds. You must first show a dog what you want from him and then associate a command.

Some puppies learn the Quiet on Command exercise with just a few repetitions. Other pups seem to need a hundred. Just remember that all puppies, like all people, are individuals. Be consistent and persistent with these techniques. You *will* achieve results.

Part Seven

Puppy Care

----

*A*re you prepared to provide your puppy with good health care and basic grooming? This section will give you guidelines on how to do a good job at both. It also describes how to find the right training program for your pup as he approaches his four-month birthday. And finally, parting thoughts on raising a well-behaved, lovable dog.

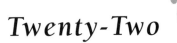

Twenty-Two

Health Issues

I'm often asked health-related questions by new puppy owners, but I'm careful not to assume the role of medical expert. Even though I worked as a veterinary technician for many years, I don't have anywhere near the same medical knowledge that a veterinarian has. But I do know health care basics, which all dog owners should be aware of.

This chapter is intended as an information source and as a guideline to providing good care for your puppy. It has been written with the input and guidance of a wonderful veterinarian, Chuck Noonan, D.V.M., who practices in Weston, Connecticut. If you have a specific medical problem with your puppy, you should seek professional help from a licensed veterinarian. Nothing can substitute for the eyes, ears, and hands of a trained veterinarian when you are trying to solve a medical problem, especially a serious one. With that in mind, let's explore some of the health issues related to young dogs.

Emergencies

These are the most serious situations that you and your puppy will have to deal with, so let's cover them first. What is a canine medical emergency? How can you recognize one? What do you do if one occurs?

The first thing all puppy owners should do—before an emergency ever happens—is to know where to turn for help at any time of the day or night. When you got your puppy, you probably selected a vet (see the section below on this subject). Do you know if the vet is "on call" for emergencies at all times? Understandably, most are not. They may share "on call" duties with other vets in the community or may refer their clients to an animal emergency center. Some vets (sadly) even turn away emergencies unless the dog is brought in by a regular, paying client. If your puppy became seriously ill *right now,* who would you call? Do you know where a regional emergency center is located? Do you know how to get there? Do you know where your vet's "on call" colleagues have their offices? Before you read any further, check into these questions. You will be less likely to panic or do the wrong thing if you have an emergency plan of action all figured out.

Assessing an emergency in a puppy or adult dog can be difficult because they can't talk. It's like trying to figure out why a human baby is sick. Clues such as unusual behavior or a change in body fluids will help tip you off, but only a veterinarian can accurately diagnose and treat the problem. Here is a list to help you learn to recognize a medical emergency.

Ten Common Emergency Situations Requiring Immediate Veterinary Care

1. Difficulty breathing
2. Seizuring
3. Blood in urine, stool, vomit, or nasal discharge
4. Hit by car
5. Staggering
6. Temperature above 102.5 degrees Fahrenheit
7. Ingestion of any possibly toxic substance, especially pesticides, insecticides, prescription medications, cleaning fluids, automotive antifreeze, sharp or jagged objects, etc. Puppies might eat *anything.*
8. Severe lameness in any limb
9. Inability to pass urine or stool
10. Repeated vomiting

In an emergency situation, your job as a responsible pet owner does not end with a phone call and a middle-of-the-night car ride to the veterinary hospital. There are a number of other steps you can take to help your puppy receive an accurate diagnosis and appropriate care. These steps do not apply to all situations, but you should be aware of each one so that you can do your best in a crisis.

Ten Steps to Aid Your Veterinarian in an Emergency Situation

1. Keep your pet's records readily available. Bring these records with you.
2. Be a good observer. Be able to tell the veterinarian when the pet last ate, drank, urinated, or defecated.
3. Bring a sample of any stool, vomit, or urine to the veterinarian.
4. Time the episodes of seizuring and/or fainting.
5. Control bleeding with firm, direct pressure on the way to the veterinarian.
6. Start cooling overheated pets with water or ice packs on the way to the veterinarian.
7. Bring containers of any possible ingested toxins to the veterinarian.
8. Do not give any home remedies or human medications before checking with your veterinarian.
9. Be aware that a pet who is in pain may bite even its owner.
10. Above all, remember to keep your head. Now is the time to be calm, be a good listener, and most important, be an advocate for humane and caring treatment for your pet.

Emergencies can be frightening, upsetting experiences for both owners and puppies. I hope you and your pup never have to deal with one. If you do, you will handle it better and improve the odds for effective treatment if you have a game plan and you follow the guidelines listed above.

Choosing a Veterinarian

Depending on where you live, you may have one or two—or more than a dozen—veterinarians to chose from for your pet's care. If you have never owned a pet before, you may not know which veterinarian you are going to use. Here are a few tips on finding the vet who is right for you.

• If possible, start with a few recommendations. If all your pet-owning neighbors love taking their animals to Dr. Noonan, then give him a try. If your breeder swears by someone else, consider that vet, too. Then it's up to you to make the final decision (which, of course, can be changed if you run into difficulties).

• Plan to visit the vet within a day or two of bringing your puppy home. That will accomplish several things. First, any illness or problem that appeared in early puppyhood will be detected and treated. Second, it will allow your pup to meet the veterinarian and become familiar with the veterinary hospital. And third, it will give you an opportunity to assess the hospital and evaluate the staff.

• What should you be looking for? A facility that looks and smells clean. A helpful, pleasant receptionist. A reasonably short time in the waiting room. A sense of orderliness and calm. A surgical area and basic X-ray equipment, at the minimum.

Not every veterinary office will fit this description. Be prepared to look elsewhere if you come away with a feeling that the place needs a lot of improvement. Trust your instincts.

• The same is true of the staff. Is your pup handled roughly? Are you given a little extra time during that first visit for a thorough exam? Are your questions answered? Are treatments explained clearly? Keep in mind that you and your veterinarian are really a team in providing medical care to your pet. Your own observations and descriptions of your puppy help your veterinarian provide an accurate diagnosis and effective treatment. A bond of trust will develop between you and your vet, provided you are happy with his or her facility, the support staff, and the vet's own demeanor.

Vaccinations and Other Preventive Measures

Like human babies, puppies need protection against life-threatening illnesses. Modern veterinary science has provided numerous vaccines and medications that have been saving canine lives for many years. Don't be lulled into thinking, Dogs never get that disease anymore, or I've never heard of that disease. You may not be familiar with all of the diseases that your puppy should be protected against. This does *not* mean that your puppy is safe without treatment! The minimal time and expense of administering these drugs will be recouped many times over during your pet's lifetime.

Below is a recommended vaccination schedule for puppies, along with other steps your veterinarian may take during your pup's first few visits. It will give you some idea of what to expect during each appointment. Don't be afraid to ask your veterinarian about any of the items you want more information about. Informed owners give their puppies the best chance for long, healthy lives.

First Office Visit: Eight-Week-Old Puppy

1. Physical exam, including puppy's weight
2. Discussion of puppy's diet and fencing to create a safe yard
3. Stool sample
4. Preventive medication for heartworm (a potentially fatal parasite) if appropriate to your geographic region
5. Worming to eliminate roundworms (common in puppies)
6. Vaccination for distemper, Corona virus, parvovirus, parainfluenza, hepatitis, and leptospirosis (these are combined in one injection)

Second Office Visit: Twelve-Week-Old Puppy

1. Physical exam, including puppy's weight
2. Discussion of diet, housebreaking, and reproduction plans (spaying/neutering versus breeding)
3. Stool sample
4. Preventive medication for heartworm appropriate for pup's weight
5. Worming to eliminate roundworms
6. Repetition of the distemper combination vaccine
7. Vaccination for rabies and Lyme disease, if appropriate to your geographic region

Third Office Visit: Sixteen-Week-Old Puppy

1. Physical exam, including puppy's weight
2. Discussion of diet, housebreaking, fencing to create a safe yard, reproduction plans, plus flea and tick control

3. Preventive medication for heartworm appropriate to pup's weight, and provision of enough heartworm preventive for the coming year
4. Repetition of the distemper combination vaccine
5. Vaccination for Lyme disease, if appropriate

If your puppy will be spending a great deal of time with other dogs, either in a kennel or on the breed show "circuit," you may want to consider boostering his distemper combination vaccine and also vaccinating him against kennel cough (a common respiratory ailment). Otherwise, you won't need to schedule another preventative "checkup" until your puppy is about one year old.

A Positive Vet Experience

Even the healthiest of dogs needs occasional veterinary care. After the puppy vaccinations are complete, your pet should visit a veterinarian *once every year* for a general checkup and heartworm test (a simple blood test to check for heartworm parasites).

A dog who misbehaves during visits to the veterinarian may not receive timely care—all because his owners dread the unpleasant experience. During the Puppy Preschool phase, you can help your puppy learn to tolerate medical attention. It goes without saying that this skill is a lifelong asset.

One of the things you can do to lay the foundation for a positive vet experience is to practice lots of handling. Chapter 19, "Handling Your Puppy," describes this technique in detail. A puppy who is used to having his feet touched, mouth examined, and ears looked into will be much less likely to react badly when the veterinarian does these same things. Also, practice your "Stay" exercises. A puppy who can sit or lie down and then stay in place is a pleasure to work with. Not only does it help the vet examine the pup, it also gives the puppy a familiar job to do, which provides a bit of reassurance in the unfamiliar setting of a veterinary office.

If your pup does squirm, growl, or resist during a medical exam, you should react the same way as you would at home—by growling. Owners so often try to reassure the pup with gentle strokes and soothing words, such as "It's okay, puppy. Dr. Noonan will make you feel better." Keep in mind that petting and soft talking are actually *praise* from the pup's point of view. You never want to praise resistant or aggressive behavior. Instead, praise the pup only when he is accepting the vet's examination or procedures. If your puppy is frightened, simply say nothing (you don't want to reinforce a fearful response). With time, many puppies become less upset by the routine poking and prodding of a medical exam.

Finally, assess your choice of veterinarian after several visits. The best veterinary reputation in the world means nothing if you and your pup do not have a good experience with that vet. Sometimes personalities clash, sometimes vets have prejudices against certain breeds, sometimes offices are too crowded or overbooked to allow for a calm, pleasant visit. Your satisfaction and your pet's comfort and good health are what count the most. Don't be afraid to make a change if you need to go elsewhere to find satisfactory care.

Spaying and Neutering

Spaying and neutering is a health-related issue that will be an important decision during your puppy's first year. While you won't have to take action during the Puppy Preschool phase, you will just a few months beyond it. With that in mind, start thinking about this subject now. Here are some important points to consider.

As described in Chapter 4, "Finding Puppies," all sorts of people breed dogs. By reading that chapter, you should have some idea how much time, effort, and money it takes to do it responsibly. In my opinion, the average pet owner has no business breeding dogs. It's hard to do it right! Even if you think your dog is the greatest dog who ever lived, that's not a good reason to create more dogs in the world. Many thousands of wonderful, unwanted animals are put to death in pounds and shelters every year. I believe that responsible dog ownership extends to caring about the canine population as a whole. And that means *don't* breed your pet.

The medical procedures used to spay a female dog and neuter a male dog are simple and effective. They have been performed millions of times over the years and pose minimal risk to the animal. In fact, both males and females reap health benefits from the surgery. For example, a life-threatening condition called pyometra—an infection of the uterus—can occur in unspayed females. Unneutered males have much higher chances of developing infected prostate glands and cancerous anal growths.

Numerous myths are associated with spaying and neutering. People think the procedures cause obesity, create "wimpiness" (especially in males), or are unnatural. Talk to your veterinarian if you have such concerns, or read the thorough coverage of this subject in my book, *Dog Talk: Training Your Dog Through a Canine Point of View.* You will learn that spaying and neutering provide many benefits to a dog, its owners, and the canine population as a whole. I highly recommend both procedures.

Dog Breeds and Health Care

Some dog owners have to deal with more veterinary care for their pets than others. Luck seems to play a part as does physical soundness of the individual dog. Careful supervision also can make a difference in your pet's health, such as keeping the dog away from roads and locking up toxic substances.

But even the most responsible owners may end up with a dog who needs frequent medical care. That's because the breed of the dog itself may contribute to this situation. In an informal survey, several veterinarians contributed their thoughts on which common breeds they see more frequently than average. During their lifetime, dogs of these breeds are more likely to require more than the usual amount of veterinary care. The most frequent medical complaints that generate each vet visit are shown in parentheses.

Ten Popular Breeds Most Likely to Need More than the Usual Amount of Veterinary Care

1. English bulldog (breathing difficulties, skin problems, cesarean section when giving birth, lameness)
2. Cocker spaniel (problems with ears, skin, eyes)
3. Shar-pei (skin problems, digestion problems)
4. Chow chow (skin problems, digestion problems)
5. German shepherd (problems with eyes and skin, lameness, gastrointestinal difficulties)
6. Boxer (skin problems, heart ailments, gastrointestinal difficulties)
7. Dalmatian (skin problems, urinary tract disorders, deafness)

8. West Highland terrier (skin problems)
9. Doberman pinscher (heart ailments, prostate problems, skin problems)
10. Collie (blindness)

If you own one of these breeds, do not panic and assume you will end up with a sickly dog. Instead, use this list to heighten your awareness about potential medical problems. Remember, early intervention can improve your odds of curing or minimizing many illnesses.

If you know where your puppy was bred, ask the breeder about these health issues. Good breeders are acutely aware of health problems in their breed, and they make every effort to breed only the healthiest animals. Also, ask your veterinarian to assess your puppy for potential problems. While no one has a crystal ball and can predict the future, an experienced vet may be able to tell you if there are any signs indicating an increased risk.

Twenty-Three

Home Grooming Tips

Depending on the breed (or mix of breeds) of your puppy, you will have minimal, moderate, or extensive grooming requirements throughout your pet's lifetime. The puppy's coat of fur is what can take the most work. For example, a traditionally groomed poodle needs regular visits to a professional groomer for washing, shaving, clipping, combing, and so on. A Labrador retriever just needs brushing and an infrequent soaping-up and rinsing off in your family's bathtub. Let's hope you thought about grooming requirements before you chose your puppy. There's nothing worse than a matted, smelly coat on a long-haired dog whose owners are too lazy or disinterested to take care of it.

Even if you have a low-maintenance breed, your puppy will still need some basic grooming. Toenails grow, fur sheds, fleas and ticks hop aboard, and muddy puddles always appear after a rainstorm. So you should know some basics about how to care for your puppy's appearance.

Just as important, your puppy should know how to accept your grooming procedures. Start with general handling skills described in Chapter 19. When you are ready to introduce some specific grooming steps to your puppy (don't wait too long!), the descriptions in this chapter will show you how.

Brushing and Combing

This is probably the most important—and easiest—grooming procedure you will do. One obvious benefit of brushing and combing is that you remove dead hair from your puppy's coat, which will give his fur a nice, healthy shine. Brushing and combing also give you the opportunity to check over your puppy on a regular basis. A regular "body check" is essential to good health. It allows you to find small problems before they turn into big ones.

Is there a right way and a wrong way to brush a puppy? In a sense, yes. The *wrong* way is to make the brushing session a tense struggle between you and the pup. Not only will the puppy grow up hating a brushing session, you will hate to do it and probably *won't* do it very often. That's not good for either of you.

Brushing should feel good to your puppy, both physically and emotionally. Introduce brushing when your puppy is relaxed. Choose a brush with blunt, pinlike bristles that will reach through his fur and massage the skin. Sit on the floor with your pup or—if necessary—put him on a sturdy, slip-proof surface above the floor.

Gently brush your puppy's coat for just a few minutes to start. Tell him what a good-looking puppy he is. Tell him how good that feels to have brush strokes under his neck, along his back, and over his shoulders. Keep up a steady stream of pleasant conversation, which soothes and reassures most puppies. I started my dogs this way, and as adults they now love to be brushed. I'm not sure which they like more—all the loving praise or the brush strokes! Either way, it's a relaxing, pleasant time for both of us. (I also have absolutely no doubts about the medical findings that stroking a pet can lower a person's blood pressure. So think of brushing your dog as good *human* care, too!)

Some puppies get overly stimulated at first by the feel of the brush on their skin. They may try to jump away or bite at the brush. This is not uncommon. You will need to use your judgment to overcome this without a huge struggle. Was your puppy exercised and relaxed to start with? Were you in a relaxed, patient mood? Have you practiced general handling skills so that your puppy is familiar with being handled? Certainly it's okay to give a few tough growls ("*Nhaa!*") to tell your puppy to stop biting or squirming. But if it turns into a battle, start over from scratch. Work on handling skills for a few days. Then introduce the brush, but just stroke the backside of it (without the bristles) over the puppy's coat. Then use the bristle side, but don't press down too hard. There's nothing relaxing or pleasant about a brush being pulled roughly through the fur.

Combing is a nice follow-up to brushing, as it pulls out more dead hair and smooths the coat. Use a comb whose teeth are wide enough apart to penetrate the fur. Be careful that you don't pull too hard at a knot or matted area of the coat. (Mats are dense, knotted sections of hair. Depending on your dog's type of fur, mats may form around a burr or a twig in the coat, or they may form where the hair is especially long and thick, such as behind the ears and below the rump.) Yanking out hair can hurt, so try to work knots free with your fingers or carefully cut out the matted section with a pair of scissors. More frequent brushing and combing will help prevent these tangles from forming.

Owners of some breeds may find that their puppy comes with specific grooming instructions for coat care. This may include certain kinds of brushes and combs to use. Certainly follow an experienced breeder's recommendations. If you have doubts, ask your veterinarian or schedule a consultation with a professional groomer (with you present). He or she can show you the best way to provide weekly coat care for your special breed.

When your puppy is used to being brushed and combed, plan to do it at least once a week—for the rest of his life! With many short-haired breeds, that's about all the grooming of the coat you'll need to do on a frequent basis. I have found that if the dog brush is stored in a convenient place, such as near my favorite chair, I'll pull it out more frequently and brush the dogs while I listen to music, watch TV, or talk to my family. That helps keep this important grooming step part of the weekly routine.

Trimming Your Puppy's Toenails

You should learn how to trim your dog's nails—it's not hard at all. Most dogs need their nails trimmed *at least once a month*. Some dogs require a nail trimming as often as every other week. Twice a year during a veterinary office visit is not enough. Even if your dog goes to the groomer every six weeks, this may not be enough. Trimming nails is something that owners are able to do—and should do—on a regular basis at home.

Excessively long toenails create many problems for dogs. They can catch on things and rip off, giving your dog a very sore foot. Also, long nails will cause the dog's feet to splay. This means that the cartilage between the toes spreads and eventually weakens. This cartilage can potentially break down, causing serious foot problems as your dog grows older. I have seen dogs with nails that were so long that the nail actually grew around and back into the dog's foot! This causes the dog serious pain, and the risk of infection is high.

The trick to success when trimming your dog's nails is to try *not* to do too good a job. That's because inside the nail is a small blood vessel. This blood vessel is sometimes referred to as the "quick." If you trim the nail back too far, you will cut the quick and it will bleed. Your dog will not bleed to death, but it will certainly hurt your dog. If you hurt his feet he is not going to want you near them. The trick is to just "nick the tips" of the nails. Do this frequently instead of an occasional nail-chopping session. Here's why: As a dog's toenails grow longer, so do the blood vessels. As the blood vessel grows longer, there is less nail that you can trim off. But every time you trim the nails, the blood vessels recede back slightly. If you take a little bit off on a regular basis, you will keep the dog's nails at a good length without cutting into the quick.

Do not try to clip your dog's toenails with human nail clippers. These do not work well, and there is a much greater risk of hurting your dog. Many different brands and styles of canine toenail clippers are available. While some brands are of better quality than others, style is subjective to individual taste. The best way to check for quality is to ask a professional dog groomer or a veterinarian what they use. Pros rarely use cheap equipment.

The chances are much greater that you will cause a nail to bleed if you are wrestling with a wiggle-worm as you try to trim toenails. When you first start trimming your puppy's nails, you may find that it is a two-person job. One person holds the pup while the other clips the nails.

It's very hard to hit a moving target, so get your puppy still before you start cutting. I keep my dog in a sitting position while I do his front feet. My helper (Barbara McKinney) kneels next to him, reaching over his back with one arm. Her other arm reaches across the front of his chest. Then both her hands help hold out the dog's front leg and foot to steady them. A good technique she uses is to cup the dog's elbow in the palm of her hand, so he cannot flinch and pull his arm back. I then hold the front paw with one hand to help keep it still and proceed to trim the nails.

For the back nails I have the puppy lie down. Barbara slides one hand through the collar to keep him in place. She holds the rear leg with her other hand at the top of the hock. Some dogs do not need the hand through the collar, so she will use that hand to rub his chest. I hold his rear paw with one hand to steady it and trim with the other.

Growl "*Nhaa!*" if the pup wiggles or fights you. Although it is important to hold the puppy still, minimize restraint. Heavy restraint will have a backlash effect and cause the puppy to resist. If your helper can gently rub the pup, this seems to help distract his attention. We do not praise the puppy while we trim his nails because it usually makes the puppy wiggle more. Praising may also inadvertently reinforce the puppy's nervousness. So don't say anything until the job is done—then lavish on the praise and perhaps give a biscuit reward.

Most dog groomers and veterinarians will be happy to give you a quick lesson on trimming technique. It is to their advantage, too, that you keep your dog's toenails trimmed on a regular basis. When dogs come into their grooming parlors and medical offices, they cannot trim long toenails back too far because of the long quick. In order for a groomer to get overly long toenails back to the proper length, you would have to schedule your dog for a weekly trimming over a period as long as eight weeks. This could cost you more time and money than you want to spend on toenails! Some veterinarians may suggest putting your dog under general anesthesia. After knocking your dog out, they can trim the nails way back and then bandage the feet. This also proves to be expensive—not to mention risky and traumatic to your dog. And then if you did not start keeping your dog's nails trimmed, you would find yourself facing the same dilemma again before very long.

Fleas and Ticks

This short section is not a medical discussion about fleas and ticks. Your veterinarian certainly can answer any detailed, technical questions about these common pests. Instead, this section describes a few basics that people who have never owned a dog or cat before may know nothing about.

Fleas are tiny insects that spend part of their life cycle feeding on the blood of warm-blooded animals. Dogs are a perfect food choice, which explains why fleas are such a common canine pest. Nourished with a fresh supply of blood, fleas can reproduce incredibly fast. Their eggs and larvae (an intermediate stage before adulthood) will infest your home, soon maturing to adulthood and ready to feed again.

A few signs that your dog may have fleas are scratching, nibbling on his coat, and licking around his rectum or genitals. If you find tiny brown or black crumbly matter in your dog's coat (especially around the base of the tail), you may be looking at "flea dirt." This is the fecal matter of the fleas and is actually digested blood. Put some on a paper towel or napkin and drop a few drops of water on it. Does it turn red? That's digested blood—and a confirmation of your suspicion about having fleas.

Fleas bite humans, too, although we are not an ideal long-term host (perhaps because we lack a covering of dense fur). Flea bites often occur around the ankles or up the legs if exposed. The bites resemble a small mosquito bite or spider bite and itch terribly on some people. They are definitely not something you want to experience—or have your house guests experience.

Flea Prevention and Control

The very best way to deal with fleas is to prevent them from invading your dog and your home. Don't bring your dog to visit a friend who is fighting a flea problem. Pay a few extra dollars for a flea bath for your dog before he comes home from a kennel stay. Use flea-prevention products, such as sprays, powders, and dips, to kill any fleas that by chance hop onto your dog. (But always follow the manufacturer's instructions! Pesticides are strong, potentially dangerous substances.) If a flea infestation gets out of control, professional exterminators can even fumigate your home.

I'm frequently asked about flea collars, which many dogs wear to prevent flea problems. I personally do not use them on my dogs. I've had several veterinarians tell me that many dogs are simply too large or too long for the collars to work effectively over the entire animal. Fleas that are forced to avoid the dog's neck and ears are perfectly happy living around the dog's hind end. And yes, they do crawl into the rectum, into the ears, between the toes, and any other place they can find to hide out when necessary. That's why you don't need to necessarily *see* fleas to have a flea problem.

Flea combs are useful on most breeds. These are fine-toothed combs that will "catch" fleas as you comb through the dog's coat. (An especially thick, long, or curly coat makes using a flea comb difficult.) After each stroke of the comb, dip the comb into a deep bowl of hot water as you pull the hair out of the comb. Hot water (as hot as your hands can comfortably stand) kills fleas quickly. Each flea you catch is one less flea that will feed and reproduce. When you are fighting a flea problem, a daily combing is essential.

I have also found that compulsive vacuuming makes a big difference. By compulsive I mean every day or every other day. That's a lot of effort for most people who have busy lives. But believe me, your busy life will be miserable if it is complicated by a flea infestation. Take twenty minutes and vacuum the house. It really helps. Don't forget to vacuum the dog's crate or bed. That's where a lot of eggs and larvae will accumulate. A hot, soapy wash of the bedding kills fleas, too. Do it at least once a week.

One other thought on the vacuum: Fleas that you suck up (including eggs and larvae) will crawl right back out of the vacuum cleaner after you turn it off and set it aside. So have a system for preventing this. You can dispose of the vacuum bag each time you clean (an expensive option). You can cut up a flea collar and put it in the bag, or you can spray a facial tissue with your dog's flea spray and put it in the bag. These last two options will kill whatever enters until the bag is full and you dispose of it away from the house. We even cover the bag's round opening with masking tape before putting the bag in the trash. "Take no prisoners!" is an absolutely necessary flea-fighting attitude.

A relatively new product available through your veterinarian is a once-a-month medication for your dog that breaks the flea's life cycle. After an adult feeds on your dog's blood, the eggs it lays are unable to mature to adulthood. This means that your dog still may get a few flea bites from time to time, but there's little chance of an infestation in your home, unless you have other animals that can keep the life cycle going. Ask your veterinarian about this interesting product.

In fact, I recommend relying on your vet whenever a flea problem gets out of hand. In my experience, inexpensive, discount-store flea products don't compare to the products you can get at most veterinary hospitals or high-quality pet supply stores. Take flea-fighting seriously and you will minimize or eliminate the problem from your pet-owning experience.

Ticks—Yuck!

Most dog owners I know are "grossed-out" by ticks. Ticks are little blood-sucking animals that look like insects but are actually relatives of spiders and scorpions. Like leeches, they bite and then hang on, drawing blood painlessly from their victim. Unlike fleas, ticks do not typically complete their life cycle in your home, so you don't have to worry about an infestation.

What you do need to worry about is the diseases that ticks can carry, which are transmitted when they bite. Rocky Mountain spotted fever and babesiosis are two examples. The disease that has received the most attention in recent years is Lyme disease, named after Lyme, Connecticut, the town where the disease was first identified. It seems to be getting more and more widespread each year.

Not all kinds of ticks carry Lyme disease. Of those ticks that do (most notably the deer tick), not every tick is infected. Interestingly, both dogs and humans are susceptible to this disease. In dogs, lameness is a characteristic symptom, often due to the inflamed joints caused by the infection. Usually the lameness comes on rather suddenly. One of my dogs had Lyme disease. He was fine one day and barely able to climb the stairs the next. A trip to the veterinarian and a course of antibiotics cured him just fine. Now all my dogs are vaccinated against the disease. Reports are mixed whether the vaccine is 100 percent effective, but I live in a high tick area and have never again had a problem.

Lyme disease produces a wide variety of symptoms in humans, many of which appear flulike. Examples of symptoms include headache, stiff neck, fever, the chills, or fatigue. Sometimes a reddish ringlike rash appears on the skin. What is so annoying about this disease is that it's hard to know if you've got it. The good news is that blood tests for Lyme disease have been improved (there used to be a lot of false readings). The *really* good news is that Lyme disease is highly treatable with antibiotics, especially if caught early.

So your job as a dog owner is to inspect your dog for ticks on a daily basis. The ones that are clinging to your dog pose no threat to you. Grasp the tick close to your dog's skin, twist, and pull. The twisting motion helps unlock the mouthparts, and pulling removes the pest. To avoid touching the tick with your bare hands, you can protect your fingers with a facial tissue, which can then be used to wrap up the tick and flush it, burn it, or otherwise destroy it. Don't simply toss the tick into the trash—it will crawl out!

Ticks that have been on your dog for a while start to fill up with blood. They will look like small (or possibly large) gray marbles. Care is needed when removing them, because the blood-filled body can break open. That's why using a facial tissue when you grasp the tick is a good idea. If you are adept with tweezers, you can use them to grasp the tick. Use pointed tweezers and reach in from the side of the tick, close to the dog's skin, to avoid bursting the body.

The ticks that you may find *walking* on your dogs are the ones still looking for a warm place to settle down and feed. By cuddling that puppy in your lap after a hike in a grassy field, you may find a tick wandering up your arm. *So be vigilant.* Check yourself and your pup after an outing. Change your shoes and clothing if necessary. Run your fingers through your hair, feeling over your scalp (warm heads and necks are good feeding places). Don't panic if you find a tick. If it's still walking around, dispose of it as described above. If it's attached, remove it and, if possible, save it (between two pieces of transparent tape works well). Watch for symptoms, especially the characteristic reddish ringlike rash. If symptoms do appear, which may be days or weeks after the bite, call a doctor and tell him or her the situation. A blood test may be required to confirm your suspicions, but you will probably be given a course of antibiotics to fight the infection. Take all your pills as directed and you should be fine.

One final word on ticks: When in doubt, ask your veterinarian. From just about anyone else you may hear all sorts of ridiculous advice and old wives' tales associated with ticks. For example, mouthparts left beneath the dog's skin will *not* burrow into the dog's body on their own. (They may cause a small swelling or infection, but they will eventually be expelled, as a splinter would.) Burning a tick off your dog's skin with a hot match is cruel and unnecessary. (Use the techniques described above or ask your vet for help.) Covering a tick with nail polish is irritating, messy, and unnecessary. (Again, simply twist it off and flush it away.) You've probably heard others. Ignore them all and learn to handle ticks right—even if you still think they're yucky.

Time for a Bath

Now for the fun part of home grooming—bath time! As mentioned earlier, your puppy's breed will influence how often (if ever) you bathe him at home. Your own physical abilities will also be a factor as will the facilities in your home for giving a bath. Certainly a tiny shower stall is no place to wash a Saint Bernard. And a bad back won't make it very easy to lean over the tub to soap up your dachshund. In such cases, you should rely on a well-recommended grooming shop to help you keep your pooch smelling and looking his best.

But . . . if you decide to give a bath at home, here are a few tips. If your puppy is small enough and your kitchen sink is large enough, introduce his first bath there. The sink brings your puppy to waist-height, which makes it easier on you. Plus, a kitchen is warm and familiar, a good place to start something new. Wear old clothes or a plastic apron. You *will* get wet.

Use warm water, a gentle canine shampoo (never human shampoo—it's too harsh), and lots of soothing praise—as long as your pup remains calm. Use your tough-sounding growl ("*Nhaa!*") to correct unruly behavior. Have a helper keep the puppy in place if you have an especially wiggly or jumpy pup. After a few bath-time experiences, most wiggly pups learn to stand relatively still and accept being washed.

Groomers always remind me that it's important to rinse, rinse, and rinse some more. Soap left in the coat can itch, irritate, and cause dryness. Towel-dry your puppy with one or more towels to remove as much moisture as possible. Let him play in a warm room or sunny backyard to finish drying.

Some dogs don't mind a little bit of a blow-drying with a handheld blow-dryer. My black Lab loves the warm air moving around on his coat (but never held too close or in one place long enough to burn his skin). My other Lab is frightened by the sound of the blower, so trying to blow-dry him just creates a stressful experience. Groomers use dryers, so ideally, it's great to help your puppy learn to tolerate it. As with most everything else, start short and easy. You and your pup are not entering a beauty pageant. Clean and dry is all that's necessary.

Other Grooming Tasks

You may find that you enjoy fussing over your puppy's appearance. That's fine as long as you maintain your common sense. A bath every few days is a terrible idea (unless prescribed by a veterinarian). The constant soaping and rinsing will remove the natural oils that keep your pup's coat healthy. Toenail trimming every day is too compulsive—and unnecessary. Even human nails don't grow that fast. Daily brushing coupled with a flea and tick inspection *is* a good idea. Not many owners find time to do it every day, but if you are one that does—that's great.

Cleaning your pup's ears and teeth are additional grooming tasks that many owners overlook. Teeth can be wiped with a gauze pad wrapped around your finger. (Don't forget to growl if the pup tries to bite you!) I've even tried a specially designed dog toothbrush and canine toothpaste (on my dog, that is!). Adult teeth in a puppy are so white and healthy that it's hard to imagine the need for cleaning them. But as with all puppy training, efforts you make now will have numerous benefits down the road. A healthy canine mouth will last into old age, so getting a puppy used to periodic cleanings will set the stage for a lifetime of good dental care.

Make an effort to check your puppy's ears every few days. If they seem to produce wax, which many long-eared breeds do, you can wipe it out from the area that you can see and easily reach. A gauze pad, cotton ball, or facial tissue is really all you need. Be gentle wiping around the fleshy folds inside the ear—they are relatively tender. Do *not* use cotton swabs to go digging around for buried ear wax. It's unnecessary, and the risk of injuring your dog is too great. If there's a deep-seated problem, a veterinarian should deal with it.

Pet supply stores and catalogs are filled with an incredible variety of grooming products. You don't need a cabinet full of these items to take good care of your dog. Keep on hand a good comb and brush, a pair of toenail clippers, canine shampoo, a flea comb and spray or powder if you start to have a flea problem, and some gauze pads. Those are the basics that every dog owner should own to keep Fido looking and feeling his best.

Twenty-Four

Time for Formal Training

Dog owners often ask me, "When is the ideal time to begin training my dog?" If you have read through most of this book, you know that teaching a puppy begins the day you bring your little canine bundle home. Housebreaking, how to wear a collar and leash, accepting handling, stopping mouthing, and all sorts of other useful behaviors are introduced to a puppy during Puppy Preschool. These behaviors lay the groundwork for a smooth and successful transition into the more structured approach of formal training.

What is so different about formal training? Not a whole lot if you have been teaching your puppy good behaviors during Puppy Preschool. That's what is so great about starting early. By teaching your puppy how to learn and follow direction from you, he's bound to be an eager and willing student in obedience class.

School Days

When is the right time to start formal training? I have found that the ideal time for owners to enroll a puppy in obedience class is at four months old.

This is comparable to enrolling a six-year-old child in first grade. During the first six years, parents use the human version of Puppy Preschool. They teach their children some basics, like how to use the bathroom, how to feed and dress themselves, perhaps some numbers and the ABCs. Then the children enter the structured classroom. Of course, children who are learning reading, writing, and arithmetic at six years old are not as proficient with these skills as they will be when they're adults. However, all individuals will reach a higher potential as adults if they begin their education early in life.

The same is true with a dog. Starting a puppy with obedience training at four months old does not mean that in just a few months the pup will respond to commands as well as a trained adult dog. However, puppies—like children—will reach a higher potential at adulthood if they begin their education at the ideal time. So when is the ideal time?

Canine behaviorists have determined that the optimum learning period in a canine's life is between the ages of seven and twenty weeks old. EEGs (electroencephalograms) of seven-week-old puppies have been shown to be identical to those of two-year-old dogs. This means that by the time your seven-week-old puppy arrives in your home, his brain is fully developed and the pup has his full capacity for learning. All that is lacking is experience, which the puppy gains on a daily basis.

If your puppy were a wild canine, such as a wolf or coyote, during this phase in his life he would start following adult pack members into the woods to learn behaviors essential to his survival. For example, he would learn to avoid porcupines and poisonous snakes and to trail rabbits. It is *instinctive* to follow direction at this point in a canine's life.

The same is true of your domestic pup. He is going to learn during this period regardless of whether you supervise what he learns or whether he learns haphazardly on his own. That's exactly why I use this time frame for Puppy Preschool and then use the last few weeks for the transition into formal training. It's when your pup is mentally and emotionally "ripe" for learning!

Unfortunately, many trainers, breeders, and veterinarians still recommend waiting until a dog is six months old to begin obedience training. By the time puppies reach this age, the instinctive, optimum learning period has passed, and canines enter a phase in which they begin to assert their independence. In the wild, wolves and coyotes begin wandering off with littermates to explore their environment without adult supervision.

Owners of domestic dogs often find that their six-month-old puppy—
"who has *never* left the yard"—is now down the street at the neighbor's.
Puppies at this age become less and less dependent on the security and
safety of the den (your home) and on the guidance of adult pack members
(you and your family).

In addition, by allowing six or more months to pass before obedience
training begins, owners run the risk of letting unwanted behaviors, such as
chewing furniture and jumping on people, develop into bad habits.

When a canine is eighteen months to two years old, he will have
achieved his full adult personality. It is at this point in your dog's life that if
he has done whatever he pleased—whenever he pleased—he may have as-
sumed the role of boss (pack leader). If this has happened, your dog may
interpret attempts to obedience train him as a direct challenge to his as-
sumed pack leadership role. He may resist this challenge in much the same
manner an old wolf would resist being ousted by a subordinate in the
pack—by growling, biting, snapping, etc.

This is what can make training an older dog very difficult if not impossible. However, the cliché, "You can't teach an old dog new tricks," is a fal-
lacy—unless your dog has reached a stage where he is violently resistant to
learning. Clearly, it is to the owner's advantage to start obedience training
early.

Lessons to Learn

In a formal obedience class, your puppy will learn a number of behaviors,
several of which you introduced to him during Puppy Preschool. He will
learn to sit and lie down on command, how to stay in place (sitting, standing, or lying down), and how to come reliably when called. Depending
on the trainer's abilities and program, your puppy may also learn how
to greet people without jumping, how to walk on a loose leash without
ever pulling, and how to heel, which means to walk directly at your left
side.

Step-by-step techniques for teaching each of these useful exercises are
found in my book, *Dog Talk: Training Your Dog Through a Canine Point of
View.* Even if you find a good trainer and an enjoyable training class, this
book will give you many additional insights into training.

You will find a step-by-step training program in my book, *Dog Talk: Training Your Dog Through a Canine Point of View*. It's filled with lots of practical guidelines for handling older puppies and adult dogs.

Choosing a Qualified Obedience Instructor

Now you and your puppy are both ready. Where do you begin? Finding the right instructor is an important first step. Don't let the convenience of a nearby "hobby trainer" sway you into choosing an unqualified person or an ineffective program. Dog training is not a licensed profession, nor are instructors state-certified. All of your Puppy Preschool efforts will go to waste if you work with an incompetent or abusive trainer. It's sad to say, but there are a lot of them out there.

Here are some tips on finding a qualified obedience instructor and an effective training program for your special pup.

• First and foremost, check the credentials of the dog trainer before enrolling your pet in a particular program. How did the obedience instructor learn to train dogs? He or she may have worked for a guide-dog organization, training dogs to lead the blind and then teaching their new owners how to handle their dogs. Or he or she may have worked in the military or police force training guard dogs or bomb- and drug-detection dogs. A person can also gain experience training dogs by competing in American Kennel Club obedience trials, Schutzhund trials, tracking tests, or field trials.

• Valuable knowledge and experience can be gained by working for a veterinarian as a pet handler or technician, teaching canine patients to behave while they are being treated or examined. Working as a dog groomer or on the staff of a boarding kennel can also provide handling experience. Only by handling hundreds or thousands of dogs can a trainer truly understand canine behavior and temperament.

People with a background in one or more of these fields—if they have been dedicated and successful—have a great foundation to teach dog obedience. However, a great trainer of dogs is not necessarily a good teacher of people. What kind of teaching background does the instructor have?

• Many excellent dog obedience seminars and clinics are held in many states each year. Effective teaching skills are learned and practiced at these functions. Does your dog trainer attend them?

Teaching skills can also be developed in jobs that require working and communicating with people. Evaluate your own interactions with this trainer. Is he or she articulate and able to express ideas clearly? This is an absolute requirement for a good teacher. In addition, a great number of helpful books are available on the subjects of training dogs and teaching people how to train their dogs. A qualified obedience instructor should be familiar with most of these books.

• Experience helps make a good trainer. How long has the trainer been training dogs? How long has he or she been teaching people to train their dogs? Neither of these skills is developed overnight. Be sure your potential instructor has some experience under his or her belt.

• Ask if the instructor owns a dog (not all of them do!). If so, evaluate for yourself how well the dog obeys. If the instructor's own dog is not obedient, chances are the instructor will not be successful teaching you to train your dog. Also, ask how many different breeds of dogs the trainer has owned or worked with closely. If the answer is one or two, you may find that this instructor will have trouble relating to your particular dog or to your dog's particular training requirements.

• This is important: Ask the instructor if you can observe one of his or her group classes. What training techniques do you see? Do any of them seem unreasonably harsh? Examples would be "hanging" dogs by their training collars, whipping dogs with the end of the leash, or jerking excessively until the dog yelps. You do not need to be an expert on dogs to know that these procedures—which I've actually seen used—constitute cruelty. There is no reason in the world to abuse a dog in order to train him.

On the other hand, how creative is the group class? Do owners walk in endless circles doing nothing but heeling? Are a variety of exercises part of the program? Use your critical judgment to evaluate what you see.

• An additional point about the instructor's class: Is it designed to teach the owners or the dogs? A group class of any size is not an ideal environment for untrained canines to learn. New smells, new faces, and a new setting are overwhelming distractions, especially for energetic and curious young dogs.

Imagine what it would be like if you tried to learn a new foreign language while listening to loud rock-and-roll music—and someone reprimanded you every time you made a mistake! That is what some beginner group obedience classes can be like. In reality, a dog is best trained in a quiet, familiar environment where he can concentrate and learn. In a properly run group training class, the emphasis should be placed on the owner's handling, not on the way a dog is carrying out the exercises in class.

If an owner (1) understands how to carry out a technique, (2) understands the purpose of the technique, (3) has a written reference to look back on that describes what was learned in class, and (4) is motivated to go home and work with the dog, then dog and handler will be successful.

Finally, ask if the instructor does obedience work as a professional. As in many other lines of work, only an experienced professional may be able to provide you with professional results. The "hobby dog trainer" who teaches to make a little extra money or because he or she enjoys dogs may not be qualified to give you the expert help you need—and to help you effectively and efficiently achieve your goal of an obedient dog.

Also, do not be afraid to ask for references from people this instructor has taught. A qualified professional will be happy to provide them, primarily because he or she should have a long list of satisfied clients who own well-behaved dogs.

A qualified obedience instructor also will help you make the most of your Puppy Preschool efforts. Whether you enroll in a group class or take private instruction, you are bound to make great progress.

A final thought: Some dog owners are lured into thinking that "sending the dog off for training" is the way to go. Don't believe it. Good training is based on communication between you and your dog. No one can create that for you! Dogs are not computers that simply need programming. They are living creatures with a brain and a personality, and they form attachments to the people around them. Dogs respond reliably only to whoever trains them. If you want your dog to respond to you, *you* must train your dog.

In addition, training your dog yourself teaches him to fit into your life—which is what you have been doing during Puppy Preschool. At a trainer's kennel, your dog would sit in a crate or be confined to a dog run many hours each day. That's not helping him learn to live with you.

So stick with the good work you have already started. Get an effective training program (like my own in *Dog Talk: Training Your Dog Through a Canine Point of View*), seek out a qualified trainer, and dive into formal training. The relatively short investment of your time and energy will pay off many times over with the lifelong love, companionship, and good behavior of your canine best friend.

Twenty-Five

Spoiled Brat or Spoiled with Love?

If I were to give just one bit of training advice about puppies it would be this: Make the puppy do all the things he hates to do! That is assuming, of course, that the things you want your puppy to do are for his own good and for the good of your family. Remember that I also suggest you eradicate the sentence "He doesn't like it" from your vocabulary when dealing with your puppy—and later, your adult dog. Only you and the other adults in your family have the big picture of what your puppy must do to be safe, healthy, well-fed, and properly exercised. Certainly a dog of any age does not.

Here are some examples from my own household of what I mean. My black Lab, Byron, hated to have his toenails clipped. If I had let him have his way, his nails would have grown to all lengths and he would have developed serious foot problems. My springer spaniel puppy, Crea, hated having her floppy springer ears cleaned. Too bad! Dirty ears can become infected—and a painful mess. Drifter, my Australian shepherd, hated a bath, but he loved to roll in goose poops at the edge of our pond! Whenever he did this smelly behavior, he got his bath. When my child tells me, "Daddy, I hate brushing my teeth," my response is the same. "Too bad. You need strong, healthy teeth. Let's go brush them."

Think of this example: Your puppy barks and whines every time you crate him. How obedient will your dog ever be if, as a young puppy, he's

Puppies are cute and lots of fun when raised right. They grow up fast, so enjoy!

telling you, "I'll throw a fit if you crate me"—and then you let him out? That doesn't give a very strong message that you are in charge.

Suppose your puppy growls or snaps at you when you try to take away a sock or glove—and you let him keep the stolen item? Clearly, your actions tell the puppy that he is in charge. Even worse, you communicate to your puppy that snapping and biting are effective ways to maintain his dominant position. That's not what you want to teach *any* dog.

If you think I sound unbending and stern, you are only half-right. Rules are rules, and I believe in enforcing them for the good and safety of my dogs and household. But I don't act like a drill sergeant. Pack leaders can be loving and caring while remaining in control.

In fact, I'll admit that my dogs are some of the most indulged dogs in America! They are fed high-quality food, their exercise needs are a daily priority, they receive regular groomings and expert veterinary care, they have a big basket of fun toys and chews, and they often go on special outings and get special treats. My dogs may be spoiled, but they are spoiled with love—not spoiled brats. Good training and good pack leadership are what make all the difference.

Index

abusive treatment, 12, 83, 121, 179
  dog with history of, 6, 97
accidents (of housebreaking), 136
adopting
  adult dogs instead of puppies, 6, 10
  from pounds and shelters, 35–36
adult dogs
  abused, 6
  adopting, instead of puppies, 6, 10
  personality of, 245
  possible problems they bring, 6
  untrained, obnoxious ones, 5
afternoon visits, leaving puppy alone on,
    105
aggression, not teaching to puppies, 99
airport, visit to, 107
allergies to dogs, ways to alleviate,
    11–12
alone, dog, 105, 148, 151
American Kennel Club (AKC), 40
angry tone, avoiding in commands, 84
anticipating commands, 198
attention, dog's craving for, even negative,
    215–16
authority, dog testing you, 79

babesiosis, 239
babies, and puppies, 122
  difficulty of raising both simultaneously,
    8–9
baby gates, 160–61
baby talk, avoiding, 85
balls, 74–75, 112
  too small, swallowing, 74
barking, controlling, 218–19
basset hounds, 113
baths, 241
  first, 102
  professional, 241
bed
  dog's, 70
  dog sleeping in your, 150–51
behavior chains, 197–98
belly up
  handling the puppy, 180–81
  as submissive behavior, 143–44
Bentley, 99–100, 108
biting
  dog's, when in pain, 225
  early signs of a future problem, 58–59
  fearful, 41–42

biting (*cont.*)
  by older dog not properly trained, 176
  unacceptable, 154, 167–69
bladder and bowel control, 137, 140
bleeding, controlling, 225
blood in urine, etc., 224
body, dog's, knowing your, 183–85
body language of dogs, 171
bonding, puppies with each other, instead
    of to you, 119–20
bonding, puppy with you
  best at 7 to 8 weeks, 6–7
  need to spend much time together, 11
bonding, you with puppy, 89–95
  at home, 90–91
  out and about, 92–93
bones
  kitchen, don't give to dog, 76
  natural, 76–77
boxers, health care of, 230
brain, puppy's, compared to adult dog's, 244
breathing difficulties, 224
breeders, backyard, 33–35, 229
  business practices in supplying puppies,
    34
breeders, professional, 29–32
  business practices in supplying puppies,
    32, 40
  and socializing puppies, 97–98
  standards of, 31
breeding
  irresponsible, 29, 33–34
  your own dog, 35
breed rescue organizations, 37–38
breeds
  particular, health care of, 230–31
  standards of, 30
brushing, 11–12, 233–34
bulldogs, 113
burglars and intruders, 140
Byron, 22, 185, 250

canine separation anxiety, 141–52
canine thinking, 22–24
  about being a new dog in the family,
    142–46
  about growing up in a pack, 142–43
  learning to imitate your dog's, 81–84

learning to "read" your dog, 21
about people, 7
about separation, 141
Canine Triangle, 151
car
  pet hit by, 224
  putting on leash and collar before getting
    out of, 104
  rides in, 103, 104
care (of puppy), 223–51
  formal training, 243–49
  health issues, 223–31
  home grooming, 232–42
  spoiling a puppy, 250–51
cats, and puppies, 123–25
chasing your dog (trying to catch him), not
    a game, 211
chewing
  destructive, 144, 153, 158
  not tolerating it, 15
  rawhides, 75–76
  toys, 156–58
  unwanted, 57, 144, 153–61
  urge to chew, 57–58, 153, 155
  when not at home, 158
child development, stages in, 49
children
  developmental stages of, 5
  older, and puppies, 9
  preschooling of, 244
  puppies and, 3, 120–21
  puppies meeting, 102
  young, and puppies, difficulty of raising
    both, 8–9
"choke" collar, 169
choosing the right puppy, 3–13, 29–45
  evaluating a puppy, 41–45
  finding puppies, 29–40
chow chows, health care of, 230
clippers, toenail, 235
coats, brushing, 11–12
cocker spaniels, health care of, 230
collar
  fit of, 67–68
  guidelines for choosing and fitting,
    162–63
  learning to wear, 163–64
  See also leash and collar; training collar

collies, health care of, 231
combination vaccine, 227
combing, 234
  for flea control, 238
come on command, 17, 210–11
  body language and verbal tone,
    211–12
  do not correct dog after he does it,
    210–11
  don't run after dog if he fails to come,
    211
  how to teach it, 214
  practicing not coming, a lesson to avoid,
    213–14
commands, training puppy not to antici-
    pate, 198
command tones, 83–84
  angry tone, avoiding, 84
command words
  choosing, 84, 198–99
  saying only once, 191–93
  timing of, 196
communication in dogs
  body and verbal, 171
  dogs with each other, 81–84
  you with your dog, 81–84
compulsive training, 187–90
conditioned avoidance, 19
conditioned responses, 19–20
  need for practice and reinforcement of,
    25
  repetitions and time needed to form, 20
  when they fail, 25
consistency
  in corrections, 172–73
  essential to dog ownership, 12–13
  and forming conditioned responses, 20
  in obedience commands, 213
cooling overheated pets, 225
Corona virus, 227
corrections
  best time for, when unwanted behavior
    is about to happen or is happening,
    20–21, 24, 156–57
  consistency in, 172–73
  don't make, after dog comes on com-
    mand, 210–11
  verbal, 83

cow hooves, as toys, 80
crate training, 39
Crea, 118–19, 250

dachshund, 113
Dalmatians, 44
  health care of, 230
dangers, puppy-level, 161
designated spot for elimination, 131
destructive behavior, due to canine separa-
    tion anxiety, 141–42, 147–48
destructive chewing, 144, 153
  learned in first year, 158
developmental stages, of children and
    dogs, 5
diagnostic tests, 39
diet, discussion with vet about, 227
digging, 70
diseases
  of other dogs, exposure to, 100
  spread by pet stores, 38–39
distemper, 38
distemper combination vaccine, 227,
    228
Doberman pinschers, health care of, 231
dog bag of essential supplies, 104
dog friends, 93
doggy day care, 148
dog runs and kennels, 69–70
dogs
  being "given away," 11–12
  of opposite sex, 118
  overpopulation problem, 32, 35, 229
  as pack animals, 7, 141, 147
  returned to shelter, 147
  ways to love them for those who can't
    own one, 12
  you know what's best for, 250–51
dog sitters, 148
dog-sitting, better than owning a puppy,
    for some people, 10
Dog Talk: Training Your Dog Through a
    Canine Point of View, 246
dominance, 119
  making clear that you are dominant,
    195–96
  puppy testing your, 175–76
dominant dog, 42, 54

doors
    dog jumping out of, 201
    keeping closed, 160
down on command, 15–17, 193–96
    misuse of, 199
down-stay, 206–9
    maximum time of, 208
    and pack leadership, 209–10
dragging a puppy on the leash, 167
Drifter, 3, 17, 22–23, 74, 94, 124, 159–60,
    201, 250
dryers, for hair, 241

ears, cleaning, 242
elderly people, puppies and, 10, 122–23
electrical cords, 161
electric fence system, 70
elementary school, visit to an, 105–6
elimination
    on command, 135–36
    outdoor place for, 107–8, 132–35, 137
    puppy telling you his need, 140
emergencies, medical, 223–25. See also vet-
    erinarians
English bulldogs, health care of, 230
equipment, 63–85
    essentials, 63–71
    extras, 70–71
    safe (and fun) toys, 72–81
euthanasia
    of dogs in pounds and shelters, 36
    of unwanted adult dogs, 6
evaluating a puppy, 41–45
    household and, 43–44
    looking for subtle differences in puppies,
        44–45
exercise
    excessive, harmful, 110
    before leaving puppy alone, 151
    need for, 109

family matters, 116–25
    puppies and babies, 122
    puppies and cats, 123–25
    puppies and children, 120–21
    puppies and the elderly, 122–23
    a second dog, 116–19
    two puppies at the same time, 119–20

farm, visit to a, 106
fear
    felt by puppy, is not "guilt," 21
    overcoming, 107–8
fear biting, 41–42
feet, dog's
    care of, 235
    handling them, 182
fencing, yards, 227
flea collars, 71, 237
fleas
    control of, 227, 236–38
    life cycle of, 236
flight instinct, 211
floor
    don't leave baby on, with dog, 122
    don't sit on, while teaching obedience,
        208
food, words for, that dogs can learn, 95
food bowls, 67
formal training, 243–49
freedom in the house, unsupervised,
        159–60
    dangers to puppy in, 161
Frisbees, 20, 79–80

games, 109–15
    eight weeks to six months, 110–11
    six months to one year, 111
genitals, diseases of, 229
German shepherds, 58
    health care of, 230
gift of a puppy, 29
golden retrievers, 34, 112
greeting, without jumping, 215–18
groomers, 247
grooming
    professional, 105
    tips, 242
group classes, observing, 247–48
growl
    mother dog's, 54, 83, 171–72
    your turn ("Nhaa!"), 173–75
    See also "Nhaa!"
guarantees, on purebred puppies, 31

hair, brushing and combing, 233–34
handling the puppy, 178–85

belly-up, 180–81
  getting puppy used to it, 15
  teaching puppy to accept, 178,
    181–83
hand signals, 207
health care, cost of, 39
health issues, 223–31
  being observant, 225
  of particular brands, 230–31
heartworm, 180
  medication, 227, 228
hepatitis, 227
hereditary problems, of dogs from pet
    stores, 39–40
high-pitched praise, 82
hikes, 92–93
hip dysplasia, 34, 39
hit by car, 224
hobby dog trainers, 248
home exploration, 100
home grooming, 232–42
homeless dogs, good qualities of, 36
home remedies, do not give without
    checking with veterinarian, 225
house, puppy-proofing, 160–61
housebreaking, 14–15, 129–40
  accidents, 136
  before you start, 131
  discussion with vet about, 227
  of dogs from pet stores, 39
  and kennel crates, 137–40
  setting the pattern, 132–35
  telling you "I need to go out,"
    140
  tricks of the trade, 135–36
households
  bonding with puppy in, 90–91
  evaluating a puppy for fitting into,
    43–44
  puppies growing up in, 34–35
  right for puppies, 7–13, 43–44
human medications, do not give without
    checking with veterinarian, 225
hunting dogs, 44

identification tags, 71, 164
immunities, 100
impregnation, accidental, 33

indoors
  not a place for puppy to eliminate, 135,
    137
  supervising puppy while, 135
inducive training, 187–90
ingestion of toxic substances, 224

Jena, 113
jumping on people, discouraging,
    215–18

keeping your head, in an emergency situa-
    tion, 225
kennel cough, 228
kennel crates, 132–35, 149
  furnishing, 66
  guidelines for size, etc., 63–66,
    137–39
  and housebreaking, 137–40
  length of time to keep puppy in, 139,
    148
  safety, 139–40
  size of, 65, 138–39
  substitutes for, such as partitions in
    rooms, 64
  when you're not at home, 158
kitchen, noises of, 101
kneeing a dog, danger of, 215

Labrador retrievers, 73, 113, 232
lameness, 224
leader, pack, 12–13, 54–55
  puppy testing you, 175–76, 190,
    209–10
  you as, 85
leash
  expandable, drawbacks of, 164
  guidelines for choosing and fitting,
    164–67
  introducing, 164–67
  size and type of, 68–69
leash and collar, 67–69, 162–70
  before getting out of car, 104
  biting on the leash, 167–69
  dragging a puppy on, 167
  eliminating while on, 135
  introducing to puppy, 15
  walking on, learning to, 167

leaving puppy alone, 148
  on afternoon visits, 105
  exercise before, 151
left side, trainer's, 193
leptospirosis, 227
licenses, dog, 71
lineage, tracing, for responsible breeding,
  33–34
love, 89n.
Lyme disease, 239
  in human, treatment, 239–40
  vaccination, 227, 228, 239

mastiffs, 112
McKinney, Barbara (co-author), 3n.
memory, dog's, 24
middle-of-the-road temperament, 42
moral code, dog's lack of, 24
mother dog
  calling her puppies, 82
  enforcing obedience, 209–10
  growl of, 54, 83, 171–72
  puppies learning from, 54
  snapping by, 171–72
motorcycles, fear of, 107
mouth, dog's
  inspecting, 182–83
  stick wedged in, 183
mouthing, 58, 122, 190
  of the leash, 167–69
  not tolerating it, 15, 175–76
mutts (mixed-breed dogs), 35

nails, quick of, 235
name (puppy's), 174
  to get his attention, 203
  teaching him it, 84
nasal discharge, blood in, 224
natural bones, 76–77
neutering. _See_ spaying/neutering
new dog, canine thinking of, 142–46
Newfoundlands, 112
"Nhaa!" (use of), 42, 83, 84, 171–77
  before an accident, 136
  for corrections, 156–57
  learning to say, 173–75
  means stop immediately, 177, 199

nighttime, outdoor bathroom runs at, 138,
  150
nipping, not tolerating it, 15
noises
  fear of, 108
  introducing puppy to, 99
  negative impact of, 101–2
nursing home, visit to a, 106
nylon toys, 78

obedience
  based on dog's respect for you, 190
  basics of, 15–18
  mother dogs enforcing, 209–10
obedience classes
  and bonding, 93–94
  enrolling puppy in, 243–45
  group classes, 247–48
  lessons learned in, 245–46
  minimum age for, 186
  observing, 247–48
  visit to a, 106
  when to start, 57
obedience commands
  basic, 186–219
  beginning, 190
  behavior chains, 197–98
  choosing your command words, 198
  consistency in, 213
  inducive vs. compulsive, 187–90
  practicing and reinforcing them, 25
  starting early, 205
  training tips, 196–97
  See also preschool training
obedience instructors
  checking credentials, 246–47
  choosing, 246–48
observant, being, of dog's health, 225
other dogs, exposure to diseases of, 100
outdoors, place for puppy to eliminate,
  107–8, 132–35, 137
outgoing puppies, 41
overheated pets, cooling, 225
overnight trips, 104
overpopulation, dog, 32, 35, 229
owner
  as leader of the pack, 13

matching dog to, 43–44
and obedience instructor, 248
temperament of, 12–13

pack life, 7, 54, 141, 142–43, 147
dominance and submission in, 175
parainfluenza, 227
parks, where dogs are allowed, 92
parvovirus, 38, 227
people
canine thinking about, 7
introducing puppy to, 99
personality
as adult, when puppy achieves it, 245
and evaluating a puppy, 43–44
pet industry, money made in the, 29
pet stores, 29, 38–40
socializing puppies from, 39
petting and soft talking, considered praise
by dogs, 228
physical exam, 227
physical limitations, owner's, and difficulty
of raising puppies, 10
picking up the house, 160
pigs' ears, as toys, 80
playing, 72
poodles, 11–12, 232
pound, 71
adopting a dog from, 35–36
praise
high-pitched, 82
petting and soft talking considered as, by
dogs, 228
when to give, when teaching commands,
203–4
preschool training, 129–219
basic obedience commands, 186–219
canine separation anxiety, 141–52
handling your puppy, 178–85
housebreaking, 129–40
leash and collar, 162–70
"Nhaa!" (use of), 171–77
unwanted chewing, 153–61
See also obedience commands
"problem" dogs, 129
puppies
charm of, 3

difficulty of raising, in some household
circumstances, 8–11
making yours feel like a valued pack
member, ten ways, 152
price of, 34, 40
quality of, from backyard breeders,
33–34
puppy, choosing the right one for you,
3–13
intuition and, 44–45
the right household, 7–13
what does owning involve, 7
puppy crazies, 57
puppy development, 49–60
birth to three weeks, 51–52
three to seven weeks, 52–55
seven weeks to four months, 55–56
four to six months, 56–57
six months to one year, 57–58
one to two years, 58–59
two years and beyond, 59–60
puppy energy, 109–11, 118, 122
puppyhood, owner living through, 3–5
puppy mills, 39
puppy parties, 104
puppy preschool, a period before formal
obedience training, 14–18
puppy-proofing the house, 160–61
puppy teeth, 154–55
purebred puppies, 30–31, 35
from breed rescue organizations, 37–38
guarantees on, 31
registration of, 40

quiet on command, 218–19

rabies vaccination, 227
raising puppies, difficulty of, in some
household circumstances, 8–11
rawhides, 75–76
"reading" the dog, 21, 94
reclusiveness, and evaluating a puppy,
41–42
records, pet's, bringing to veterinarians,
225
registration of purebreds, 40
release word ("Okay," "Go!," etc.), 199, 208

reproduction plans, 227

retinal atrophy, 39

retrieving, 111–12

right and wrong, dog's lack of sense of, 24

roaming dogs, 71
   perils to, 70

Rocky Mountain spotted fever, 239

Ross, John (author), 3n.

roundworms, 227

routines, important to puppies, 90–91

samples, urine, etc., bringing to veterinarians, 225

schnauzers, 11–12

second dog, 116–19

seizure episodes, 224, 225

senior day care center, visit to a, 106

seniors, and dogs, 10, 122–23

separation, canine thinking about, 141

sex of dogs, and getting along, 118

shampoo, 241

shar-peis, health care of, 230

shelter, 29
   adopting a dog from, 35–36
   dog returned to, 147
   downside of dogs adopted from, not knowing the background of the dog, 36
   and socializing puppies, 97–98

show champions, 32

shyness, 41–42, 100, 119

sit on command, 15–17, 19, 191–93

sit-stay command, 199–204

sitting position, dog greeting you from, 215–18

sleeping
   in bed with you, 150–51
   in same room with you, 91, 139–40

snaps, mother dog's, 171–72

socialization of puppies, 17, 96–108
   from breeders, 97–98
   of older puppies, 103–7
   from pet stores, 39
   problem of dog's failing to have been socialized as puppy, 99–100
   from shelters, 97–98
   starting small and gently, 96–100

of young puppies, 100–103

soiling their den, dogs' aversion to, 39, 137

Sophie, 148

sound shyness, 44

spaying/neutering, 118, 227, 229
   health benefits of, 229–30

spoiling a puppy, 250–51

squatting on puppy's level
   to greet puppy, 215–16
   to teach come on command, 211–12

squeaky toys, 72–74, 95

staggering, 224

stairs, going up and down, 100–101

starting off right, 89–125
   bonding with your puppy, 89–95
   family matters, 116–25
   games puppies play, 109–15
   socializing your puppy, 96–108

stay on command, 17, 19–20, 199–204

stool
   blood in, 224
   inability to pass, 224
   samples, 225, 227

stop immediately, "Nhaa!" command to, 177, 199

stores and malls, visits to, 102

strangers, meeting, 104

stuffed toys, 78

submission, dog's to you, 193

submissive dog, 43, 54, 85

swimming, 113–15
   how to teach, 114

tags on collar, 164

talking to your dog, 94–95

teaching an old dog new tricks, 59–60, 245

teeth
   adult, 155
   cleaning, 242
   puppy, 154–55

temperament (puppy's), and evaluation, 41, 43

temperament (yours), and owning a puppy, 12–13

temperature (puppy's), high, 224

terriers, 11–12, 70, 79

ticks
control of, 227, 239, 240
diseases carried by, 239
timing, of corrections, 20–21, 156–57
toddlers, 102, 120
toenail trimming, 234–36
professional, 236
tone of voice, to teach come on, 212
touching, important to puppies, 91
toxic substances
ingestion, 224
taking samples to veterinarian, 225
toys, chewing on, 80, 156–58
training
formal, when to start, 243–45
a philosophy of, 19–25
of puppies, to become well-behaved
adults, 5–6
three-phase approach to, 187
See also obedience classes
training collar, 169–70
cautions, 170
fitting, 170
introducing puppy to, 170
travel schedule, and difficulty of raising
puppies, 10–11
tugging games, 79
tug toys, 78–79
tumors, 184–85
two-ball retrieve, 111–12
two puppies at the same time, 119–20

unwanted behavior
repeating of, don't allow, 159–60
timing of corrections of, 21, 24, 156–57
unwanted dogs
euthanization of, 6
giving them a second chance, 38
returned to shelter, 147
urine
blood in, 224
inability to pass, 224
samples, 225

vaccinations, 100, 226–28, 239
vacuum cleaners, 99, 101–2
for flea control, 238

veterinarians
aiding them in an emergency situation,
225
asking advice of, 71
choosing, 224, 225–26, 229
in emergencies, 223
experience working for, 247
first visit (eight-week-old), 227
for flea control, 238
follow-up visits, 229
a positive experience at, 228–29
second visit (twelve-week-old), 227
staff and offices, evaluating, 226
third visit (sixteen-week-old),
227–28
trust your instincts, 226
what to look for, 226
vicious dogs, 175
visitors, and puppies, 102
visits with puppy, to stores, schools, etc.,
105–7
voice, your (as training tool), 81–84
vomiting, 103
blood in vomit, 224
repeated, 224

walks
on leash, 167
to town, 103–4
in wildlife sanctuary, 106
water bowls, 67, 139
West Highland terriers, health care of,
231
wildlife sanctuary, walks in, 106
wolves, behavior in the wild, 244
words and phrases, that dogs can learn,
94–95
work schedule, and difficulty of raising
puppies, 9–10, 148
worming, 227
worms, 100

yards, 69–70, 92–93, 99
designating a spot to eliminate in, 131
fencing, 227

zooms, the, 57